Milton and the Poetics of Freedom

Medieval & Renaissance Literary Studies

General Editor:
Rebecca Totaro

Editorial Board:

Judith H. Anderson	Jonathan Gil Harris
Diana Treviño Benet	Margaret Healy
William C. Carroll	Ken Hiltner
Donald Cheney	Arthur F. Kinney
Ann Baynes Coiro	David Loewenstein
Mary T. Crane	Robert W. Maslen
Stephen B. Dobranski	Thomas P. Roche Jr.
Wendy Furman-Adams	Mary Beth Rose
A. C. Hamilton	Mihoko Suzuki
Hannibal Hamlin	Humphrey Tonkin
Margaret P. Hannay	Susanne Woods

Originally titled the *Duquesne Studies: Philological Series* (and later renamed the *Language & Literature Series*), the **Medieval & Renaissance Literary Studies Series** has been published by Duquesne University Press since 1960. This publishing endeavor seeks to promote the study of late medieval, Renaissance and seventeenth century English literature by presenting scholarly and critical monographs, collections of essays, editions and compilations. The series encourages a broad range of interpretation, including the relationship of literature and its cultural contexts, close textual analysis, and the use of contemporary critical methodologies.

Foster Provost	Albert C. Labriola	Richard J. DuRocher
EDITOR, 1960–1984	EDITOR, 1985–2009	EDITOR, 2010

Milton and the
Poetics of Freedom

SUSANNE WOODS

DUQUESNE UNIVERSITY PRESS
Pittsburgh, Pennsylvania

Copyright © 2013 Duquesne University Press
All rights reserved

Published in the United States of America by
DUQUESNE UNIVERSITY PRESS
600 Forbes Avenue
Pittsburgh, Pennsylvania 15282

No part of this book may be used or reproduced,
in any manner or form whatsoever,
without written permission from the publisher,
except in the case of short quotations
in critical articles or reviews.

Library of Congress Cataloging-in-Publication Data

Woods, Susanne, 1943–
   Milton and the poetics of freedom / Susanne Woods.
     pages cm
   Includes bibliographical references and index.
   Summary: "Offers new readings of Milton's major works, including Areopagitica, Paradise Lost, Paradise Regained, and Samson Agonistes, highlighting how Milton shifts the parlance of freedom and liberty from the arena of civic order to that of the individual conscience engaged in the process of choosing; this, in turn, invites readers to consider alternatives even to Milton's own positions"—Provided by publisher.
   ISBN 978-0-8207-0466-1 (cloth : alk. paper)
   1. Milton, John, 1608–1674—Criticism and interpretation. 2. Liberty in literature. I. Title.

PR3588.W66 2013
821'.4—dc23

2013021238

∞ Printed on acid-free paper.

Contents

Acknowledgments		vii
Introduction		1
One	Early Modern Liberty: *Tenure of Kings and Magistrates,* English Cultural Self-Definition, and Divine Right	13
Two	The Poetics of Freedom: "The Poet Collingbourne" and Sidney on Politics and Poetics	39
Three	Milton's Early Poetics of Choice: The 1645 *Poems, Doctrine and Discipline of Divorce,* and *Areopagitica*	72
Four	Knowledge, Choice, and Freedom in *Paradise Lost*	103
Five	Freedom and Vocation in *Paradise Regained* and *Samson Agonistes*	144
Six	*Areopagitica*'s Reception History and Modern Contestations of Freedom	172
Notes		199
Works Cited		255
Index		277

Acknowledgments

This book had its origins so far back it is embarrassing to admit the length of its gestation, but, more sadly, that also makes it impossible to fairly represent all the very kind colleagues and friends who have cheered it on. The topic grew out of one of my earliest professional assignments, from the late John Steadman, to write the *Areopagitica* and "Tyranny" articles for the *Milton Encyclopedia*, and kept returning as an interest even as I wrote on prosody and poetic form in the 1970s and 1980s and on Aemilia Lanyer and other early women writers in the 1990s. Over the past 20 years, between larger projects and administrative responsibilities, I published several articles on freedom and tyranny in early modern literature, including on Milton, and cite them where appropriate, although the work in this book recasts and amplifies considerably that previous work.

Though it is not possible to mention everyone who has helped along the way, some friends have been around for all or almost all of the ride, and I want to thank them warmly for their patience and constant encouragement. Foremost are my colleagues from many years of the Northeast Milton Seminar, including but by no means limited to Barbara Lewalski, Mary Ann Radzinowicz, Joseph Wittreich, Stuart Curran, John Rogers, and Julia Walker. I owe David Loewenstein for his rigorous editing of what became a seed essay for this book, "Elective Poetics in Milton's Prose: *A Treatise of Civil Power and Considerations Touching the Likeliest Means to Remove Hirelings Out of the Church,*" included in the book he co-edited with James Grantham Turner, *Politics, Poetics, and Hermeneutics in Milton's Prose* (1990), and Mario di Cesare for insisting I write about Milton and Italy, which produced "'That Freedom of Discussion Which I Loved': Italy and Milton's Cultural Self-Definition," for his *Milton in Italy: Contexts, Images, Contradictions* (1991). Those two essays started me thinking about Milton's ideas of liberty even as some splendid work by historians, including Patrick Collinson, Quentin Skinner, and Blair Worden, advanced the field considerably, and literature colleagues, including David Loewenstein, David Norbrook, Annabel Patterson, Nigel Smith, and Sharon Achinstein, kept scholars engaged in issues of Milton, liberty, and the complexities of seventeenth century thought and literature.

Over the years I have had many occasions to thank the wonderful staff of the Huntington Library, not least for this book; a summer Mellon fellowship there in 2007 finally got me started on the project in a serious way. Roy Ritchie, as always, was a particular friend and guide. I have also used the good services of the British Library, the Bodleian Library, the Folger Shakespeare Library, and the Newberry Library, friendly and helpful places all, for which I am grateful. Mihoko Suzuki, Jeffrey Shoulson, Pamela Hammons, and other colleagues made me welcome in South Florida with a courtesy appointment at the University of Miami, and their encouragement and excellent library were important to this project. I am also grateful to Virginia Tufte, Wendy Furman-Adams, and Eunice Howe for rediscovering the artist and Milton illustrator Carlotta Kennedy Petrina.

The readers for this book were actively helpful in shaping the final version. I am grateful to them, to the staff of

Duquesne University Press, especially Kathleen Meyer, and to Rebecca Totaro, the editor of Duquesne's series on Medieval & Renaissance Literary Studies, who encouraged me to submit the manuscript. It was her predecessor, the late Al Labriola, who first asked me to consider developing my work on Milton and the poetics of freedom into a book for review by Duquesne. I hope the result, at last, will honor the request as I honor the memory of the requestor.

I dedicate this book to Anne Shaver, who endured its development over the years, stayed a cheerful companion, and read through the draft manuscript, catching a number of infelicities. Remaining flaws are, of course, my own.

Introduction

This book presents John Milton as an important voice for defining freedom within the contestations of English-speaking culture, for making it central to individual and cultural self-definition, and for creating a poetics that invites his reader to enact the freedom he defines. In our culture, "freedom" is a powerful term with plastic meanings and contradictory uses. Along with its cognate "liberty," it has both driven rebellion and justified empire.[1] Milton's world, like our own, struggled with the concept within what was already considered a heritage of political and personal liberty, compounded in the seventeenth century by theological questions of freedom.

It is commonplace among Miltonists to see freedom and liberty as central concepts in both the author's poetry and prose. Over the course of critical history there has been less agreement, however, in what Milton means by those terms, and considerably less discussion of how his rhetoric and poetic may embody, as well as convey, what Milton means by freedom and liberty. Scholars consider whether Milton's idea of freedom is primarily political (as Quentin Skinner and others argue) and derived from a "neo-Roman republicanism" generated by early sixteenth century humanists, or something more radically individual, deriving from Milton's theology.² These categories are not necessarily opposed, but they do tend in different directions: is freedom a function of the social contract, or is it a theological imperative? For Milton, as I hope to show over the course of this book, freedom is fundamentally about human choice, which is a God-given mandate that underlies all other kinds of freedom.

This in itself is not a surprising claim, but it leads to an interesting problem for a master rhetorician. Both as a partisan and an idiosyncratic presence during the political and theological debates of the mid-1600s, Milton built on a strong tradition of English political liberty, Reformation Christian liberty, and the liberties of poetic speech to launch a radical vision of individual freedom, famously expressed in *Areopagitica:* "when God gave [Adam] reason, he gave him freedom to choose, for reason is but choosing; he had been else a mere artificiall *Adam*.... We ourselves esteem not of that obedience, or love, or gift, which is of force: God therefore left him free, set before him a provoking object, ever almost in his eyes; herein consisted his merit, herein the right of his reward, the praise of his abstinence." At this point Milton adds an invitation to his reader to join him in seeing opportunities for choice: "Wherefor did [God] creat passions within us, pleasures round about us, but that these rightly temper'd are the very ingredients of vertu?"³

Milton is clear that if choice is truly to be free it cannot be coerced. This creates a powerful enigma: how can the author teach his readers personal freedom—that is, teach them to rely finally not on received authority but on their individual reason and conscience? One commentator unconsciously highlights the paradox by saying that Milton's prose style "exemplifies and forces upon his reader an awareness of the intrinsic liberty of the human spirit."⁴ But how can *forcing* exemplify human liberty? Milton was apparently aware of the problem and sometimes addressed it directly. "A man may be a heretick in the truth," he asserts in *Areopagitica,* "and if he believe things only because his Pastor sayes so, or the [Presbyterian Westminster] Assembly so determines, without knowing other reason, though his belief be true, yet the very truth he holds, becomes his heresie" (YP 2:543).

Milton's rhetorical challenge is to persuade his readers to think for themselves. If you believe something to be true merely because John Milton tells you so, you have no truth. What establishes true knowledge for any person, and at the same time, Milton believed, fulfills God's will, is that person's careful attention to a wide range of learning and a thoughtful approach to experience followed by the use of reason and the act of choosing. Milton, more than any previous English writer, centers freedom in the act of rational, knowledgeable choice. In this he set out to change how his readers thought about freedom and liberty, and to change not only the meanings associated with the terms themselves, but to invite a more questioning and individually assertive habit of mind. Milton pushed for his vision of liberty across the entire span of his career, despite an increasingly lower opinion of the public in general.[5] As Daniel Shore demonstrates, from his earliest days as a writer Milton used what may be called the "fit-though-few" trope to designate the elite and responsive audience who would understand and actively consider what he was trying to say.[6] Yet in inviting (and presumably, therefore, helping to form) an audience worthy to understand and even to challenge him, Milton did not simply offer the possibility of several interpretations. To the extent that he was manipulating his audience through defining them, that manipulation, I will argue, was toward an ethics of freedom enacted through making informed and thoughtful choices.

Milton's ideas about freedom emerged with increasing nuance and complexity over the course of a life spent variously in service to poetry, radical politics, reformed religion, and especially to his understanding of God's call to the individual conscience. By 1659, following his experience of civil and pamphlet wars and his uneasy and sometimes disappointing participation in Cromwell's government, Milton's view of Christian liberty had become radically individual and insistent upon the separation of religion and state. "No man or body of men in these times," he writes in the pamphlet *Of Civil Power*, "can be the infallible judges of any other mens consciences but thir own" (YP 7:243). What follows from this view is a rhetoric that invites rather than demands, entices toward individual choices rather than asserts unwavering authority.

Milton's rhetorical habit began earlier than his most fully developed affirmation of the importance of individual conscience and choice, and though it thrives within metaphorical language, it holds for prose as well as poetry, secular as well as theological discourse. In his prose writings it most obviously pervades *Areopagitica*, but it even appears (as I have argued elsewhere) in his plainest prose style.[7] Through both the prose and the poetry Milton develops characteristic constellations of rhetorical and poetic techniques that constitute the "poetics" of this book's title. These include metaphoric language, for which Milton has a natural turn of mind and which I will later argue is inherently invitational, and such schematic devices as double negatives, interrogative constructions, and a language of surmise.[8] The power of this rhetoric resides not in "forcing" his vision of freedom, but in beckoning his reader to affirm a common vision.

Areopagitica (as I show further in chapter 3) is a virtual laboratory of these techniques and processes. It also seeks to give the impression of a political tradition of English free speech on which later polemicists might build, a point I will examine in the course of chapters 1 and 2. At the same time, Milton sets his ideas of freedom not in a settled tradition or definition, but in a process of learning and choosing. Consider *Areopagitica*'s direct invitation to the English people to remember "*Wicklef*" and recognize that God is again revealing "Himself to his servants, and as his manner is, first to English-men," however unworthy they may show themselves to be:

> Behold now this vast City; a City of refuge, the mansion house of liberty, encompast and surrounded with [God's] protection; the shop of warre hath not more anvils and hammers waking, to fashion out the plates and instruments of armed Justice, in defence of beleaguer'd Truth, than there be pens and hands there, sitting by their studious lamps, musing, searching, revolving new notions, as with their homage and their fealty the approaching Reformation: others as fast reading, trying all things, assenting to the force of reason and convincement. What could a man require more from a Nation so pliant and so prone to seek after knowledge. What wants there to such a towardly and pregnant soile, but wise and faithfull labourers, to make a knowing people, a Nation of Prophets, of Sages, and of Worthies. (YP 2:553–54)

In this invitational exhortation ("Behold now") are a compound of biblical allusions ("City of refuge," "faithfull labourers"), metaphoric language, in this case analogical ("anvils and hammers" are to righteous defensive war as "pens and hands" are to the intellectual defense of "beleager'd Truth"), and, in one of his typical questions at once both rhetorical and genuine, the appeal to national pride, past, present, and future ("to make a knowing people"). That "Nation so pliant and so prone to seek after knowledge" is one always in process, not settled or static but always enacting or being responsive to "musing, searching, revolving new notions." Milton will invite his readers to enact the choices that define his understanding of freedom, and, in the process, to enact their own freedom by choosing.

Throughout this book I refer to Milton's poetics of freedom as an "invitational poetics," which expects and in some cases requires a thoughtful, active engagement with the ideas the text presents. I came to this terminology in preparing an essay that anticipated this book.⁹ In the past I have referred to Milton's rhetorical tendencies as "elective poetics," in which the reader's choices effect her response to God's (and Milton's) call to exercise free will in the formation of her own life. While I still believe this to be a reasonable description of Milton's project, particularly in the two major works that focus on vocation, *Paradise Regained* and *Samson Agonistes*, I have preferred the term "invitational poetics" as it better describes what Milton's rhetoric seeks to accomplish, and also because it suggests a certain humility not often ascribed to Milton but which I see implicit in many of his strategies, including his attentiveness to his supposed audience.

One can see elements of underlying humility even in some of Milton's apparently most self-aggrandizing moments. In *An Apology against a Pamphlet* (1642), for example, the heated end of his anti-episcopal publications, Milton takes on the satirist and bishop Joseph Hall, defending himself against Hall's accusations of loose morals by telling the story of his love of poetry and the ideals it demands. As Milton relates his early perception that he was himself a talented poet, he seeks to define and engage an appropriate reader ("let rude eares be absent") even as he recognizes that readers may variously perceive his longing for personal virtue and poetic fame: "For although these thoughts to some will seem virtuous and commendable, to others only pardonable, to a third sort perhaps idle, yet the mentioning of them now will end in serious" (YP 1:890).¹⁰ Milton's impulse in this pamphlet, as in *Areopagitica*, is essentially democratic in its recognition of multiple perspectives, and though he moves rapidly toward more meritocratic views, he maintains a lifelong conviction that no one, not even John Milton, can prescribe another person's God-given conscience.¹¹ The free conscience is the underlying message of *Areopagitica*: "Give me the liberty to know, to utter, and to argue freely according to conscience, above all liberties" (YP 2:560). Or again from *Civil Power*, much later, "no man, no synod, no session of men, though calld the church, can judge definitively the sense of scripture to another mans conscience" (YP 7:242–43, 247–48). This conviction, basic to Milton's understanding of the Protestant religion as he affirms it, leads almost inevitably to a poetics of persuasion rather than assertion, of invitation rather than affirmation.

Of course, Milton does assert and affirm, as in his vigorous argument for unlicensed discourse and a free conscience. As Shore argues, even Milton's "professed withdrawals" from worldly motives are part of his strategy to persuade.[12] What I claim throughout this book, however, is that Milton seeks to engage his reader in asserting and affirming the realities Milton presents, but never from the mere assumption of authority and always with a sense that alternative positions should be part of one's consideration. Let me illustrate the point with two examples of Milton's use of the invitational interrogative, one example taken from prose and one from poetry. These may be set against the more usual expectation of how the interrogative is used in rhetoric. In her summary of syntactic artistry, for example, Virginia Tufte describes "two common interrogative forms...the *leading question*, designed to imply and elicit the answer it intends, and the *rhetorical question*, formed strictly for effect and therefore making any answer at all superfluous."[13] She goes on to describe the effect most of us expect from interrogative constructions: "If the interrogative is employed to direct us specifically toward the resolution of some problem, the leading question takes us directly there.... The rhetorical question is what might be called a question after the fact, an announcement that we have arrived at an answer. It celebrates that forming a question in the face of such certainty is simply for ironic emphasis."[14]

Taking the latter first, consider the apparently rhetorical question I earlier cited from *Areopagitica:* "Wherefore did

[God] creat passions within us, pleasures round about us, but that these rightly temper'd are the very ingredients of vertu" (YP 2:527). Unquestionably, Milton would like his reader to affirm that passions and pleasures, "rightly temper'd," are the constituents of virtue. This conclusion, however, is scarcely obvious, and certainly not ironic, particularly in the context of Protestant discourse that describes postlapsarian humankind as totally depraved and unable to choose toward salvation. Implicit in Milton's rhetorical question is the view that humankind is able to temper rightly the passions and pleasures, a subject of considerable debate during the Reformation, as I note further in chapter 1. The rhetorical question is an invitational one, asking the reader to consider a set of complex issues in the hope that the reader will come to Milton's conclusion, but by no means assuring it.

Or consider the even more complicated leading questions (to use Tufte's term) the Serpent offers Eve in book 9 of *Paradise Lost*, as he encourages her to eat of the forbidden fruit:

> Wherein lies
> Th'offence, that Man should thus obtain to know?
> What can your knowledge hurt him, or this Tree
> Impart against his will if all be his?
> Or is it envie, and can envie dwell
> In Heav'nly brests?   (*PL* 9.725–30)

The narrator goes on to emphasize that these words are "replete with guile" (733), but the process of the questions themselves illustrates the task these invitational techniques place on Milton's reader. On the one hand, we know this is a temptation scene, and Eve is much less able than the experienced, fallen reader to recognize the guile. As we read we are prepared to counter the Serpent's arguments, not to be led by them. On the other hand, from Eve's perspective, and even to some degree from that of the fallen reader, these seem like fair questions. How could Adam and Eve's knowledge be harmful to an all-powerful God, and how could anything betray the divine will? The poet's narrative, though in the voice of the tempter, invites us to consider these difficult theological questions and to see the ironic underpinning that the duplicitous language suggests. It is not God, but Adam and Eve who will be hurt. Envy does not, presumably, reside with God, or at least in the sense the Serpent appears to use the term (though it is a question worth pondering), but it certainly resides in the formerly "Heav'nly brests" of Satan and the fallen angels, here speaking through the descended form of the Serpent. The reader of this passage is not simply a bystander watching the tragedy of Eve's bad choices, but a participant in the full complexity of the human condition, where choices are always before us.

It is perhaps worth noting that whether human choice is a fact or an illusion is a longstanding debate unlikely to be settled by speculations past or present. Long before there was an Enlightenment or Immanuel Kant or the presumed imperatives of evolution and genetics or of computational linguistics there was, as C. S. Lewis points out in a classic essay on the Renaissance, the opposition of the magicians and the astrologers, those who would control nature and those who believed nature controlled us.[15] The question of free will was central to Reformation and Counter-Reformation arguments about human nature. For Milton, as this book will illustrate more fully in what follows, God gave humankind genuine free will, with reason and the light of conscience to enable choice, with true freedom coming from who one *is*, formed and asserted by the choices one makes.[16] This is true for the reader as well as the author, Milton believed, and the result is invitational poetics. The following chapters examine those poetics on several levels: as they develop in Milton's prose and early poetry, in theory as well as practice, with some precedent in his Elizabethan predecessors; as they are expressed within prose sentences and lines of poetry through Milton's choices of diction and syntax; and as they inform character, plot, and genre, especially in the last works.

Milton's ideas and methods have a heritage, and the first two chapters of this book outline elements of that heritage and suggest some of its applications to Milton's thought and practice. In chapter 1, I connect Milton's most famous statement about his ongoing interest in liberty with debates that preceded him. In chapter 2, I show Milton's Elizabethan predecessors grappling with the possibilities and limits of poetic indirection; Sidney, in particular, provides an underappreciated rhetorical and theoretical foundation on which Milton's invitational poetics could build. These background chapters are intended as a platform for seeing Milton's own evolution toward a poetics of choice, followed by their confident manifestation in the great poems. In chapter 4, I consider *Paradise Lost* as Milton's grand disquisition on knowledge, choice, and freedom; and in chapter 5 I look at *Paradise Regained* and *Samson Agonistes* in relation to the ambiguities of choice and vocation. Chapter 6 briefly situates Milton in relation to the most influential seventeenth century political thinkers, Thomas Hobbes and John Locke, and examines the influence of *Areopagitica* on political culture since Milton's time, placing Milton's ideas in a tradition that leads to modern contestations of freedom.

My methodology is historical, in that I try as much as possible to read dated materials within their own contexts, and interpretive, as I read Milton in relation to his larger oeuvre and with some attention to poetic theory and the conventions of poetic form. I am in general agreement with the current strain of Milton criticism that, as Richard DuRocher and Margaret Thickstun put it, rejects the effort "to find coherence and control in Milton's poetry" in favor of recognizing, instead, a "radical incoherence and openness," although I see that openness as part of a larger ontology and epistemology.[17] Similarly, Peter Herman and Elizabeth Sauer propose to contest a "paradigm of imposing certainty" about Milton's work and intentions, which they argue has created a false "unifying imperative." This willingness to acknowledge uncertainty has the effect of opening up interpretive space, and is, in that sense, consistent with my view that Milton sought to invite active reading.[18] This should not be seen, as I sometimes think it is, as a license to invent Milton or his ideas out of whole cloth. It is clear to me, as it is to most Milton critics, that Milton operated within the Christian context that he inherited, and even his heterodoxies had a history and authority within the turbulent context of Reformation and Counter-Reformation thought.[19]

In my acknowledgments I give thanks for the work of the historians and literary critics who have done so much over the past 20-plus years to show Milton's active involvement in the politics and history of his time, and I will have occasion to cite most of them over the course of this book. They provide another way of situating contemporary Milton studies, as Shore in the introduction to *Milton's Art of Rhetoric* sets the "worldly" critics, who see Milton engaged in the history of his time, against the "otherworldly" critics, most notably Stanley Fish, who see Milton stepping away from the challenges of his time toward universals and metaphysics. Shore adds: "Perhaps because of Milton's own deep-seated beliefs about human freedom, his worldly critics are less likely than historicists of other stripes to adopt a deterministic view of causality. Even while weaving the poet ever more fully into the fabric of history, they do not look to dissolve his individuality or to render him a mere effect or epiphenomenon of the world in which he lived."[20] This seems to me a commonsense recognition of the author's right to his or her work, even as it acknowledges the influence of historical and social forces on anyone engaged in public discourse.

Accordingly, throughout this book I refer to authors as if they really did intend and write the works I discuss. For almost a generation this was unfashionable ("fetishizing the author") because the production of a work of literature is a complex relationship among a person or persons, the culture from which they came and the society for which they wrote, the materiality and economics of producing a book, the unspoken inhibitions and longings that inform both the text and the reader, and a fluid indeterminacy in language itself. Milton provides a particularly complex case because he, more than any other writer before the Romantic period, insisted on the relation between author and work, and yet was actively buffeted by the storms of his own time.[21] Even so, in this book I do talk about writers as if they were real and intentional people, which seems reasonable in a book about freedom, even if it begs the question. I do not claim to understand fully their personalities or their intentions, but I do propose that their writings are interpretable, and that whatever conditions restrained what they were able to produce or inhibit what we are able to understand, enough remains of meaning on the one hand and interpretive possibility on the other to enlarge the picture of what it means to be human.

ONE

⚜

Early Modern Liberty
Tenure of Kings and Magistrates, English Cultural Self-Definition, and Divine Right

"There are, in all, three varieties of liberty without which civilized life is scarcely possible, namely ecclesiastical liberty, domestic or personal liberty, and civil liberty," Milton famously asserts in his second Latin *Defence of the English People*.[1] With these categories Milton in mid-career described the focus of his vocation as a pamphleteer and controversialist during and immediately after the English civil wars of the 1640s, the result of which, at the time, seemed to be an end to monarchy in England. In 1654, when the *Second Defense* was written to respond to European denunciations of regicide, Milton was serving in Cromwell's government as Secretary for Foreign Tongues, a position that made him the chief defender of the English republic to the rest of Europe. He had recently gone completely blind in service to the cause of liberty, he believed, but the tone in this and other controversialist writings from the late 1640s and early 1650s is optimistic and assured. Milton was not alone in pushing ideas of freedom and liberty and centering them in English cultural self-definition, but his words continue to resonate, in part because of their rhetorical force and intellectual power and (as a result) in part because of the continuing popularity of *Paradise Lost* and *Areopagitica.*

Milton's campaign on behalf of his vision of civilized life emerged from a rich political, theological, and linguistic history inherited from traditions of freedom and liberty that emerged from tensions in medieval and early modern England. In *Tenure of Kings and Magistrates* (1649), perhaps the clearest statement of his political views, Milton outlines a radical vision of civil governance as he pushes to justify the trial and execution of Charles I.[2] Far from receiving a divine right to power, "kings and magistrates" are entirely subject to the laws and covenants that "free persons" entrust them to execute on behalf of the common good. It is not the king or magistrate but the individual who has the divine sanction: "No man who knows ought, can be so stupid to deny that all men were borne free, being the image and resemblance of God himselfe, and were by privilege above all the creatures, borne to command and not to obey." Since the Fall, however, people have banded together for their own protection and established rulers by their consent, "not to be thir Lords and Maisters," but rather to be "thir Deputies and Commisioners, to execute, by vertue of thir intrusted power, that justice which else every man by the bond of nature and of Cov'nant must have executed for himself, and for one another." This is the only conceivable reason why, "among free Persons, one man by civil right should beare autority and jurisdiction over another." Laws under which the rulers must govern, and covenantal oaths to help prevent the rulers from their tendency toward "injustice and partialitie," allow these "free Persons" to "limit the autority of whom they choose to govern them." Further, groups of men, counselors and Parliaments, are able to act on behalf of the people as a whole, with or without the king, when danger threatens.[3]

Tenure was a work both polemical and personal. It was written during the trial of Charles I in January 1649 and probably was finished and published shortly after the king's execution on January 30, with a slightly enlarged edition published a year later.[4] It makes the general case for deposing and executing a tyrant, relying on classical, biblical, and Reformation sources for establishing natural rights that infer contractual governance, and for defining tyranny. In this sense it is not, or not merely, as some have argued, a treatise in support of neo-Roman republicanism, but rather, as Thomas Fulton notes, "first and foremost an argument about justice.... arrived at [not] by an appeal to the glorious days of Rome, but through a description of the natural condition of humanity and a comparative analysis of European constitutional history."[5] As a polemical treatise it seeks to do for the English people what Milton would later do for all of Europe (in his first Latin defense, *Pro populo anglicano defensio*, 1651): argue on behalf of the people's right to depose a lawless tyrant.

By personal, I mean that *Tenure* affirms the highly individualized vision of freedom that underlies Milton's political and religious thinking. The work begins by appealing first to individual reason in the face of external pressures of "Custom" and internal ones of "blind affections" and goes on to assert the Platonic theme that runs throughout his work, that individual virtue is the basis of all right governance: "If men within themselves would be govern'd by reason, and not generally give up thir understanding to a double tyrannie, of Custom from without, and blind affections within, they would discerne better, what it is to favour and uphold the Tyrant of a nation. But being slaves within doors, no wonder that they strive so much to have the state conformably govern'd to the inward vitious rule, by which they govern themselves. For indeed none can love freedom heartily, but good men; the rest love not freedom, but licence." "Licence"—that chaotic and unruly behavior based on personal whim rather than right order—Milton sees as a boon to tyrants, as "bad men" are all "naturally servile" (YP 3:190).

Useful summaries of the historical and intellectual background to Milton's mature political views as he expresses them in *Tenure* exist,[6] but I want to place his views in the context of what may be called the popular tradition of English freedom and contrast them, as Milton developed them, with the most pertinent of Milton's predecessors on the theory of kingship, James I. The chapter will conclude with a look at the Reformation problem of free will, exploring more fully Blair Worden's thesis that "Milton brought to politics the ideal of freedom that he had worked out in religion."[7] Milton's radical individualism, which underlies his idea of freedom and its rhetoric, may seem normal enough looking backward through the Romantic period, but its heterodoxy in its own time, while not isolated, evolves from an interesting tradition of English popular thought.

In fact, the bases of Milton's assertions, if not the extent to which he pushed them, had a long history in England.[8] The English people were proud to be free, not slaves to others or to the land they tilled. The English word "freedom," like the Greek *eleutheria* or the Latin *libertas*, had from ancient times defined the position of the citizen as opposed to the slave, and it is this status as citizens that the English understood themselves to hold generally, unlike their European counterparts.[9] English writers also proclaimed pride in a tradition of parliamentary government that placed all men under the rule of law.[10] One of Milton's sources for *Tenure* was Sir Thomas Smith, whose much-cited *De republica Anglorum* (1565), translated and printed posthumously as the *Commonwealth of England* (1583), discusses the relationship between prince and Parliament and suggests the fundamental value placed on a kind of representative democracy, however limited it may appear to a modern critic.[11] Smith, a scholar and Protestant clergyman trained at Queen's College, Cambridge, at the height of the "new learning," served Edward VI and Elizabeth I as secretary of state and also spent four years as Elizabeth's ambassador to France, where he wrote his Latin treatise on the English commonwealth.[12] In a letter to a friend, Smith cites homesickness as an impetus for writing, along with the desire to show how England's form of government "differs from the others."[13]

While careful to include the role of the monarch, Smith makes representative government the principal seat of power in England. "The most high and absolute power of the realme of England," Smith asserts, "consisteth in the Parliament," whose transactions involve all ranks of men including the monarch, so that prince, lords, and representatives "consult together," and every bill becomes the "whole realms deede." No one, therefore, may complain of parliamentary actions: "For everie Englishman is entended to bee there present, either in person or by procuration and attornies, of what preheminence, state, dignitie, or qualitie soever he be, from the Prince (be he King or Queene) to the lowest person of Englande, And the consent of the Parliament is taken to be everie mans consent."[14] The prince, according to Smith and common law tradition, has absolute power in foreign policy and in authorizing "mony" and coinage, but parliamentary law is absolute within the kingdom.

The question of what distinguishes true monarchy from tyranny and whether a Parliament or a people has the right to overthrow a tyrant was, of course, critical in the 1640s. Smith, writing almost 100 years earlier, hedges the second point as Milton would note in *Tenure*,[15] but follows Aristotle and others in defining a tyrant, as one who comes to power "by force...against the will of the people," abrogates laws already in place and makes new ones "against the will of the people," and rules not for the benefit of the people but to his own advantage and that of his party.[16] Sir Thomas More had served the Tudor dynasty by painting King Richard III as a type of tyrant, a portrait that Shakespeare would then borrow and imprint indelibly in his *Richard III*.[17] In his manuscript Commonplace Book, Milton would cite both Smith and Aristotle in his own notes on "the tyrant" and use *Richard III* to good effect in *Eikonoklastes*, his attack on Charles I's posthumously published (supposed) self-exculpation, *Eikon Basilike* (YP 1:454).[18]

Well before the events of the civil wars, then, Parliament and king might be seen in an uneasy balance. English common law can be traced back to before 1215, when disgruntled barons forced King John to sign the Magna Carta, a document that affirmed some basic rights for themselves along with the principle that not even the king is above the law.[19] The Model Parliament of 1295 established that body's ongoing form, which included representation from the nobility, clergy, and commons, with representatives settling by the mid-fourteenth century into the two houses of Parliament, Lords and Commons. A frequently translated Latin treatise from around 1465 by John Fortescue, England's lord chief justice and chancellor in exile, advised King Henry VI that laws "are made not onely by the Princes pleasure, but also by the assent of the whole royalme: so that of necessitye they must procure the wealth of the people, and in no wyse tende to their hynderaunce. And it cannot otherwise bee thought, but that they are replenished with much witte and wysdome, seeing they are ordained not by the devyse of one man alone, or of a hundred wise Councellers onelye, but of more than three hundred chosen menne."[20] The right of free speech in Parliament was apparently secure by the mid-fifteenth century, and the particular importance of the House of Commons had become well established by the time Smith wrote his treatise.[21] In the sixteenth century, issues of civic freedoms represented by Parliament and the common law became complicated further by the Reformation debate over free will.

Parliament's importance to English ideas of political freedom, including a rudimentary form of free expression, finds literary manifestation in *A Myrrour for Magistrates*, a collection of stories in verse. This enormously popular work was first published in 1559 (although there was a suppressed, earlier edition in 1555 during the reign of Queen Mary) and went through seven editions by 1587, most of them adding stories along the way.[22] The tales are explicitly in the tradition of Boccaccio's *Fall of Princes*, translated and popularized by John Lydgate around 1440, but drawn from English examples. Most are told in the voice of a ghost whose fall from high to low provides a cautionary tale. Their stated intention was to entice moral behavior by providing negative examples, but the appeal was surely the same as it is now: pleasure in watching other people's misery, especially the collapse of the mighty.

The *Myrrour's* first "tragedy," "The fall of Robert Tresilian chiefe Justice of Englande, and other his felowes, for miscontruying the lawes, and expounding them to serve the Princes affections," is of precisely that sort, but makes a case for Parliament at the same time. Tresilian, chief justice under Richard II, was tried for treason by Parliament and hanged in 1388. The author of the tragedy is probably George Ferrers, who worked early and closely with William Baldwin, the original compiler of the *Myrrour* and the person responsible for much of the prose dialogue that connects or introduces the stories. Ferrers had been a member of Parliament under Henry VIII, Edward VI, and Mary, and the disputatious times in which he lived (and survived) may contribute to his expression on behalf of English law.

The Tresilian story invokes English freedoms threatened by corrupt judges in the reign of Richard II and cheers the restoration of those freedoms in the form of a revived judicial system.[23] The point of the story, as the figure of William Baldwin says in introducing it, "is to warn all of his authorytie and profession, to take heed of wrong Judgementes, mysconstruyng of lawes, or wrestying the same to serve the princes turnes, which ryghtfullye brought theym to a miserable ende" (71).

Tresilian and his fellow judges are accused of taking bribes and perverting justice in individual cases, and, more generally, of ignoring the intent of the law in order to enact the capricious will of the king: "So wurkyng lawe lyke waxe, the subjecte was not sure / Of lyfe, lande, nor goods, but at the princes wyll" (85–86). This rule by what was called "policy," or the monarch's personal whim, rather than by law, was a sign of tyranny to the English, and in this story Parliament rises up to address it. Although theoretically only the king can call together a Parliament, the two houses ("Baronye" and "commons") agree to meet on their own:

> The Baronye of Englande not bearyng this abuse,
> Conspyring with the commons assembled by assent,
> And seynge neyther reason, nor treaty, could induce
> The king in any thing his Rygor to relent,
> Mawgree all his might they called a parlyment
> Francke and free for all men without checke to debate
> As well for weale publyke, as for the princes state. (99–05)

The product of this particular "free" debate is not a direct attack on the king but removal of the corrupt judges, with Tresilian "dampned to the gallowes most vyly as a thiefe" (119). The ghostly Tresilian warns his listeners to avoid temptation and stay firm in the law: "The favour of a prince is an untrusty staye, / But Justice hath a fee that shall remayne alwaye" (125–26). Justice is, notably, a function of the common law rightly enacted, and case law, including trials by juries of peers, is one of the principal areas in which Englishmen (though not yet women) of all classes maintained a sense of their personal participation in the commonweal.[24]

Milton directly evokes this understanding of English law. In *Tenure*, he uses the example of Richard II to support his position that kings are not above the law, and that Parliament has a right to take action, reflecting much of the sentiment in the Tresilian story: "our Ancestors who were not ignorant with what rights either Nature or ancient Constitution had endowd them, when Oaths both at Coronation, and renewd in Parliament would not serve, thought it no way illegal to depose and put to death thir tyrannous Kings. Insomuch that Parliament drew up a charge against *Richard the second,* and the Commons requested to have judgement decree'd against him, that the realme might not be endangerd" (YP 3:220–21).[25] As I will argue in more detail in the following chapters, the double negatives that shade this passage are typical of the invitational, rather than assertive, poetics characteristic of Milton's rhetoric of freedom, even as he places his views firmly into a particularly English tradition of the "ancient Constitution."

Although by the sixteenth century the English generally were considered free under the laws of England and through representation in Parliament and participation in the judicial system, some groups had very specific "liberties." Towns, guilds, and universities were granted rights to make choices on behalf of their own institutions, a situation under some threat with the Tudor centralization of power, particularly after the break with Rome in 1533. In one example, John Young, vice chancellor of Cambridge University (and later bishop of Rochester and Edmund Spenser's patron), responded to a threat from the centralized ecclesiastical commissioners who wanted to investigate the presence of papist books and opinions at Corpus Christi College. Writing to Elizabeth's chief minister, William Cecil, Young assures him that the university can handle the situation internally: "And we think that proceeding thus in these matters effectually that the college will thereby in all respects be brought into good order; and so we shall do what the high commissioners would have done, and we will save our university liberties from prejudice."[26]

In this case special liberties were in conflict with the new urgencies of the English Reformation. In theory, Reformation theology separated the spiritual and political realms.[27] In practice, a monarch or (as in Geneva) a theocracy might replace the religious authority of the pope. When Henry VIII's bishops proclaimed him head of the English church they may have simplified the governance of church and state but complicated issues of civil liberty. James Simpson argues that the Reform position on free will not only challenges the idea of individual agency but leads to more general restrictions on civil liberties. He describes a tendency from the time of Chaucer through the mid-sixteenth century to centralize and simplify both political and religious power, leaving the individual dependent on the "grace" or undeserved generosity of God or monarch. "The many sixteenth-century calls for absolute obedience to the royal will represented not only a practical political necessity but also the coherent result of an evangelical conception of divine grace, whose overwhelming force etiolates the Church to the profit of the State."[28] *The Myrrour for Magistrates* pushes back against centralized power and the arbitrary grace which, when the monarch uses it to trump the justice system, becomes that abhorred rule by policy instead of law. The popularity of the *Myrrour* and its initial Tresilian story suggests an English taste for free speech and righteous communal action.[29]

Nonetheless, Vice Chancellor Young recognized that he needed to crack down on what we might call intellectual freedom in order to preserve the prerogatives of the university, and under the early Stuarts Parliament would find itself caught among the various claims of religion, authority, and civil liberties. James I challenged limits on monarchal power in both theoretical statements and in the legal disputes where jurisprudence made common law. His conflicts with Parliament are well documented and stem at least in part from James's published assertions of royal authority coming up against the purported primacy of Parliament in the English tradition. In addition, the House of Commons was increasingly the voice of English Puritanism and the property interests of the mercantile class as well as of traditional gentry. If Parliament saw itself as primary or at least co-equal to the king in its law-giving power, James saw it as an agent of his own absolute authority, a vehicle for supporting the policies of divinely ordained monarchy.

While Milton's *Tenure* emerged from a complex tradition of political freedom and specific liberties, it also responded to theories of absolute monarchy, most pertinently expounded by James.[30] These theories help to clarify the complex relation between the rights of monarch and subject as they were generally understood and also to illustrate the arguments against which Milton and his reform-minded contemporaries sought to establish a new understanding of individual and political freedom.

James wrote two treatises on monarchy while still king of Scotland but with clear anticipation that he and his eldest son (at the time, the ill-fated Prince Henry) would inherit the throne of England. The first, *The Lawe of Free Monarchies; or, The Reciprock and mutuall dutie betwixt a free King, and his naturall Subjectes*, was published in Edinburgh in 1598 and in London after his ascension to the English throne in 1603.[31] James's "Advertisement to the Reader" cites the purpose of the work: "The profite I would wish you to make of it is, as wel so to frame all your actions according to these grounds, as may confirme you in the course of honest and obedient subjects to your King in all times coming, as also, when ye shall fall in purpose with anye that shall praise or excuse the by-past rebellions that brake forth either in this countrey [i.e., Scotland], or in any other, ye shall herewith be armed against their Sirene songs" (A3–A4). In the main text he argues that monarchy is the best form of government, "as resembling the Divinitie, [so it] approcheth nearest to perfection, as all the learned and wise men from the beginning have agreed upon" (A5); that it is ordained by the Christian God as his own regency on earth, since "Kings are called *Gods* by the propheticall King *David*, because they sit upon God his throne in the earth, and have the [ac]count of their administration to give unto him" (A7); that by "the law of Nature the King becomes a naturall Father to all his Lieges at his Coronation [and] as the Father, of his fatherly dutie, is bound to care for the nourishing, education, and virtuous government of his children, even so is the King bound to care for his subjects" (A8v); and "the other branch of this mutuall, and reciprock band, is the dutie and allegeance, that the lieges owe to their King" (B), which duty is absolute obedience.

The *Lawe of Free Monarchies* expresses an apparent contradiction at the heart of later confusions: on the one hand, the royal coronation oath requires the monarch "to maintain all the [al]lowable and good Lawes made by their predecessours, to see them put in execution, & the breakers, and violaters thereof, to bee punished, according to the tenour of the same: ... [and] to maintain the whole Countrey, and every state therein, in all their ancient priviledges and liberties, as well against all forraine enemies, as among themselves" (A7v–A8). This derives clearly enough from traditions established by the Magna Carta and seems at first to support the role of Parliament as a law-making body, with the people's "ancient priviledges and liberties" inherent to their condition as English subjects. On the other hand, as (James claims) the Old Testament model of kingship shows, "What shameless presumption is it to any Christian people now a dayes to claime to that unlawfull libertie, which God refused to his owne peculiar and chosen people" to challenge the rule of the king (C). In the English tradition, Parliament (theoretically including the king) makes the laws, so a coronation pledge to enforce them would seem to grant Parliament its co-equal role. But James insists, from Scottish precedent, that a new king must uphold valid laws because they were made, not by any legislative body, but by his kingly predecessors: "Kings were the authors and makers of the lawes, and not the lawes of the Kings" (C3). In fact, so far is Parliament from being the maker of laws, "general lawes, made publikely in Parliament, may upon knowne respects to the King by his authoritie be mitigated, and suspended on causes onely knowne to him" (C5v). Further, the "ancient priviledges and liberties" a subject may inherit, like the laws, are equally the gift of a monarch, since no subject may claim the "unlawfull libertie" to rebel against even the most tyrannical king.

In this view, there is no contradiction between the subject's liberties and the monarch's absolute power. Since that power is the foundation of civil order, the subject's right to act within the framework of an orderly community, safe from violence and foreign domination, is the first basis of liberty. Since order is the first rule of freedom under this configuration, the people must even endure a tyrant, as the alternative is inevitably disorder: "a king cannot be imagined to be so unruly and tyrannous, but the common-wealth will be kept in better order, notwithstanding therof, by him, than it can be by his way-taking" (D2). In a phrase that begins with an observation similar to one Milton would later make in *Paradise Lost*, James sees a tyrant as a scourge of God: "I graunt in deed, that a wicked king is sent by God for a curse to his people, & a plague for their sinnes. But that it is lawful for them to shake off that curse at their owne hand, which God hath laid on them, that I deny, and may do so justly" (D3).[32] In a well-known passage in book 12, Milton's Archangel Michael tells an Adam horrified by Nimrod, the first tyrant, that Adam's own original sin has paved the way for tyranny:

> since [man] permits
> Within himself unworthy Powers to reign
> Over free Reason, God in Judgement just
> Subjects him from without to violent Lords;
> Who oft as undeservedly enthrall
> His outward freedom: Tyrannie must be,
> Though to the Tyrant thereby no excuse.   (12.90–96)

Milton meant no divine right of monarchs to lie behind this reasoning. Adam is "fatherly displeas'd" at the vision Michael gives him of Nimrod, the son who is "execrable" in taking authority on himself, "from God not giv'n." God gave humans equal authority over the lower animals, "but Man over men / He made not Lord; such title to himself / Reserving, human left from human free" (12.64–71). James would not agree. Even though the *Lawe of Free Monarchies* emphasizes the monarch's duties more than the subjects', the latter's primary responsibility is total obedience to the "head" of which they are the body politic (C7v), a traditional metaphor that also anticipates Hobbes's *Leviathan*.[33]

Much of Milton's *Tenure* responds to the arguments found in the *Lawe of Free Monarchies*, although his only references to James in that work surround praise of the Scots nation for deposing James's mother, Mary, and so declaring themselves a "free Nation, made King whom they freely chose, and with the same freedom unkingd him if they saw cause, by right of ancient laws and Ceremonies yet remaining." The only mention of James by name cites the warning in 1586 by Scots Puritan James Gibson to then James VI that "he should be rooted out, and conclude his race, if he persisted to uphold Bishops." Milton goes on to suggest that the stamp on the coin at James's Scots coronation, "*Si Mereor in me, Against me, if I deserve*, not only manifested the judgement of the State, but seem'd also to presage the sentence of Divine Justice in this event upon his son" (YP 3:225–26).[34] In the core of his argument, though, Milton might well be responding to James. "To say Kings are accountable to none but God," he asserts, in direct contradiction of James's view of laws and covenants, "is the overturning of all Law and government. For if they may refuse to give account, then all cov'nants made with them at Coronation; all Oathes are in vaine, and meer mockeries, all Lawes which they swear to keep, made of no purpose; for if the King feare not God, as how many of them doe not? We hold then our lives and estates, by the tenure of his meer grace and mercy, as from a God, not a mortal Magistrate" (YP 3:204).

Milton utterly rejects James's argument that a monarch's divine sanction is shown by God's interaction with biblical kings. Scripture shows that the people desired a king, Milton says, and "though their changing [from other governance] displeas'd him, yet [God] that was himself thir King, and rejected by them, would not be a hindrance to what they intended" (YP 3:207). This is not an example of the divine right of kingship, but of God's gift of free will and his support for his people even when they err. While James sees even bad rule as better than rebellion, citing a chaos that inevitably ensues, Milton is intent on defining the tyrant and endorsing tyrannicide. The right of inheritance is no safety, since a tyrant "whether by wrong or right comming to the Crown, is he who regarding neither Law nor the common good, reigns onely for himself and his faction" (YP 3:212).[35] Milton supports the right of the people to make and retract decisions about governance, and God's power resides not in the monarch, but in the individuals who come together to dictate their own form of governance. For Milton, those who break the laws or their covenantal oaths, as he and his colleagues in the commonwealth government were firmly persuaded King Charles had done, are subject to judgment.

Basilikon Doron, James's treatise to his eldest son, Henry, follows and extends the earlier treatise in emphasizing the responsibilities of the monarch.[36] In the long humanist tradition of treatises on the education of princes, James would have his son educated in virtue in order to make him fit to rule, beginning with rule over himself.[37] The lessons of prudence and care for his subjects that James conveys (along with his absolutist assumptions) appeared to have taken some hold. Henry was a very popular prince, and by the time he developed his own court (as Queen Anne had hers), there are indications that he had somewhat more liberal views than his father. He was a patron of Sir Walter Ralegh's *History of the World*, a work published two years after Henry's death with a lament for his passing. (James I tried unsuccessfully to suppress the work.)³⁸ Ralegh, a meritocrat with republican leanings, became a favorite with parliamentarians after his execution in 1618, and when Milton chose to put together some admonitions from various sources that may have been intended as a warning to Cromwell, he attributed the work to Ralegh.³⁹

James's theories of absolute monarchy were well known and seldom directly challenged. When they were, there was usually trouble for the challenger. One result of his assertion of absolute royal prerogative in his dealings with the law courts was conflict with England's leading jurist, Sir Edward Coke, whose downfall in 1616 was engineered by the machinations of ambitious courtiers (including Sir Francis Bacon).⁴⁰ In that same year the king published the last of his treatises on monarchy, his *Remonstrance... for the right of kings, and the independance of their crownes* (1616), in which he argues again for the divine right of kings, "the Soveraigne Magistrate ordained by nature, and confirmed by succession," to rule independent of other authority.⁴¹ It is in some ways the most interesting of the treatises, touching as it does on the freedom and independence of nations.

At first glance the *Remonstrance* seems an extension of James's earlier claims, and another challenge to the English parliamentary tradition inherited from Fortescue and Smith, but the issue is more complex. The explicit challenge in this work is not to parliamentary but to papal authority. James's treatise is in response to a French cardinal's assertion of papal power over monarchies, a sensitive issue for Protestant monarchs in general and James in particular; in 1570 Pope Pius V had released the English from loyalty to Queen Elizabeth in favor of James's Catholic mother, Mary, Queen of Scots, a complicated history for Protestant James, Elizabeth's designated heir. More immediately and directly, James's treatise responds to the assassination in 1610 of the popular Henry IV (the former Huguenot, Henry of Navarre) and to a conviction that James himself faced "dangers" from "conspiracies flowing from the same source" (Ar).

James's preface announces his work as a reply to a speech by the French Cardinal Jacques du Perron, supporting the Catholic disciplines of the Council of Trent. James claims that the cardinal's speech prevented the French Third Estate (essentially the French House of Commons) from passing an article that would have liberated the French monarchy from papal authority. In this context James does not dismiss parliamentary power; in fact, it is the power of the Third Estate[42] that he invokes in his treatise. James says that an action before them had given him hope that "the people would be unwitched of this pernicious opinion: that Popes may tosse the French King his Throne like a tennis ball, and that killing of Kings is an act meritorious to the purchase of the crowne of Martyrdome." After Perron's speech in the Estates General, however, this "Article of the third Estate" did not rid France of papal authority over monarchy, but rather "like a sigh of libertie breathing her last, served only so much the more to enthrall the Crowne, and to make the bondage more grievous and sensible than before" (A2r).

In denying papal authority over monarchy, James asserts his right to be the designated and legal heir of a legitimate prince, his cousin Elizabeth, a well-established but still volatile claim in a Europe split between Catholic and Protestant countries.[43] At the same time, he invokes both his right as the absolute lawgiver within his own realm and the "freedom" of monarchs from any foreign interference. For himself, "it hath more congruitie with Royall dignity, whereof God hath given me the honour, to prescribe Lawes at home for my Subjects, rather then to furnish forraine Kingdoms and peoples with counsels" (Ar). Yet he does just that, in admonishing the Estates General of France not to give in to a theory of papal eminence over monarchy, "as a defendant of honour, [insisting] that my brother-Princes and my selfe, whom God hath advanced upon the Throne of Soveraigne Majesty and supreame dignity, doe hold the Royall dignity of his Majesty [God] alone" (Pp4r).

The *Remonstrance* is a good example of James's view of the supremacy of kings as God's regents on earth, yet it is based on the king's recognized legal responsibility (as in Smith) to keep the kingdom independent from foreign influence and safe from foreign powers. Through the *Remonstrance* James also declares his own and his country's Protestantism, a popular stance with Parliament's varied and restive reformers. As a result, James's portrait of his absolute prerogatives is larded with terms like "free" and "liberty." Further, as he had asserted in *Lawe of Free Monarchies*, and admonished Henry in *Basilikon Doron*, it is the monarch's duty to protect the liberties of his subjects. Despite the language of absolutism and his run-ins with both Parliament and the English courts, the modern estimate is that James was a reasonably good politician who knew how the system was supposed to work.

Milton would certainly have approved James's stance on behalf of Protestantism and independence from the pope, and it is useful to remember that when he was 17 he wrote 226 lines of Latin verse celebrating the deliverance of "pious James" from the Gunpowder Plot.[44] At the same time, Milton would argue that a native tyrant is no better than a foreign one. If, as Milton and his colleagues believed of Charles, a prince breaks "all the Covnants and Oaths that gave him title to his dignity, and were the bond and alliance between him and his people, what differs he from an outlandish King, or from an enemy? For look how much right the King of *Spaine* hath to govern us at all, so much right hath the King of *England* to govern us tyrannically" (YP 3:213–14).

Most consider it a tragedy that Prince Henry died suddenly in 1612, and the title of Prince of Wales fell to James's second son, Charles. When James died in 1625, the year that Milton matriculated at Cambridge, Charles was not the son who had been trained from birth to be king. Historians tend to agree that the shift from the dogmatic but pragmatic James to the dogmatic but less compromising Charles was an unhappy one for Britain.[45] There was certainly substantial dissatisfaction, apparent in the upheavals of the 1640s, with what were perceived as the monarch's trampling on English freedoms.[46]

Milton's claims in *Tenure*, then, have a background in an English cultural self-definition much complicated not only by the inevitable tensions among differing views of civil power, but by the cross-currents of the Reformation throughout Europe and most specifically in England and Scotland. One central complication impinges dramatically on Milton's other two forms of liberty, "ecclesiastical, and domestic or personal": the question of free will. *Tenure* is one of many places in which Milton's view of free will emerges. The quick summary is that Milton believes strongly that even fallen humankind can and must make choices, and *Paradise Lost* is the most vivid evidence of free will's importance to his vision of human nature and divine providence. But a more difficult question is whether, after the Fall, a person's apparent ability to make choices indicates an ability to choose one's own salvation.[47]

Early Reformation leaders, including Luther and Calvin, were adamant that the fallen condition made salvific free will impossible. The core argument goes something like this: if Adam and Eve chose to disobey God and so separate humankind from the source of all freedom, and if humankind is now entirely dependent on God's grace for any hope of redemption, how can we have free will? Some biblical passages seem to say that all are predestined to heaven or hell, and the basis of this predestination is unknowable, as is the outcome in any particular case: "No one can come to me unless the Father who sent me draws him" (John 6:44).[48] Other passages seem to say that human beings have choices and must make the right choices in order to achieve salvation: "Blessed is the man who endures trial, for when he has stood the test he will receive the crown of life which God has promised to those who love him" (James 1:12).[49]

The contest was set out in the 1520s in a series of pamphlets between Desiderius Erasmus, church critic but loyalist, and Martin Luther. Luther argued that the Fall rendered humankind helpless to choose salvation, and therefore utterly without agency where it matters. Luther calls reason "human folly," and claims that "Christians are not led by free will but driven by the Spirit of God." The passivity of the human will is absolute, as "to be driven is not to act or do oneself. But we are so seized as a saw or an axe is handled by a carpenter."[50] Erasmus set the stage for the Counter-Reformation Catholics (and, later, some Protestants, such as the Dutchman Jacobus Arminius), arguing from multiple biblical texts that God had left the light of reason in humankind and that human beings were therefore empowered to choose toward or away from God's grace. "Now, if man could do nothing [i.e., have no power of free will], there would be no room for merit and guilt; consequently also none for punishment and reward. If on the other hand man were to do all, there would be no room for grace....Man is able to accomplish all things, if God's grace aids him. Therefore it is possible that all works of man [can] be good."[51]

For reformers such as Luther and Calvin, the Fall produced a humanity so depraved that it is incapable of doing anything to ameliorate its condition. There was no way to earn salvation, nor any way to be worse than we already are. It was a great relief that God in his unfathomable mercy saved even a portion of an otherwise hopeless humankind. This did not, of course, mean that the faithful Lutheran or Calvinist could (or would) behave wickedly or irresponsibly, as the Catholics accused. On the contrary, the gift from God of faith and salvation would inevitably display itself appropriately, offering a "Christian liberty," or freedom from the strict provisions of

Old Testament law, that was the opposite of licentiousness.[52] Good works are the fruit of faith, and they are performed in the light of a freedom bestowed by grace. Even so, according to Calvin and other early reformers, not good works but rather one's direct relationship to God signals salvation: "there are twoo thinges wherat wee must chiefly ame, and whereuntoo it behoveth us too apply all our wittes and indevers, and they bee the very summe of all the thinges which God teacheth us by the holy scripture. The one is the magnifying of God as he deserveth, and the other is the assurednesse of our salvation, that wee may call uppon him as our father with full libertie. If wee have not these twoo thinges, wo woorth us, for there is nother fayth nor religion in us."[53] To be free to call upon God "with full libertie" does not mean that one has free will to choose salvation of one's self, but rather that Christian liberty is God's gift to the faithful whom he has called. Calvin's catechism insists that "all such works as we do of ourselves, by our nature are utterly corrupt, whereof it followeth necessarily that they cannot please God, but rather procure his wrath, and he condemneth them every one." Not works, but "faith only," itself a gift from God, is acceptable to God.[54]

The Catholic response favored the biblical passages that required people to participate in their own salvations, and that made good works a continuing imperative. Some of the more questionable good works, including those in response to extortionist practices of the church or its representatives, fueled the Reformation in the first place. Counter-Reformation Catholics were willing to concede the excesses but not the principle. God requires individuals to accept God's offered grace and so choose and participate in their own salvations. Cardinal Robert Bellarmine's Counter-Reformation catechism, in contrast to Calvin's, insists that "Christ has satisfied for the sins of all men, but it is necessary to apply this satisfaction in particular to this man and to that man, which is done by faith, by the sacraments, by good works."[55]

The English Reform Protestant tradition from which Milton emerged sought to make a clear distinction between Protestant and Catholic thought on freedom of the will. William Perkins (1558–1602), whose work Milton admired, does it more colorfully than most:

> The Church of Rome sets forth the estate of a sinner by the condition of a prisoner, and so doe we: marke then the difference. It supposeth the said prisoner to lie bound hand and foote with chaines and fetters, and withall to bee sicke and weake, yet not wholly dead but living in part: it supposeth also that being in this case, he stirreth not himself for any helpe, and yet hath abilitie and power to stirre. Hereupon if the keeper come and take away his bolts and fetters, and hold him by the hand, and helpe him up, hee can and will of himselfe stand and walke and goe out of prison.... We in like manner graunt, that a prisoner fitly resemb[l]eth a naturall man, but yet such a prisoner must he bee, as is not only sicke and weake, but even stark dead: which cannot stir though the keeper untie his boltes and chanes, nor heare though hee found a trumpet in his eare: and if the said keeper would have him to moove and stirre, he must give him not onely his hand to helpe him, but even soule and life also.[56]

Despite this total rejection of salvific free will, Perkins (like Calvin before him) recognizes that a semblance of free will, though it may be diminished, remains in the ordinary course of a person's daily life. "In the will, the remnant of Gods image is a free choice. First, in every naturall action, belonging to each living creature, as to nourish, to engender, to moove, to perceive. Secondly, in every humane action, that is, such as belong to all men; and therefore man hath freewil in outward actions, whether they concerne manners, a family, or the commonwealth, albeit both in the choice and refusall of them it bee very weake."[57]

Whatever the debates about human depravity after the Fall, the imprisoned will, predestination, and the role of grace, there remains in England, even in the Reform tradition, the assumption that a man can act freely in the political realm, and that the commonwealth allows and requires him to do so. Even if what we might call personal freedom remained problematic in Reformation England, and even if the centralization of the court tended to overshadow some of the traditional medieval liberties of cities, towns, guilds, or other institutions, English cultural self-definition nonetheless included a vision of political freedom. From Milton's earliest pamphlets, and dramatically by 1644 in *Areopagitica*, it is easy to see that he inherits the English self-conceit of political freedom and interprets it broadly. How early he came to believe in a fundamental and even salvific free will is not clear, but his propensity to Arminianism appears to expand over the course of his career as a controversialist.[58]

One can see the process, not inconsequentially, in connection with Milton's view of biblical interpretation. In the early antiprelatical pamphlets Milton establishes his lifelong principle that the Bible alone offers divine authority, and goes further to assert the Bible's clarity, as in *Of Reformation* (1641):

> To inferre a generall obscurity over the text [of Scripture], is a meer suggestion of the Devil to disswade men from reading it, and casts an aspersion of dishonour both upon the mercy, truth, and wisedome of God.... The very essence of Truth is plainnesse, and brightnes; the darknes and crookednesse is our own. The *Wisdome* of *God* created *understanding*, fit and proportionable to Truth the object, and end of it, as the eye to the thing visible. If our *understanding* have a film of *ignorance* over it, or be blear with gazing on other false glisterings, what is that to Truth? (YP 1:566)

This puts the problem of biblical obscurity squarely on the shoulders of the fallen reader. The controversy over his divorce tracts in 1644, on the contrary, forced him to consider the need for interpretive decisions in biblical reading, which would argue that human choice necessarily contributes to the salvific process. I will have more to say on this in chapter 3. In any case, by about 1660, when he had mostly completed his *De doctrina Christiana*, Milton's position was firmly Arminian. As Maurice Kelley describes it: "Arminianism...rejects both the autonomous man of Pelagius, independently working out his own salvation, and the arbitrary God of Augustine, Calvin, and Beza, unconditionally impelling man to an end predestined from eternity. For these it substitutes a synergism wherein the human will cooperates with divine grace to attain an earned rather than a bestowed election to eternal life" (YP 6:80).

By the time Milton published his last pamphlet on issues of individual freedom and conscience, *Of True Religion* (1673), he was confirming a long-held view that religious freedom and pluralism are essential to God's call to the free conscience. He supports all (except, as always, Catholic) Christian controversialists, including some toward whom he clearly leaned. Along with the Arminians, these included Arians and Socinians, who challenged Trinitarian doctrine in ways evident in Milton's own thinking in *De doctrina* and (most modern critics would agree) *Paradise Lost*. While not claiming for himself any sectarian affiliation, Milton insists on toleration toward these and other schismatics, such as Anabaptists and Quakers. In *True Religion* Milton argues that many different groups do not, as the papists claim, constitute heresies, so long as there is a Bible-focused, thoughtful effort to act in accordance with conscience:

> All of these [Protestant groups] have some errors, but are no Hereticks. Heresie is in the Will and choice profestly against Scripture; error is against the Will, in misunderstanding the Scripture after all sincere endeavours to understand it rightly.... It is a humane frailty to err, and no man is infallible here on earth. But so long as all these profess to set the Word of God only before them as the Rule of faith and obedience; and use all diligence and sincerity of heart, by reading, by learning, by study, by prayer for Illumination of the holy Spirit, to understand the Rule and obey it, they have done what man

> can do: God will assuredly pardon them, as he did the friends of *Job*, good and pious men, though much mistaken, as there it appears, in some Points of Doctrin. (YP 8:423–24)

Here Milton tacitly acknowledges the difficulty and individuality of biblical interpretation, a far remove from his earlier claim that "the very essence of [scriptural] truth is plainnesse and brightness."

If one is able to make a choice "profestly against Scripture," one has the will and agency to choose otherwise, and therefore to choose toward one's own salvation. It is still possible to make errors against one's will, despite reading the Bible and praying; that is the human condition after the Fall. Milton's increasing emphasis on the inviolability of the individual conscience put him out of the mainstream of Reform theology and toward the beginning of a new tradition that would shift the idea of liberty from the polity to the individual, increasingly centering notions of freedom on the individual rather than on institutions.

An early framework for the primacy of the individual comes from Milton's insistence on the separation of church and state, from the antiprelatical tracts of the early 1640s through the last pamphlets of the 1650s, such as *Likeliest Means to Remove Hirelings*. Even in the *Second Defence*, where Milton makes his case to Europe for the freedom of a people to oppose a tyrant, he includes an aside on the separation of church and state: "Men at first united into Civil Societies, that they might live safely and enjoy their Liberty, without being wrong'd or opprest; that they might live Religiously, and according to the Doctrine of Christianity, they united themselves unto Churches. Civil Societies have Laws, and Churches have a Discipline, peculiar to themselves and differing from each other. And this has been the occasion of so many Wars in *Christendom*; to wit, because the Civil Magistrate and the Church confounded their Jurisdictions."[59] This distinction between civil and religious jurisdictions was as important to Milton as it was in different ways to Thomas Hobbes and John Locke. A common insistence on the inability of religion to prescribe individual beliefs forms one of the contexts out of which a theory of individual rights emerged in English political philosophy.

In general, and like other Protestants, Milton abhorred "custom and superstition" as replacements for careful reading of Scripture and contemplative thought. But Milton's vision of freedom was of an ongoing process of provisional thinking, the thinking self always making choices—in the light of Scripture, of course, but also from what God reveals through conscience about one's experience in the world. For this process, Milton relied on the power of language to reveal as well as persuade. There is for Milton, then, another kind of freedom, beyond his triad of civil, ecclesiastical, and domestic, that enables and enacts the others: freedom of expression. This last may depend on the others for viability, but it is central to poets and writers.[60] A desire for personal freedom, often in the face of perceived social or political limits, often motivates expression, and free expression almost inevitably has a public dimension. The feminist mantra of the 1970s, "the personal is political," is another way of saying that individual expression has political consequences. Professional writers may have other motivators, such as fame or financial reward, but most literary vocations, certainly including Milton's, include some version of what George Orwell called "political purpose."[61] In the early modern period there are very few safe avenues for free expression outside the confines of Parliament and a few other venues, such as the universities and the law courts (and those only up to a point), except perhaps in poetry and fiction.[62]

Two

⋈

The Poetics of Freedom
"The Poet Collingbourne" and Sidney on Politics and Poetics

Milton was born during one of the richest eras of experimentation with the English language, producing among other things a greatly expanded vocabulary. According to Norman Blake, "although many words were being borrowed from 1400 onwards, the period of greatest borrowing was between 1530 and 1660, with the peak in the decades on either side of 1600. This period is thus unique in the history of the language."[1] In addition, the new learning's focus on classical texts and rhetoric gave special attention to figurative language, itself a way to extend and elaborate meaning and of particular interest to poets. This chapter will seek to connect poetic language with the aspiration toward modes of freedom by looking at how poetic freedom and its limits were understood by some of Milton's Tudor predecessors. Most important to this investigation is that first great English literary critic, Sir Philip Sidney, whose work shows some parallels with how Milton portrayed poetic freedom in his early polemics. The central argument of this chapter is that sixteenth century English literary culture, both popular and courtly, illustrates tensions among free expression, interpretive license, and hegemonic authority, out of which Milton would build his more radical invitational poetic.

All poetry has a radical undercurrent, linguistically if not politically. Poets depend on language that challenges normal usage, takes risks, and departs from expectations that the poets themselves may have created. Effective poets are therefore often agents of change, beginning with how they handle language and extending to how they present the world. Metaphors, as one cognitive linguist observes, "operate as mediators between the human mind and culture. New metaphors change both the ordinary language we use and the ways in which we perceive and understand the world."[2] Poetic language has thus long been understood as a vehicle for pushing against social and political limits, as well as against the limits of language itself.[3]

This last point was clear from earliest times, as Brian Cummings reminds us.[4] When Erasmus in the first book of *De copia* (1512) defines metaphor as *translatio*, he is harkening back to Quintillian, for whom metaphor serves as a way to borrow from a "proper" place a word that will help express or extend a concept that has insufficient "proper" vocabulary. Similarly, Winifred Nowottny argues that devices of comparison—metaphor in its broadest sense—extend a poet's vocabulary through a process of analogy, *"speaking of X as though it were Y"* (emphasis hers), but to be effective "there has to be a similarity between two things sufficient to hold them together and a disparity between them sufficient to make their comparison exciting."[5] Metaphor, then, has a middle space, a Z that makes the translation possible, and this is the space in which individual interpretation takes place. As Cummings explains, the figure known as metalepsis represents this "intermediate step" in the *translatio* of metaphor: "The figure does not signify in itself, but [according to Quintillian] it 'provides the transition.' For a moment, we have come face to face with the deepest mystery in metaphor altogether: the hinge between the term transferred and 'the thing to which it is transferred,' or that between word and thing."[6] The metaphoric process brings *res* and *verba* together in new ways, and at the same time opens up space for new ideas to emerge. Richard Lanham comments on the twentieth century interest in the idea of metaphor: "perhaps it is metaphor's intrinsic *instability* which has attracted so much recent attention: to appreciate the metaphoricality of a metaphor we must posit a nonmetaphysical, normative 'reality' against which to project the metaphorical transformation. The oscillation of the two reality states, normative and transformative, provides the essential bounded instability of a bistable illusion."[7] On a larger scale, Philip Sidney's "nature" and "second nature," which I discuss later in this chapter, possess exactly this sort of interactive relationship.

Metaphor broadly considered, then, has two important characteristics for a poetics of freedom: it challenges the normative and it opens up interpretive possibilities. I have said that Milton has a metaphoric cast of mind; this allows him to make an array of connections between *res* and *verba* that in turn extend his capacity for describing a rich imaginative vision. In the passage from *Areopagitica* (YP 2:553–54) cited in the introduction, authors' "pens and hands" are like the "anvils and hammers" fashioning armor to defend "beleaguer'd Truth"; Milton is able to elevate his ideas (here, on behalf of a free press) from a normative focus (heresy needing censorship) to a wider vision ("wise and faithfull labourers, to make a knowing people, a Nation of Prophets, of Sages, and of Worthies"). Against cultural conformity he sets the image of a heroic nation leading the "approaching Reformation." Even as they alter their environment, figures of speech in general and metaphoric language in particular lean toward the invitational, as the reader or listener enters the metaleptic space where he finds the Z that will connect the metaphoric vehicle with its tenor. It also leans toward the subversive, as the writer aspires toward what cannot or should not be said in plain speech. In what ways are pens and hands like hammers and anvils, or the activity of the studious like a defensive war? But also, why are multiple efforts (like multiple forms of armor, perhaps) better than a single enforced orthodoxy?

Victoria Kahn suggests that Milton's metaphorical habit of mind comes from reading Scripture.[8] As I will argue in chapter 3, when Milton confronts biblical texts in the effort to make his case in favor of divorce, he comes to understand the crucial role of interpretation in a rhetoric that moves a reader toward greater personal freedom. But he also inherited a culture that tended to combine notions of freedom with the virtues of eloquence, recognizing the potential for indirect speech to say what in plain language would be dangerous.

As I illustrated in the previous chapter, Milton's Tudor predecessors had an idea of freedom and a sense of how it particularized English society. The English people saw themselves free of the villeinage or serfdom that still plagued Europe, and they took pride in their systems of government. These included a (more or less) representative parliament but also the jury system and other vehicles, such as town councils, through which they might participate in the public order. Free expression, however, was another matter. The Tresilian story shows how parliamentary free speech was viewed, in theory, as inviolate, although members of Parliament along with everyone else were held accountable for their published views if they were deemed seditious or libelous, and until the dominance of Parliament during the mid-seventeenth century there remained tension between monarch and Parliament over what topics could be freely discussed in that body.[9] Speaking or writing one's mind could be dangerous. In one famous Tudor era example, Protestant John Stubbs had his hand chopped off for a 1579 pamphlet against the possibility of the queen's marriage to the French Catholic Duc D'Alençon.[10] Even so, poets in the sixteenth century saw themselves in a special role, as Renaissance humanist education elevated literary study along with the humanities more generally.[11]

George Puttenham in *The Arte of English Poesie* (1589) summarizes the Elizabethan exaltation of language, rhetoric, and poetry, following classical models in making it the first civilizer of humankind. Poetry defines and organizes human experience, persuading people toward civil society: "for speech it selfe is artificiall and made by man, and the more pleasing it is, the more it prevaileth to such purpose as it is intended for: but speech by meter is a kind of utterance, more cleanly couched and more delicate to the eare then prose is, because it is more currant and slipper upon the tongue, and withal tunable and melodious, as a kind of Musicke, and therefore may be tearmed a musicall speech or utterance, which cannot but please the hearer very well."[12] At the same time, Puttenham recognizes the transgressive quality of poetic language: "as figures be the instruments of ornament in every language, so be they also in a sorte abuses or rather trespasses in speech, because they passe the ordinary limits of common utterance....what els is your *Metaphor* but an inversion of sence by transport; your allegorie by a duplicities of meaning or dissumlation under covert and darke intendments."[13] Throughout his book, as he celebrates poets and poetry, Puttenham seems particularly to enjoy ways in which poetic language challenges expectations and changes words from their usual meanings. "Figures sensible," for example, "by alteration of intendments affect the courage and geve a good liking to the conceit." So a figure of "*transport*....is a kind of wresting of a single word from his owne right signification, to another not so naturall, but yet of some affinitie or conveniencie with it, as to say *I cannot digest your unkinde words*, for I cannot take them in good part."¹⁴ With the apparent delight Puttenham and others take in the "wresting" of language, it is unsurprising that the queen's most trusted peer, William Cecil, Lord Burghley, was famously suspicious of poets, which did not keep Puttenham from dedicating this work to him.

Burghley distrusted even the queen's most famous blazoner, Edmund Spenser. The tension between peer and poet appears in some of Spenser's satiric writings, which may have been meant to attack Burghley. In turn, Burghley probably held up payment on some patronage Elizabeth awarded Spenser for *The Faerie Queene*. In any case, the poet blamed court "wicked tongues" for bringing his work "into a mighty Peres displeasure," and there is little doubt about the identity of the "mighty Pere."¹⁵ From this relationship, and no doubt others, Spenser understood the value of indirect speech. In the letter to Sir Walter Ralegh appended to *The Faerie Queene* Spenser describes his work as, first of all, "a continued Allegory, or darke conceit [which the poet has] thought good...for avoiding of gealous opinions and misconstructions" (407). This understanding, that poetry thrives best when it uses conventions of disguise, is not new in early modern England, nor is the impulse to negotiate court disapproval in order to speak freely.¹⁶ *The Myrrour for Magistrates* again offers a useful early Elizabethan example.

The Myrrour's one "tragedy" about a poet, "Howe Collingbourne was cruelly executed for making a foolishe rime" (*Myrrour*, 346–58), claims free expression as an ancient privilege of poets. In the prose introduction to this story, one of the discussants dismisses an objection to a preceding story of the Duke of Buckingham by noting that "it is a Poesie and no divinitye, and it is lawfull for poetes to fayne what they lyst, so it be appertinent to the matter." To this the figure of William Baldwin replies, "in deede my thynke it should bee so, and ought to be well taken of the hearers: but it hath not at all times been so allowed." The illustration Baldwin offers is of "The Poet Collingbourne," presented as the ghostly voice of a rhymer who penned a riddle that enraged Richard III: "The Cat, the Rat, and Lovel our Dog, / Do rule al England, under a Hog" (*Myrrour*, 69–70).

The doggerel rime attributed to Collingbourne, and the relative lowliness of the poet compared with the aristocratic norm of the *Myrror*'s other ghostly protagonists, at first suggests comic relief. Baldwin sets up the story by inviting his listeners to imagine his ghostly speaker as a parody of the courtier poet: "you must ymagin that you se him a mervaylous wel favoured man, holdinge in his hand, his owne hart, newely ripped out of his brest, and smoking forth the lively spirit" (*Myrrour*, 346). Nonetheless, this ghost's arguments serve to illustrate the premise of Baldwin's preface, that it is "lawfull" for poets to have particular liberties, just as guilds and universities do. How far those liberties extend is a matter, quite literally, of interpretation, and in Collingbourne's case there may have been too little feigning rather than too much. The central question the poem addresses, and not always indirectly, is how free is poetic expression and what are the conditions that liberate it?

Collingbourne acknowledges that his rime *was* a criticism of Catesby, Ratcliffe, Lovel, and King Richard III, but he justifies himself by invoking intention and tradition: he meant to show off his wit in the cause of warning those at fault, he explains, and poets, in the tradition of Horatian satire, have a special right to exercise their wit freely as an honest form of criticism and warning:

> Theyr lawles dealynges al men dyd lament,
> And so dyd I, and therfore made the rymes
> To shewe my wyt, howe well I could invent,
> To warne withal the careles of theyr crymes,
> I thought the freedome of the auncient tymes
> Stoode styll in force....
> Belyke no tyrantes were in Horace dayes,
> And therefore Poetes freely blamed vyce.
>
> ("Collingbourne," 92–100)

The ironic last two lines exemplify a poetic indirection that could lead to trouble. The speaker implies that poets could freely blame vice in Horace's time because there were no tyrants; if they can't freely blame vice now, then we must live in tyrannous times. The Poet Collingbourne insists that he names "no man outright / But ryddle wise" (104–05) and therefore his utterance cannot be taken as treasonous speech. Even if it is potentially treasonous to charge those in power directly with their tyrannies, the cloak of riddle, indirect speech, and metaphorical discourse grant special permission. He uses riddle and metaphor both to hide from the charge of directly criticizing those in power and as a traditionally recognized vehicle for precisely such criticism. In a metaphor that links the rights of poets with the rights of those who speak freely in a court of law (like Parliament, a protected venue), Collingbourne's ghost portrays poets as lawyers pleading the law against the arbitrary tyrannies of rule by the monarch's fickle will:

> I thought the Poetes auncient liberties
> Had bene allowed plea at any barre.
> I had forgot howe newfound tyrannies
> Wyth ryght and freedome were at open warre,
> That lust was lawe, that myght dyd make and mar.
> ("Collingbourne," 197–201)

The wise and learned, he goes on to insist, can tell the difference between genuine argument, whether at law or in poetry, and can dismiss the inept or outrageous for the nonsense it is. Presumably the Elizabethan reader is meant to affirm Baldwin and his colleagues safe under the legitimate Tudors in a way that Collingbourne could not have been under a tyrannous Plantagenet. This appeal to patriotic and presentist assumptions, that we may expect freedom in England in current times as opposed to in other countries and more wicked times, will also be the germ of Milton's argument for a free press in *Areopagitica,* where he assumes his parliamentary audience to have destroyed the tyrannies of a previous regime and contrasts free England with fettered Rome.

Collingbourne concludes by telling how he was viciously executed with great pain and indignity. He complains that the suffering he endured was excessive "for this trespas smal" (130) and that condemning a writer's words without examining his intention is unfair. The "auncient freedome" of free exchange of ideas

> ought not be debarred
> From any wyght that speaketh ought, or wryteth.
> The authours meanyng should of ryght be heard,
> He knoweth best to what ende he endyteth:
> Wordes sometyme beare more than the hart behiteth.
> ("Collingbourne," 211–15)

All expression, but especially the poet's, is capable of multiple interpretation; the poet should at least be granted a fair hearing on his true meaning and intention.

With the same balance between complaint and irony that infuses the whole, the poem concludes with Collingbourne's ghostly admonition to other poets: "Warne poetes therfore not to passe the bankes / Of Hellicon, but kepe them in the streames, / So shall their freedome save them from extreames" (278–80). The wit here provides a moderately dense example of what it urges. By staying inexplicit, in the literary and metaphorical streams of Helicon, poets will have the freedom to pursue their calling without suffering *in extremis*, as Collingbourne himself did. So, too, will the bounds of the literary occupation keep the poet in his right calling, and away from extreme raving or perhaps the extremes of inappropriate political involvement. Riddle and metaphor hide, reveal, contain, and liberate, all at the same time.

Baldwin's concluding commentary reinforces the message that poets should be seen to have special liberties, which in turn make them useful to magistrates:

> Gods blessing on his heart that made [this poem]...specially for reviving our aunceint liberties. And I praye God it may take suche place with the Magistrates, that they may ratifie our olde freedome....If kyng Richard and his counsayloures had allowed, or at the least but wynked at sum such wits, what great commodities myght they have taken thereby. Fyrst, they should have knoowen what the people myslyked and grudged at...& somought have found meane...to have stayed the people's grudge: the forerunner commonly of Rulers destruction. (*Myrrour*, 359)[17]

Even if the language of poets may be deemed offensive, it should be permitted, "wynked at." Baldwin invites the rulers to become part of the conspiracy through which hidden language provides useful, even stabilizing, information.

If poets ought to have "Free libertie to chaunt [their] charmes at will" according to a feigned voice from a past time of tyranny, speaking freely was still no easy matter in the *Myrrour's* contemporary Elizabethan world, where newer poets such as Spenser and Sidney were finding their way. Despite the *Myrrour's* occasional effort to contrast oppressions from the preceding century with a presumably more liberal Elizabethan politics, order and obedience are the enforced foundations of political freedom for the Elizabethans, as the queen's homilists everywhere insisted.[18] Nonetheless, the traditional belief in the freedom of the English citizen-subject, which included some degree of personal agency, implied a certain liberality of speech, so long as there was no incitement to disorder nor disparagement of the monarch. Renaissance humanism ("the new learning"), the normative early modern education that exalted the humanities on classical models, was preeminently a study of language and expression, through which a person may merit success and preferment, not simply inherit it.[19] Those in power were expected to have carefully parsed their Latin and Greek and to appreciate Virgil, Cicero, and Plato.

While there were a number of treatises in this period on education, including education in rhetoric and poetry,[20] Roger Ascham's *The scholemaster* (1570) offers a particularly useful example. Ascham trained at St. John's College, Cambridge under some of the finest second-generation English humanists,[21] and served as tutor to then-Princess Elizabeth in 1548 and again when she was newly queen in 1558. His posthumously published *The scholemaster*, a lively discourse on humanist educational practice, went through five editions in less than 20 years. Ascham advocates the educational technique of double translation, in which a student first translates a piece of Cicero (for example) into English, then, after a pause, translates the English back to Latin and compares it with the original Latin text. Attention to the fine points of language made the educated classes acutely aware of expression in English as well as Latin. Despite its ("new learning") focus on eloquence and an impassioned rejection of corporal punishment in teaching, *The scholemaster* is a conservative document. Ascham worries, for example, that "the quickest wittes commonlie may prove the best Poetes, but not the wisest Orators: readie of tongue to speake boldlie, not deepe of judgement, either for good counsel or wise writing."[22] Ascham's concern underscores both the value of the person brought to virtue by education and the anxiety that those who are most able may be most bold, most free in their speech.[23]

Elizabethan England had become at least partially meritocratic, with even Elizabeth implicated in the emphasis on earned authority. Although she kept her legal claim consistently the conservative one of inheritance from her royal father, she worked hard to convey the impression of accomplished as well as inherent majesty.[24] Ascham's appreciation of his royal pupil conforms with other evidence of her skills with language and her understanding of the value of nurture as well as of nature: "Yea I beleve," says Ascham, "that beside her perfit readiness, in Latin, Italian, French, & Spanish, she readeth here now at Windsore more Greeke every day, than some Prebendarie of this Church doth read Latin in a whole weeke. And that which is most praise worthie of all, within the walles of her privie chamber, she hath obteyned that excellencie of learning, to understand, speake, & write, both wittely with head, and fair with hand, as scarse one or two rare wittes in both Universities have in many yeares reached unto."[25] Elizabeth also appreciated excellence and eloquence among servants of the crown and raised up a number of courtiers from lower ranks, including William Cecil, born a mere gentleman, to become Lord Burghley in 1571.[26] Elizabeth wrote poetry herself, made eloquent speeches, and used the praise of poets as a vehicle for promoting her public image.[27] Nonetheless, she can hardly be offered as a benevolent sponsor of free debate or individual free expression, and she might not advance those who expressed themselves too freely beyond the banks of Helicon.

The most vivid example is Sir Philip Sidney. Sidney was of higher birth than the other English poets of the early modern period whom we consider canonical; his mother was a Dudley and he was the presumed heir of his uncle, the Earl of Leicester, Elizabeth's long-time favorite. He wrote at least one entertainment for the queen, "The Lady of May," for her visit to Leicester's estate at Wanstead.[28] Yet as Richard McCoy wryly notes, he "was not one of Elizabeth's favorite courtiers."[29] Blair Worden reminds us that Sidney was not knighted until 1583, and then only so he could serve as a proxy for a friend.[30] He was, in short, a mere gentleman for most of his life, albeit a very well-connected one with promising prospects. He was also a dedicated supporter of Protestantism across Europe, and among those who opposed Elizabeth's possible French marriage. Sidney's enduring if incomplete "heroic poem" in prose, *The Countess of Pembroke's Arcadia*, was apparently written in its original form (the *Old Arcadia*) during a rustication from court which stemmed from his too insistent urging of a Protestant alliance and a related quarrel with his social superior, the Earl of Oxford.[31] A heroic romance about love and honor, *Arcadia* is also a political treatise on the varieties of right and wrong rule, both political and personal, and by example and direct statement it also has something to say about poetic expression.[32]

Sidney's point of view in *Arcadia,* on the surface at least, is more aristocratic and hierarchical than Baldwin's in the *Myrrour.* When King Basilius's steward, Philanax, urges the king to return to his proper role as ruler of Arcadia, he expresses perfectly the monarchic belief that order and stability emanate from the top, and that change is dangerous: "Let the subjects have you in their eyes; let them see the benefits of your justice dayly more and more; and must they needes rather like of present sureties, than uncertaine changes."[33] But this is based on the uncontroversial premise that good order extends from all in society meeting their respective responsibilities. Basilius is the rightful king and should rightfully be playing his role in the kingdom instead of retreating to the countryside, a move based, as it happens, on his effort to read a riddling oracle. One of Philanax's concerns is that this move, which Basilius means to protect his two daughters, in fact hinders their educations, of particular importance to his elder daughter and heir, Pamela. Basilius has left her care to the uneducated shepherd Dametas, and Philanax takes him to task for it: "for the recommending so principall a charge of the Princesse *Pamela* (whose minde goes beyond the governing of many thousands of such) to such a person as *Dametas* is (besides that the thing in itself is strange) it comes of a very evil ground, that ignorance should be the mother of faithfulness. O no; he cannot be good, that knowes not why he is good, but stands so farre good, as his fortune may keep him unassailed" (*Works* 1:25–26).[34]

Embedded in this admonition is the premise that learning and experience are both necessary to the right choices that exercise—and ultimately define—virtue. Ignorance is no more the mother of faithfulness than a fugitive and cloistered virtue can invite praise. A. C. Hamilton argues that Sidney's Puritanism leads to a neo-Stoic view of "life as a prison that tests man's worth," and that implicit in his fiction and poetic theory is "the view...that man's virtue is tested by the confines of life, and the faith that virtue makes man free."[35] This may be true in the realm of faith, where Sidney may be presumed to share William Perkins's view that we are not only confined, "but even stark dead" when it comes to any ability to choose toward our salvation,[36] but it appears not to be true in the world of ordinary human affairs, where, for Sidney, both education and experience are vital. Neither Sidney's aristocratic bias nor his Puritanism lead him to value static hierarchy. Those of high birth may be of low virtue, such as Cecropia and her son Amphialus, while those of lesser birth may be among the most virtuous and wise, such as Philanax and another good courtier to King Basilius, the hospitable Kalendar, whose name suggests the ongoing processes of life even sequestered in Arcadia.

The heroes of *Arcadia*, the cousin princes Pyrocles and Musidorus, exemplify the meritocratic values of education and experience, and the importance of learning how to make right choices. Poetry, in its broadest sense of fiction (the primary sense in which Sidney uses it in *The Defence of Poesy*), plays a crucial role in this process. The princes have been educated not merely in the rules of grammar, but on stories of valor, "the delight of tales being converted to the knowledge of al the stories of worthy Princes, both to move them to do nobly, & teach them how to do nobly...so that a habit of commaunding was naturalized in them, and therefore the farther from Tyrannie" (*Works*, 1:190). Freedom throughout the *Arcadia* comes from knowledgeable choices based on learning, experience, and a magnanimous disposition (this, perhaps, a nod not only to the culture of hierarchy but also to the divine grace without which nothing else is possible), while tyranny is self-interested governance and unnatural command. Proper governance is a theme throughout *Arcadia*, with the revised version full of stories about good and bad governance of both self and of society. It is central to the work's first action adventure, in which Pyrocles and Musidorus, through their encounter on opposite sides of the Laconian civil war that is the backdrop of their separate arrivals in Arcadia, reconnect after the shipwreck that separated them. This story also provides a useful outline of the tensions between republican and aristocratic leanings that make Sidney both a model and foil for someone like Milton.[37]

It will be recalled that in this story civil war has set the rude Laconian peasant class, the Helots, against the noble class, the Lacedaemonians. The Helots, "having been of old, freemen and possessioners, the Lacedaemonians had conquered them, and layd, not only tribute, but bondage upon them," a not unusual consequence of conquest but not one of which Sidney apparently approves (*Works*, 1:39). The Helots tolerated this condition until Lacedaemonian excesses made their lot too great to bear. Although the Helots were not militarily skilled, they had numbers, the desperation of nothing to lose, and the good fortune of two excellent captains in succession, the second of them Pyrocles. Musidorus enters the fray on behalf of the ruling Lacedaemonians in order to help his Arcadian host, Kalendar, retrieve his imprisoned son, Clitophon, held by the Helots. The cousins at first only recognize a worthy opponent and offer to reduce the entire conflict to a one-on-one battle. When they do recognize each other and are joyfully reunited, they work out an arrangement of peace between Arcadia and Laconia, and between the factions within Laconia.

In resolving the Laconian civil war, Sidney's characters balance aristocratic with egalitarian and meritocratic values. The disguised prince Pyrocles, who has already educated the Helots on courage and valor by his example, draws the moral of self-rule from the Helots' near escape from destruction at the hands of the Arcadian army: "the error committed, in retaining *Clitophon* more hardly than his age or quarrel deserved, becomes a sharply learned experience, to use in other times more moderation" (*Works*, 1:46). Finally, Pyrocles effects a solution to the quarrels between the Helots and Lacedaemonians that restructures their society more fairly and offers opportunities for social mobility. The Helots will no longer rebel, he tells them, and in exchange,

> The Townes and Fortes you presently have are still left unto you, to be kept either with or without garrison, so as you alter not the lawes of the Countrie, and pay such duties as the rest of the *Laconians* doo [sic]. Your selves are made by publique decree, free men, and so capable both to give and receive voice in election of Magistrates. The distinction of names between *Helots* and *Lacedaemonians* to be quite taken away, and all indifferently to enjoy both names and privlidges of *Laconians*. *Your* children to be brought up with theirs in *Spartane* discipline: and so you (framing your selves to be good members of that estate) to bee hereafter fellows, and no longer servauntes. (*Works*, 1:46–47)

While the Helot rebellion has been squarely blamed on the tyranny of the Lacedaemonians, who conquered and oppressed a free people, the Helots' return to the status of free citizens comes only after education and effort in the noble virtues of warfare. Further, it carries with it the responsibilities of freedom—obedience to law, payment of duties, and "*Spartane* discipline"—even as it grants the essential right "to give and receive voice in election of Magistrates." The integration of Helots and Lacedaemonians into a single Laconian society is to be founded on a common education. The solution is elegant and in keeping with the evidence of Roman republicanism that Skinner and others find among the humanist-educated meritocrats of the Renaissance, and Worden lays out in his discussion of *Arcadia*.[38] Nonetheless, Laconian society has not been equalized. Rather, the oppressions of an old tyranny have been eliminated so that a new meritocracy can arise. As for rebellion itself, it has no virtue; it is a "contagion" (*Works,* 1:40), redeemed from devastating both societies by the presence of an exceptional leader. The Helots are "as much moved by [Pyrocles'] autoritie, as perswaded by his reasons," and must continue to learn the responsibilities of free citizenship under the law (*Works,* 1:45).[39]

Issues of right governance recur throughout *Arcadia* and have been amply discussed by Worden and others.[40] Sidney's efforts to balance a Tudor era abhorrence of disorder with an equal abhorrence of tyranny are notable for their reliance on speech and rhetoric as vehicles both to tell the stories and to give them their proper outcomes. Pyrocles' eloquence persuades the Helots to cease their fighting. When the melancholic tyrant of Phrygia is slain in book 2, "certaine yong men of the bravest minds, cried with a lowde voice Libertie, and encouraging the other citizens to follow them, set upon the garde and souldiers as chiefe instruments of Tyrannie" (*Works* 1:200). Musidorus resists the Phrygian crown but gives the people laws with which to construct a fair and stable society. Pyrocles similarly resists the crown of Pontus, but assures that it goes to a legitimate queen (the late tyrant's sister) who shares it with a nobleman of merit. In these and other instances, reason, persuasion, eloquence, and the consent of the people combine with a more traditional inheritance to establish right rule.[41] Further, in revising from the comic structure of the *Old Arcadia* to the heroic of the *New Arcadia,* Sidney has not only followed the narrative classicism of renaissance Aristotelian Antonio Minturno, as Kenneth Myrick showed, he has also taken license from the romance tradition and looped story after story through his main narratives.[42] The result both reveals and obscures his point of view on serious political issues, as the Poet Collingbourne would approve. One effect is to affirm that neither birth nor education is enough to merit governance. Princes and magistrates need a judicious combination of the two, and, as Richard McCoy points out, they also need experience in order to recognize the complexities of the situations they encounter.[43]

Sidney is not Pyrocles or Musidorus, both of the noble rank Sidney might hope to inherit, but, in predeceasing his uncle, never achieved. He may be seen (as Worden and others have suggested) in Philanax the wise counselor and, even more, in Philisides, one of Arcadia's humble shepherd-singers whose Ister Bank eclogue is a parable of fallen human nature and the problem of governance.[44] As Alan Sinfield points out, Sidney was, strictly speaking, a state servant, in effect a bureaucrat, and "bureaucrats, like intellectuals...occupy a special position in terms of their class affiliations and relations with power. The class from which they originate is not necessarily the same as the hegemonic class which they serve." These "disjunctions in the roles and affiliations of the bureaucracy" allow it to develop a certain degree of "political autonomy [and] may also give rise to a degree of independent political thought," which Sinfield attributes to Sidney.[45] Sidney's independent convictions led not only to his probable rustication from court in 1580, which had the happy effect of leading him to write *Arcadia*, but also to the battlefield of the religious wars in the Netherlands, where he lost his life in October 1586. His focus on kings and queens behaving badly in *Arcadia*, along with his friendship and correspondence with Hubert Languet and Philip de Mornay, place Sidney in the camp of those who believed, on some level, in republican principles, and more explicitly in government by social contract and mutual consent.[46] Law and the responsibilities of governance and citizenship are the initial and often-repeated messages of the *New Arcadia*, often complicated by human passions, amorous and otherwise. Although (for polemical reasons) Milton dismissed *Arcadia* as a "vain amatorious poem" in 1649, he also read the work carefully and approvingly enough to include passages from it in his Commonplace Book.[47] Like his great-nephew, the Restoration republican exile Algernon Sidney, Sir Philip held many views Milton would share, including the belief that international Protestantism was a bulwark of freedom against Catholic tyranny and oppression, and that government should be by consent of the governed.[48] Further, as Stephen Zwicker argues, Sidney paved the way for poets, including Milton, to become principals in political discourse.[49] What he does implicitly in *Arcadia*, Sidney makes explicit in the *Defence of Poetry* by placing poetry above history and philosophy among the formative disciplines of the new learning and also by suggesting how the poet might exemplify the powers that lie within "the banks of Helicon."

Tyranny is not only a recurring theme in the *Arcadia*, but, as Robert Stillman shows, it appears as a theme among the examples Sidney gives in the *Defence of Poesy*.[50] This work, probably written or begun in 1580 after the first version of the *Arcadia*, was posthumously published in 1595 in two editions, essentially the same but variously titled the *Defence of Poesy* and *An Apologie for Poetrie*.[51] It is the foundational work of modern literary criticism in English, surpassing by far, in a period busy with works that say something about literary art, the rhetoric handbook of Thomas Wilson, the prosody lessons of George Gascoigne, the educational treatises of Thomas Elyot and Roger Ascham, and the poetry handbooks of William Webbe, Abraham Fraunce, and George Puttenham.[52] It may have been in part a response to Stephen Gosson's *School of Abuse* (1579), an attack especially on theatrical fictions and, perhaps surprisingly, dedicated to Sidney; Thomas Lodge wrote a *Reply to Stephen Gosson Touching Plays* that same year. Sidney's *Defence* makes direct use of the classical standards, Aristotle's *Poetics* and Horace's *Art of Poetry*, and shows acquaintance with the continental neo-Aristotelians, notably Julius Caesar Scaliger.[53] We know the *Defence* was written after 1579 because it singles out Spenser's *Shepheardes Calendar* for hopeful commentary on the progress of English verse. It has not much good to say about English drama, but Marlowe and Shakespeare were still several years from appearing on the scene.

Sidney's *Defence* draws on the full range of his classical humanist education, including his reading of the Italian humanists.[54] It draws heavily on the tradition of poetry as an imitation of nature (from Aristotle's *Poetics*) meant to teach and delight (Horace's *Art of Poetry*) with the Christian humanist and Reformation overlay of biblical poetics (especially with reference to the Psalms and the Song of Songs). It remains, however, in many ways an original work. Unlike the polemics of Gosson's treatise (or, for that matter, Scaliger's *Poetices*), the tone is engaging and unassuming even as the argument displays a familiarity with a wide and rich range of texts. The *Defence* is as fine an example of *sprezzatura* as exists in English, from the humorous self-deprecation of the exordium to the parodic bombast of the peroration. What interests me here, however, is the way in which some of Sidney's most famous statements shade into self-contradiction, particularly in the light of his well-known Protestant beliefs (as Peter Herman observes), and the rhetorical techniques that he uses both to hide and reveal those contradictions.[55] Like the balance between the aristocratic and the meritocratic that Sidney strikes in *Arcadia*, in the *Defence* he offers a "right poet" who is somewhere between a "maker" (a "poet" from the Greek *poiein*) and a "prophet" (a *vates*, or "divine" poet). Although he eschews describing the latter, his whole theory of poetry demands that a poet be, at least to some extent, a divinely inspired visionary.[56]

Consider Sidney's explication of the Latin term "*vates*, which is as much a diviner, foreseer, or prophet...so heavenly a title did that excellent people [the Romans] bestow upon this heart-ravishing knowledge" (*Defence*, 98). He notes the ancient practice of opening books of poetry (notably Virgil's) arbitrarily, to find an omen in whatever verse a reader might happen upon. Although this is a "vain and godless superstition," he sees some merit even in the pagan practice, "for that same exquisite observing of number and measure in words, and that high flying liberty of conceit proper to the poet, did seem to have some divine force in it" (99). From this ambivalent nod to the classical tradition of poetic prophecy, he turns, in humble and tentative language, to affirm the poetry of the Psalms, that perfect model for Protestant poetics:[57] "And may not I presume a little further, to show the reasonableness of this word *vates*, and say that the Holy David's Psalms are a divine poem? If I do, I shall not do it without the testimony of great learned men, both ancient and modern" (99).

The rhetorical devices Sidney uses nod toward an assertion of biblical authority for the poet as prophet. He begins his discourse on *vates* in a confident and pedagogical style. As he makes the transition from the "vain and godless" practices of classical "superstition," his language becomes more tentative, full of double negatives, surmise, and interrogatory constructions. Pagan practices are "altogether not without ground," and poetry "did seem to have some divine force." Not only does he ask whether he may presume, even as he does presume, he keeps his language conditional and full of double negatives ("if I do, I shall not do it without"). The deference extends throughout this passage as he presents David as the model of the prophet poet. "For what else is" his use of the poet's techniques (invocations, meter, *prosopoeias*) through which "he maketh you, as it were, see God coming in His majesty, his telling of the beasts' joyfulness, and hills leaping, but a heavenly poesy, wherein almost he showeth himself a passionate lover of that unspeakable and everlasting beauty to be seen by the eyes of the mind, only cleared by faith?" He pulls back ("I fear I seem to prophane that holy name [of prophecy], applying it to Poetry") but then moves carefully forward, allowing that those "with quiet judgments" willing to "look a little deeper" shall find that the "end working...being rightly applied, deserveth not to be scourged out of the Church of God" (*Defence*, 99).

Sidney's discourse on the psalms, as divine poetry that Christianizes the definition of the poet as *vates*, is notable for its invitational structures. Rather than telling and explaining, he offers his own brief hermeneutic on what the techniques of poetry are able to reveal of the divine, backs off a bit, then invites his readers to become interpreters themselves. The transition between the picture of the classical *vates* and the people's superstition concedes its limitation without fully denying the prophetic power of even the secular poet. He generalizes the powers of the poet as somehow inherently divine before he appeals to the model of David and makes the case for figurative language as a means of religious insight. But the language of hesitation, double perspective, and surmise both distances readers and brings them in. Sidney hesitates to say controversial things that, after all, may not be true, but readers willing to enter more fully into this dialogue may discover things for themselves, and be more deeply engaged, rather than put off, by the narration.

The tone of the next passage is completely different. We are back to being instructed by a speaker on sure ground. "But let us see how the Greeks named it," he begins, confidently noting the origin of *poet* in *poiein*, "to make," and happily showing how England follows the Greeks ("I know not whether by luck or wisdom") in calling the poet "a maker." He then moves in the same brisk tone to assert how "high and incomparable a title it is," by focusing on other branches of knowledge and showing their limitations, again beginning with confident assertion: "there is no art [i.e., area of knowledge] delivered to mankind that hath not the works of Nature for his principal object." This is unobjectionable—Sidney is leading us toward his proposition, in which he defines poetry as "an art of imitation, for so Aristotle termeth it." But before he gets there he turns his poet as "maker" into another model of the divine, one who thrives in explicitly secular contexts but who, nonetheless, is a creator beyond the scope of any other professional. This is the familiar passage in which the poet is elevated above nature, growing "in effect another nature, in making things either better than Nature bringeth forth, or, quite anew.... so as he goeth hand in hand with Nature, not enclosed within the narrow warrant of her gifts, but freely ranging within the zodiac of his own wit" (*Defence*, 100).

This is a striking claim for originality in a period devoted to imitating Greek and especially Roman models. Sidney's originality is not a modernist iconoclasm, because the classics continue to supply the models for freely ranging "within the zodiac"—the universe, but a delimited one—of the poet's "own wit," inventiveness, imagination.[58] That imagination does not simply "build castles in the air," but rather creates substantial pictures based on the "*Idea* of the work," an idea made "manifest, by delivering [it] forth in such excellency as he hath imagined them." This manifestation is the "second nature" that makes the poet a co-partner with Nature itself. It is enticing and therefore useful because it creates solid images of virtue, as in Xenophon's portrait of the noble and virtuous Persian king Cyrus. The poet's image is more powerful than Nature's, which could make only "a particular excellency," the historical Cyrus, while the poet is able to "bestow a Cyrus on the world to make many Cyruses, if they [the poet's readers] will learn aright why and how that maker made him" (*Defence*, 101).

What follows, and immediately precedes the work's "propositio" with its reference to Aristotle's *mimesis*, is a three-part argument on behalf of the poet's divinity. By valuing the poet, one gives "right honour to the heavenly Maker of that maker, who having made man to His own likeness, set him beyond and over all the works of that second nature." The imagination (and, presumably, skill in displaying it) is a gift of God that allows the poet to exercise God's own creative powers, "when with the force of a divine breath he bringeth things forth far surpassing [Nature's] doings." At this point, the hesitation and indirection of his earlier claim for poetry's divine credentials in the Psalms returns to preface an argument for poetry derived from Genesis. As the poet's second nature surpasses Nature's own "doings," it is "with no small argument to the incredulous of that first accursed fall of Adam: since our erected wit maketh us know what perfection is, and yet our infected will keepeth us from reaching it." Our idealized "second nature" may remind us of our fallen condition since it juxtaposes our recognition of perfection with equal recognition of our inability to reach it. Or, the ability to make and to recognize perfection is left to us (in our "erected wit") even as our "infected will" sends us back to an appropriate dependence on God. Sidney is struggling here with the tension between the poetic freedom of great poets "freely ranging only within the zodiac of" their imaginations, and the complete absence of salvific free will in the Calvinist tradition that he has embraced, and he acknowledges that "these arguments will be by few understood, and by fewer granted." So he returns, finally, to asking that his reader grant that "the Greeks, with some probability of reason gave [the poet] the name above all names of learning" (*Defence*, 101).

The case for the poet's special role in God's creation, the *vates* case, is a much more difficult one than the traditional case for poetry's practical role in the secular world. Sidney is witty and compelling when he sets poetry among the other humanities. Philosophy and history are both powerful forces and would "win the goal, the one by precept, the other by example. But both, not having both, do both halt" (*Defence*, 106). Poetry, on the contrary, can not only teach but also delight, and so move its audience to virtuous action. "Now doth the peerless poet perform both: for whatsoever the philosopher saith should be done, he giveth a perfect picture of it in some one by whom he presupposeth it was done, so as he coupleth the general notion with the particular example" (107). The historian can give us particulars, but without the lessons of moral philosophy; too many historical examples are, like many fictional ones in the *Arcadia*, examples of tyranny and injustice.[59] Unlike the historian, however, who is "so tied, not to what should be, but to what is" (107) that he cannot always raise up a moral vision out of life's disorder, Sidney's fictions can introduce transformations and solutions that illustrate not only the virtues of Pyrocles, Musidorus, and other heroes of *Arcadia*, but become a "speaking picture" (101) of justice, liberty, right relationships, and right rule. This, Sidney claims, is the world of the right poets, "which most properly do imitate to teach and delight, and to imitate borrow nothing of what is, hath been, or shall be; but range, only reined with learned discretion, into the divine consideration of what may be and should be" (102).

The *poet* cannot help but partake of the *vates* in Sidney's vision. Sidney separates these right poets from those biblical models such as David, Solomon, Moses, Deborah, and Job, who "did imitate the inconceivable excellencies of God"—presumably the truest of the *vates*. "Against these none will speak that hath the Holy Ghost in reverence" (*Defence,* 101–02). Certain Greek and Latin poets, "though in a full wrong divinity," may also be included among the imitators of the divine. Sidney also separates his right poets from poets whose works, however skillful, are not imaginative, but are concerned with specific branches of learning, such as moral or natural philosophy (Tertaeus, Phocylides, Cato, and Lucretius, and Virgil's *Georgics*), astronomy (Manilius and Pontanus), or history (Lucan). On the one hand, Sidney does not claim his right poet to be divinely inspired, as were the biblical poets, but he insists on the poet not being tied down to other branches of learning or to simply describing things as they are or have been, but rather, he insists again that they are free to portray "the divine consideration of what may be and should be." Subject matter may support the distinction between *vates* and *poet*, as between those who imitate God and his actions directly and those who are concerned with the (now fallen) world of God's creation, but the ultimate resource is the same: humanity's "erected wit," made in the image of God, the creator, and enabled by that image to exercise a divine power in making a second nature.[60]

This section of the *Defence* illustrates some important tensions in the development of Protestant poetics and also shows Sidney's struggle with poetic freedom within the context of those tensions.[61] His call for what amounts to a near-complete poetic freedom is bound by the "universe" it seeks to imitate, by the limits of "discretion," and by the virtuous purposes of poetry. It is both confined and liberated, as well, by Sidney's Calvinist theology. Yet whenever he reaches a place where the tensions of either his own argument or the complexities of religion intrude, he tends to use the techniques of poetry, including metaphor and conjectural sentences and rhetorical structures, to invite his reader into the evolution of his ideas.

I have lingered over Sidney's approaches to ideas of political and poetic freedom because I do not think they have been properly credited for what they offered Milton.[62] Milton rarely cites English sources; his approving references to Spenser (YP 1:722, 2:516, 3:390, 5:20) are the major exceptions, and in each case he looks to his well-known predecessor for examples of effective poetic representation rather than intellectual support. Yet when Milton comes to write his *Art of Logic*, it is to Sidney he turns as his authority for focusing on Ramus: among philosophers "who have thought that logic was worthwhile...the most deserving, in my opinion as in the opinion of our good Sidney, is Peter Ramus" (YP 8:208). It is fair to assume that Milton knew Sidney's *Defence,* and there is much in it that anticipates Milton's strategies for advancing his highly individual and individualized case for liberty within a contentious political and theological atmosphere. I would not claim that the *Defence* was so much an influence on Milton as a model argument that consolidated classical and continental approaches to thinking about poetry and gave those arguments a particularly English exuberance, along with a Ramist suspicion of rhetoric separated from logic.

Milton, one of Europe's finest Latinists, made the choice to write in English and to follow at first the patterns available to a professional poet, for whom the preeminent living model in his youth was Ben Jonson. Yet, as Ruth Mohl notes, "the Arcadian shepherds in *Arcades* and *Comus* might have stepped out of Sidney's romance," and much of the "Renaissance atmosphere" of these and even of "*Paradise Lost* derived from [Milton's] youthful reading" of Sidney and Spenser (YP 1:361n2). Further, as Milton took what was largely a hiatus from writing poetry and sought to define himself in the polemical context of the 1640s, he began also to speak publicly about the role of poetry both in his own life and more generally. Lewalski notes that of Milton's five antiprelatical tracts, three are satirical responses to other treatises, but the other two, *Of Reformation* (1641) and *Reason of Church-Government* (1642), are more general essays that display "conscious art," including extended metaphors and Ciceronian periods balanced with looser hypotactic structures that convey "energy, vitality, and zealous fervor."[63]

Of Reformation cites poets among Milton's authorities (e.g., Dante, Petrarch, Ariosto, and Piers Plowman) (YP 1:558–60) and acknowledges the devices of poetry for polemical purposes. When he challenges the episcopacy's essentialness to a stable monarchy ("No *Bishop,* no *King*"), he uses story and metaphor to support his claim that "Royall Dignity" is not established by bishops any more than by the papacy, but rather by "the unmoveable foundations of Justice, and Heroicke vertue." Before he goes further with this argument, he is put "into the mood to tell you a tale" from "*Menenius Agrippa*," whom Sidney placed (with Erasmus) among the "smiling railers" whose satire he applauds (*Defence*, 121). "Upon a time the Body summon'd all the Members to meet in the Guild for the common good (as *Aesops* Chronicles averre many stranger Accidents) the head by right takes the first seat, and next it a huge and monstrous Wen little lesse then the head it selfe, growing to it by a narrower excresency" (YP 1:582–83). This wen, or tumor, claims excellence by merit and right to succeed should the head fail. A philosopher is summoned to argue with the wen, does so successfully, and finally concludes it to be "to the head a foul disfigurement and burden, [which] when I have cut thee off, and opn'd thee, as by the help of these implements I will doe, all men shall see" (YP 1:584).

Far contrary to their claim of being essential, Milton argues as he returns from "whence [it] was digress't," the prelates have "sore weak'nd" the "accessory causes that support Monarchy," which are "the love of the Subjects, the multitude, and valor of the people, and store of treasure" (YP 1:584–85). He has used story as one of the "implements" by which he makes his own argument for cutting off the influence of the prelates, even as, a reader might surmise by the juxtapositions of the argument, the prelates have cut off godly people from their own country. The lament that follows highlights what Milton has been doing throughout *Of Reformation:* painting a poet's picture of the tyranny of prelacy and the loss to the figurative body politic. "What numbers of faithfull, and freeborn Englishmen, and good Christians have bin constrain'd to forsake their dearest home," he complains, "their friends and kindred, whom nothing but the wide Ocean and the savage deserts of *America* could hide and shelter from the fury of the Bishops" (YP 1:585). He continues by invoking the right of the poet directly to figure forth what this should mean to all free Englishmen:

> O Sir, if we could but see the shape of our deare Mother *England*, as Poets are wont to give a personal form to what they please, how would she appeare, think ye, but in a mourning weed, with ashes upon her head, and teares abundantly flowing from her eyes, to behold so many of her children expos'd at once, and thrust from things of dearest necessity, because their conscience could not assent to things which the Bishops thought *indifferent*. What more binding than conscience? What more free than *indifferency*? Cruel then that *indifferency* needs be, that shall violate the strict necessity of Conscience, merciless, and inhumane that free choyse, and liberty that shall break asunder the bonds of religion. (YP 1:585)

The irony of this passage, particularly in light of Milton's later career, is that he is calling on poetic freedom (poets can "give personal form to"—that is, personify and make vivid—"what they please") to castigate the freedom of "indifferency," or the judgment that some elements of religious belief and practice are not necessary to salvation, and therefore may be decided by preference. In this case, however, the preference is that of the bishops, who have mandated ceremonies that Puritans considered idolatrous and even papist. Their consciences therefore send them away, both weakening the fabric of English society "and alienating from us all Protestant Princes, and Commonwealths," as England seems, rather, to prefer "the *Spaniard*, our deadly enemy before them." In this rhetoric the old quarrel between Holland and Spain for which Sidney died in 1586 is reignited, with England again in the middle. As Sidney advised Elizabeth to pursue a Protestant alliance, Milton, 60 years later, sees the weakening of that alliance as a sign of the folly of prelacy. Recently returned from his Italian journey, Milton uses his experience among the Catholic Italian academies to warn against the dangers of "the Jesuits, who are indeed the onely corrupters of youth, and good learning; and I have heard many wise, and learned men in *Italy* say as much" (YP 1:586).

The preface to the second part of *Reason of Church-Government* again draws on Milton's Italian experience, notably the applause he received from the Italian academies (YP 1:809–10), as he offers a view of his own poetic aspirations, sometimes in terms and language reminiscent of Sidney. The preface begins with a lamenting discourse on the responsibilities of vocation—of the right use of the gifts and knowledge with which a person has been blessed—that makes explicit the writer's companionship with reluctant prophets such as Jeremiah and Teresias. Like Jeremiah especially, this writer must speak, though he anticipates the words will bring no pleasure to his audience. He is "determin'd to lay up as the best treasure, and solace of a good old age, if God voutsafe it me, the honest liberty of free speech from my youth, where I shall think it so dear a concernment as the Churches good" (YP 1:804). He imagines a conversation with a disappointed God, should he refuse to use his gifts to respond to the present controversy, and offers as his hope for his work that it may lead to a "charter and freehold of rejoicing to me and my heires." He claims his motive is "neither envy nor gall...but the enforcement of conscience only, and a preventive feare least the omitting of this duty should be against me when I would store up to myself the good provision of peaceful hours" (YP 1:806). He invites "the elegant & learned reader" to bear with him as he speaks of himself and his plans, yet unfulfilled.

These passages have been discussed often,[64] but here I am interested in the way Milton picks up on the particular freedom of the poet, combining the Sidneian analysis of *vates* and poet as maker, and the language he uses to stake his claim. Like Sidney, Milton portrays the poet as free from the restraints of nature and temporality. The poet soars "in the high region of his fancies with his garland and singing robes about him," as opposed to the practical man "in the cool element of prose," confined to the circumstances he must in real time address (YP 1:808). The poet's "mind at home in the spacious circuits of her musing hath liberty to propose to herself" genres and topics, and "whether the rule of *Aristotle* herein are strictly to be kept, or nature to be followed, which in them that know art and use judgement is no transgression, but an inriching of art" (YP 1:812-13). This manner of following nature is in effect to be freed from the constraints of natural events and humankind's rules, allowing "the instinct of [a poet's own] nature and the imboldning of [the poet's study and practice, or] art...[to] be trusted" (YP 1:814).

As Milton begins to posit some actual approaches and topics that he might take, his prose takes on a tentativeness we might recognize from Sidney's locutions about the prophetic elements of poetry. By contrast, though, Milton's tentativeness is over whether to write a modern epic based on English history and myth. "It haply would be no rashness from an equal diligence [art] and inclination [poetic nature] to present the like offer [as Tasso has done for the modern Italians] in our own ancient stories" (YP 1:814). The tentative nature of this language falls away, however, as he thinks of moving from historical epic to divine drama. "Or whether those Dramatick constitutions, wherein *Sophocles* and *Euripides* raigne shall be found more doctrinal and exemplary to a Nation, the Scripture also affords us a divine pastoral Drama in the Song of *Salomon* consisting of two persons and a double *Chorus*.... And the Apocalypse of Saint *John* is the majestick image of a high and stately Tragedy, shutting up and intermingling her solemn Scenes and Acts with a sevenfold *Chorus* of halleluja's and symphonies" (YP 1:814-15). Classical dramatic models may provide a possibility ("whether...") but Scripture more definitively "affords us" examples of powerful theatricality and song.

Sidney's rhetoric turns confident when it moves from the poet as a prophetic voice to the poet as a more mundane teacher, better than the historian and the philosopher because he can teach and delight with examples untied to historical fact. Milton's voice turns more confident as it moves from secular to divine examples. Without conditional language, rhetorical questions, or the double negative constructions otherwise common to his prose, Milton asserts that the poet's "abilities, wheresoever they be found, are the inspired guift of God rarely bestow'd, but yet to some (though most abuse) in every Nation: and are of power beside the office of a pulpit, to inbreed and cherish in a great people the seeds of vertue and publick civility, to allay the perturbations of the mind and set the affections in right tune, to celebrate in glorious and lofty Hymns the throne and equipage of Gods Almightinesse" (YP 1:816–17). Even though these gifts may be commonly abused, the poet is a prophet of equal value to the preacher, or perhaps greater. The poet's ability to "paint out and describe" allows him to "teach over the whole book of sanctity and vertu through all the instances of example with such delight to those especially of soft and delicious temper who will not so much look at Truth herselfe, unlesse they see her elegantly drest" (YP 1:817–18). This election to teach and delight on behalf of God, this poetic "power beside the office of the pulpit," becomes the mandate of the poet, who may be denied a more conventional pulpit because he has been "Church-outed by the Prelats" (YP 1:823). His prophetic voice cannot be prevented, either in "the honest liberty of free speech" in addressing the issues of his day, or in the "high regions of his fancies" as he would "paint out" even the things of God.

Milton's principal model for the poet may at first seem to be Spenser, or at least the Spenserian-nationalist approach to making poems to uplift a nation and promote individual virtue. The reference to Spenser in *Areopagitica* shows that Milton did indeed count Spenser as a colleague in exploring a poetics of choice. Knowing and confronting evil is important, Milton insists, "which was the reason why our sage and serious poet *Spencer*, whom I dare be known to think a better teacher than *Scotus* or *Aquinas*, describing true temperance under the person of *Guion*, brings him with his palmer through the cave of Mammon, and the bour of earthly blisse that he might see and know, and yet abstain" (YP 2:516).[65] Yet as Milton announces his *vates* role and speculates about what sort of poems he might make, his language reflects the same tension between unease and assurance that Sidney uses to good effect to invite his own "elegant & learned reader" to participate with him in the decision process, even if they appear to differ in which sorts of topics, secular or divine, make them the most comfortable. As I noted in the introduction, Milton's prelatical tracts often display what I have elsewhere described as his elective poetics, a constellation of devices, including double negatives, rhetorical questions, the language of surmise, and, of course, metaphor, meant to encourage not merely assent but reader engagement with the choices that constitute freedom.[66] The indirection on which such a poetics relies is a crucial feature of this passage about Milton's sense of poetic vocation. So, too, is the invitation to a "knowing reader" with whom Milton may "covnant...that for some few years yet I may go on trust with him toward the payment of what I am now indebted" (YP 1:820). This is the reader Milton seeks to invite into an expanded poetic freedom, through which both author and audience make choices that enable and represent political and theological freedom.

Three

⋈

Milton's Early Poetics of Choice

The 1645 *Poems, Doctrine and Discipline of Divorce,* and *Areopagitica*

Milton published his first book of *Poems* in 1645 at a time when his energy had been devoted to prose controversy. Most of the work included is from the 1630s and suggests some interest in patronage, the usual route to success as a poet. Even some of the Latin poems in this volume hint at a poet finding it useful to praise the great, although poems to his own father or to his former tutor, Thomas Young, laud and elicit patronage of a less traditional sort.[1] Of the early poems I will touch on in this chapter, *L'Allegro* and *Il Penseroso* (written around 1632) suggest Ben Jonson's influence in their clarity, density, and elegant couplet versification with its judicious handling of enjambment, but also show the young poet stretching his powers.[2] More directly on the model of the professional poet supported by patronage (which Jonson represented to Milton's generation), Milton was commissioned to write two entertainments for the aristocracy, *Arcades* (ca. 1632), celebrating Alice, Countess Dowager of Derby, and *A Mask Presented at Ludlow Castle* (1634), a more elaborate celebration of the countess's stepson (and son-in-law), Thomas Egerton, by then Earl of Bridgewater, in his elevation to become Lord President of the Council of Wales. In the latter, and probably in *Arcades* as well, Milton collaborated with the court musician Henry Lawes, described by his biographer as a "cavalier songwriter."[3]

Despite these early opportunities, Milton's intellectual training and religious inclination made him an unlikely court poet, as Jonson was, even though the chance might have been open to him through his friendship with Lawes.[4] While on the surface Milton seems to be setting out on a typical poet's journey to success, therefore, his Reform Protestantism, along with the good fortune of his father's support, tended toward and permitted a more idiosyncratic approach to a poetic career. Milton took very seriously the public role of the poet, but the contents of the 1645 *Poems* are eclectic and mostly consistent with his dissenting views about religious and political institutions. Even if he were tempted by the lucrative patronage of the royal court, Queen Henrietta Maria's Catholic entourage was anathema to seventeenth century Puritans, and Milton's earliest prose works reflect the belief that court papists threatened not only the reformed true religion, but also English sovereignty.[5] There is a hint of that view in Milton's entertainments for the Egerton family, which serve as celebrations of English Protestant virtues in contrast to the court masques, which glorified and mythologized the royal couple.[6]

Milton's early work signals deliberate preparation for something greater than securing the praise of aristocrats, as he began to explore the opportunities and limits of poetic freedom.[7] Similarly, as he engaged the religious and political controversies of the 1640s he pushed against many of the conventions of his day, whether derived from prelates or Presbyterians, monarchists or parliamentarians. This chapter examines some of the ways Milton developed his own ideas about freedom and his own version of poetic freedom during the 1630s and 1640s, culminating in the poetic prose of *Areopagitica* in 1644. Even before that rich and evocative work, however, the poetry of the 1630s shows Milton moving toward a poetics that seeks to create a thoughtful reader, and then invite that reader to recognize and make interpretive choices.

L'Allegro and *Il Penseroso*, Milton's earliest poetic explorations of individual attitudes and choices, contrast youthful mirth and solemn study. These lyric arguments, perhaps emerging from Milton's experience with university disputations, have for decades provided a standard college exercise in poetic comparison. Formally, the poems are mostly parallel. Each is preceded by a ten-line denunciation of the alternative mode as excess, presented in alternating trimeter and pentameter lines, and then each falls into a presumably normative tetrameter in praise of its subject. So *L'Allegro*'s opening, "Hence loathed Melancholy / Of *Cerberus*, and blackest midnight born" is matched by *Il Penseroso*'s first two lines, "Hence vain deluding joyes / The brood of folly without father bred," and *L'Allegro*'s "But com thou Goddess fair and free / In Heav'n ycleap'd *Euphrosyne*" (11–12) with *Il Penseroso*'s "But hail thou Goddess, sage and holy, / Hail divinest Melancholy" (11–12). Other parallels and contrasts include *L'Allegro*'s movement from day to night, *Il Penseroso*'s from night to day; the former's preference for comedy, morning larks, "jocund rebecks" (a kind of mandolin), and social interaction; the latter's for tragedy, nightingales, organ music, and solitary walks.[8]

The poems richly describe pleasures appropriate to the different ways of experiencing the world, and both are arguably about freedom. *L'Allegro* has an exuberant sense of physical freedom and gaiety:

> Haste thee nymph, and bring with thee
> Jest and youthful Jollity
>
> ....
>
> Sport that wrinkled care derides
> And Laughter holding both his sides.
> Com, and trip it as you go
> On the light fantastick toe,
> And in thy right hand lead with thee
> The Mountain Nymph, sweet Liberty.   (25–26, 31–36)

Il Penseroso's freedom, by contrast, is of mind rather than dance, solitary rather than social:

> Or let my lamp at midnight hour,
> Be seen in some high lonely Towr,
> Where I may oft out-watch the *Bear*,
> With thrice-great *Hermes*, or unsphear
> The spirit of *Plato* to unfold
> What Worlds, or what vast Regions hold
> The immortal mind that hath forsook
> Her mansion in this fleshly nook: (85–92)

The "or" constructions in this passage are typical of *Il Penseroso*; they occur 19 times (as opposed to only four times in *L'Allegro*). The pensive one seems particularly attuned to options and aware of choices, though *L'Allegro* understands, too, that the possibilities for varying joys are conditional: "if I give thee honor due, / Mirth admit me of thy crue" (37–38), for example, and "if the earlier season lead / To the tann'd Haycock in the Mead, / Som times with secure delight / The upland Hamlets will invite" (89–92). This is not an assured description of delights to come, but a hopeful anticipation of possibilities.

It is tempting to try to decide which of these modes Milton himself may have preferred. He was unquestionably studious, and the conclusion of *Il Penseroso* seems particularly to point to the future author of *Paradise Lost:*

> And may at last my weary age
> Find out the peacefull hermitage,
> The Hairy Gown and Mossy Cell
> Where I may sit and rightly spell
> Of every Star that Heav'n doth shew,
> And every Herb that sips the dew;
> Till old experience do attain
> To something like Prophetic strain. (167–74)

Yet this is hindsight, and in any case Milton was far from the dour portrait that readers may conjure from labels such as "scholarly" or "Puritan." In early poems he celebrates springtime and beauty with energy and enthusiasm, and he must have had the capacity for great sociability; he impressed the Italians and others he met on his European journey and sustained many friends in cheerful conversation toward the end of his life.[9] This complexity underscores the fruitlessness of trying to interpret literature based on the life of the author, but it also leads to an important point about Milton's emerging poetic engagement with his audience. These early poems set choices before the reader and invite the exercise of thoughtful choosing: which is the more satisfying life—one of cheerful sociability or studious contemplation? Ultimately, too, which is the true freedom—that of the community as it works and plays together, or that of the individual as it seeks its own pleasures?

Even as these poems appear to urge differing life choices, they illustrate the limitations that one's own knowledge and disposition will place on the ability to engage in thoughtful choosing. The picture each voice paints of the other is not the one each in turn presents to us. *L'Allegro* asks for "unreproved pleasures free" and "immortal verse /...untwisting all the chains that ty / The hidden soul of harmony" (40, 137, 143–44), while *Il Penseroso* looks at *L'Allegro* and sees "toys," an "idle brain" and "fancies fond" (4, 5, 6). *Il Penseroso* asks for "the pealing Organ" and the "full voic'd choir" that "Dissolve me into extasies / And bring All Heav'n before mine eyes" (161, 162, 165–66), while *L'Allegro* assumes that the life of *Il Penseroso* brings "horrid shapes and shrieks and sights unholy" (4). Each self-portrayal is appealing, each denunciation a distortion. The reader is invited to choose, but no final choice can be fully satisfactory because each mode of being voices a biased and incomplete knowledge of the other, and because any person may at different times find either style of freedom and pleasure appealing. Taken together both poems offer glimpses of the poet's appreciation of differences within and among individuals and the value of a broad understanding of the possibilities for choosing. What they do not imply is an author-directed "right" choice.

Eric Brown sees these companion poems as interweaving and interdependent, not at all the stark choice that they seem to be, and ultimately not as separate as they appear. "The poems divulge their concern with the borders between themselves in their paradoxical imagery of limitless horizons, unbounded enclosures, and other sites of liminality," Brown points out, and adds, "The repeated dissolution of these borders creates a sense of instability between the poems, contributing to the constant flux in which one poem melts into the other."[10] In my reading, what Brown calls "instability" is an element of Milton's developing invitational poetics. We are invited to admire each mode and to see its limited vision, boundaries both undercut and clarified by the juxtaposition of the two. The poems' parallel (and perhaps interweaving) constructions and indeterminate and individualistic values create an early representation of what will increasingly become a key part of Milton's aesthetic: art is what allows the "elegant Learned reader" (YP 1:807) to engage profitably and directly, but not passively, with the artist.

Milton's aesthetic bears a direct relation to his epistemology. For Milton, knowledge comes from study, especially of the Bible, along with the willingness to bring an enlightened conscience to both study and experience. Since no single authority except God can lead the individual to his right vocation and salvation, the purpose of knowledge is the freedom to pursue truth.[11] The exercise of freedom is choice, which is the mandate of a God-given free will even after the Fall and, presumably, even toward salvation: "when God determined to restore mankind, he also decided unquestionably (and what could be more just?) to restore some part at least of man's lost freedom of the will."[12] To exercise that freedom one must be able to know and to choose, and fundamental to knowing and choosing is access to information and diverse views. All knowledge in a fallen world, however, is clouded or incomplete, and therefore no single choice can lead securely to truth or virtue. What becomes important, as *L'Allegro* and *Il Penseroso* illustrate separately and together, is the freedom to make the best choices one can within the framework (including personal disposition) one is given.

While the pursuit of knowledge assumes respect for and sometimes guidance from authority, no authority except that of God, as grounded in the Bible, is absolute.[13] Similarly, no invitation, even toward what looks like beauty or happiness, is fulfilled without the full consent of the invited. The poet's work is to teach by delighting, but also to draw the reader or listener toward active choices. In his preface to *The Reason of Church-Government*, Milton cites Plato, whose

> advice was, seeing that persuasion certainly is a more winning, and more manlike way to keepe men in obedience then feare, that to such lawes as were of principall moment, there should be us'd as an induction, some well temper'd discourse, shewing how good, how gainfull, how happy it must needs be to live according to honesty and justice, which being utter'd with those native colours and graces of speech, as true eloquence the daughter of vertue can best bestow upon her mothers praises, would so incite, and in a manner charme the multitude into the love of that which is really good as to

imbrace it ever after, not of custome and awe, which most men do, but of choice and purpose, with true and constant delight. (YP 1:746)

Milton's poetics, as well as his best rhetoric, will always seek to use "true eloquence the daughter of vertue" to "intice" and "charme" his audience, so it may embrace the good as a matter of "choice and purpose." That which is charming is not necessarily coercive; even if its purpose is to educate toward the author's perceived good, the education is only truly effective if that good is freely chosen. Increasingly (culminating, perhaps, with *Samson Agonistes*), this means leaving room for the reader to recognize alternative possibilities and to leave the right choice suspended, even if only slightly, to allow for the reader's active response.[14]

There is something of this even in Milton's two entertainments, where moral purpose and the role of poetry merge with praise for those being honored. In *Arcades* the Countess of Derby is the entertainment's centering force, clad in a circle of light. Nonetheless, the "Genius of the Wood," a figure for the poet and possibly played in the entertainment by Henry Lawes (Milton's collaborator and the Egerton family music master, who was to play the comparable Attendant Spirit role in the Ludlow *Mask*), must explain her to the enraptured Arcadians. She is the "rural Queen" (94, 108), but he is the generative force that knows how to honor her and the natural world over which she presides.[15] The power of music and song help "keep unsteddy Nature to her law," even though fallen humankind can no longer hear "the heavenly tune," the music of the spheres, that would be most fit to honor this "peerles" creature (68–75).[16] The singer will praise her, therefore, with "What ere the skill of lesser gods can show" (79). As the Countess centers and makes virtuous by her example what might otherwise be an unruly group of shepherds and rustics, music and poetry draw attention and praise to her centering virtues.

The entertainment celebrates a noble matriarch, then, and at the same time celebrates the power of art in a fallen world. The Countess herself, née Alice Spencer, was an important patron of poets and artists, including her distant cousin Edmund Spenser, who dedicated *The Teares of the Muses* to her. The "Genius" knows that the Arcadians are on a "quest" with the "free intent" to show "honor and devotion" to their "great Mistres" (34–36). He offers them (through art) knowledge that enhances their choice and enriches their experience, inviting them, finally, to come in from their pastoral world to find a better order in serving her:

"Bring your Flocks, and live with us, / Here ye shall have greater grace, / To serve the Lady of this place" (104–06). The entertainment is ceremonial, and those invited to join in praising the Countess would hardly be exercising their free will in following the Genius into her service. Even so it offers the invitational posture that Milton will later assume in his prose rhetoric as well as his more accomplished poetics, where knowledgeable choice will be a more serious and less mediated matter.

In the character of the "Lady" in the more ambitious Ludlow *Mask* Milton centers a more complicated celebration of "vertue," song, and freedom. The end of learning, as Milton would later write in *Of Education* (1644), is to regain the prelapsarian ability "to know God aright," but we must first know him through his creatures.[17] Yet, as Milton was to affirm in *Of Reformation* (1641), while God "created *understanding*, fit and proportionable to Truth the object, and end of it, as the eye to the thing visible," our fallen state assures that we must struggle with "a film of *ignorance* over it" (YP 1:566). The Lady enacts this problem, as lost in the dark wood, separated from her two brothers,[18] she hears commotion and goes toward it:

> This way the noise was, if mine ear be true,
> My best guide now, me thought it was the sound
> Of Riot, and ill-manag'd Merriment

....
                I should be loath
To meet the rudeness, and swill'd insolence
Of such late Wassailers; yet O where els
Shall I inform my unacquainted feet
In the blind mazes of this tangl'd Wood?   (169–71, 176–80)

The darkness is itself "a film of *ignorance*," and a reminder of the limits of our senses. The Lady's ear is true, and it turns out she will be able to understand and judge rightly the arguments of Comus, but she cannot at first see through the disguise of hypocrisy, what Milton would call in *Paradise Lost* "the only evil that walks / Invisible except to God alone" (3.683–84). As Comus appears to her in the guise of an honest shepherd and offers to find her brothers and guide her to "a low / But loyal cottage, where you may be safe" (318–19), she replies, at first accepting what she sees: "Shepherd I take thy word, / And trust thy honest offer'd courtesie." She is also wise enough to throw in a little prayer: "Eie me blest Providence, and square my triall / To my proportion'd strength" (320–21, 328–29).

When Comus takes the Lady not to a humble cottage where she may wait for her brothers but to "a stately pallace, set out with all manner of deliciousness" (657 s.d.) and invites her to join the hedonistic revelry of his surrounding rabble, she resists, though it means being confined to an "inchanted chair." Both eye and ear now clear, she has sufficient knowledge to understand what she is up against and to make her moral choice, contrasting inner with external freedom: "Thou canst not touch the freedom of my minde / With all thy charms, although this corporal rinde / Thou hast immanacl'd, while Heaven sees good" (662–64). In her reliance on inward rather than outward knowledge and strength, the Lady, in words Milton gives to the older of the two brothers, finds "divine Philosophy" her true pleasure, as "musical as is Apollo's lute / And a perpetual feast of nectar'd sweets" (477–78). Comus, offering a false rhetoric, cannot sway the

Lady, who responds at first by disdaining to respond: "Enjoy your dear Wit, and gay Rhetorick / That hath so well been taught her dazling sence / Thou art not fit to hear thy selfe convinc't" (789–91).

The Lady sees Comus so taken by outward appearances and hedonistic pleasures as to render him the opposite of Milton's fit audience, unable or unwilling to accept a rational argument. In this she is the channel for a younger Milton anticipating an older one. Milton is consistent in making language a vehicle for knowledge in a way that display is not, even though he is himself a master at rich rhetorical display. As a poet and the son of a musician, he may have thought truth inhered more readily in the serio-temporal than visual arts.[19] In *Paradise Lost*, Satan's self-display "High on a Throne of Royal State," designed to make others look at him, is in sharp contrast to the Father's impenetrable brightness, whose gaze on others brings them "beatitude past utterance" (*PL* 2.1–10, 3.56–62). Like other church reformers, Milton rejected the visual symbolism of Laudian services, while music remained a constant in his portrayals of the divine.[20] Milton certainly did appreciate and was attracted to physical beauty, but his tendency is always to favor poetry and song over appearance.[21]

The Lady in the *Mask* has reason, which enables her knowledge, but it is her virtue, the power attendant upon her trust in divine Providence, that guides her past physical appearances to truth. Even so, she is literally stuck without outside assistance. Milton suggests that while each individual who would be free needs to invest in an ordered understanding, salvation is only possible through providential guidance. In a Calvinist reading, the Lady is among those predestined for salvation and her "vertue," signified by her refusal of physical pleasures and her devotion to "the sage / And serious doctrine of Virginity" (785–86), is a gift of grace. Yet the *Mask* also puts forward the need for education and seeks to educate (here, in true and false rhetoric), leading to a body of knowledge (philosophy) that helps one see temptations for what they are.

As Ann Coiro argues, Milton's work shows clear indebtedness to the masque tradition, yet as Mary Ann Maguire and William Shullenberger (among others) illustrate, Milton is trying to write a new kind of masque, one that contrasts the visual show and amorous excess of the Caroline court with a story in which reason and grace invite community action and lead to freedom both personal and political.[22] The young brothers fall in with their teacher, Lawes, in his role as an Attendant Spirit, whose benevolent shepherd's disguise contrasts with Comus's malignant one. In a scene that recalls the end of book 3 of Spenser's *Faerie Queene*, the brothers chase Comus away from the Lady but miss capturing his magic wand and so cannot themselves free her.[23] The Spirit must call on the river nymph Sabrina who releases the spell, not inconsequentially through song and rhyme (890–920). Her controlled, ritualistic touch first on the Lady and finally on the "marble venom'd seat / Smear'd with gums of glutinous heat" (*Mask*, 916–17]) accomplishes what the headlong rush of the brothers cannot: the Lady is freed.

Lewalski sees Sabrina as "the good poet whose elegant songs and rituals free the Lady from the spells of the bad poet, Comus, and confirm her in her own arts of song."[24] It is true that Sabrina literally crosses the banks of her helicon, in the Poet Collingbourne's terms, leaving her watery "channell" to set her "printless feet / O're the cowslips Velvet head" (*Mask*, 897–98) in order to reach the Lady and perform her magic. Yet the Lady herself does not speak, much less sing, after the visit from Sabrina; the Attendant Spirit sends Sabrina back to her watery world with a blessing and brings the Lady to her father's house, where general singing and dancing can commence under the watchful patriarchal eye. Coiro points out the unusual centrality of women to the *Mask*'s narrative, but also finds the result disturbing: "to a degree more subtle and profound than any queen-centered masque, Milton's work balances crucially and yet uneasily on the character of the Lady.... The virgin Sabrina, the only other woman in the play, is a redemptive but also, sadly, a deadening version of the Lady."[25] This, I think, is only partially true. If, as the Attendant Spirit seems to indicate, Sabrina's river spirit defines and feeds the beautiful lands of the new lord president (she is the "Goddess" of the Severn [865]), she has her own cold fruitfulness, and it seems to reside in her ability to cross those riverbanks when properly invoked. The Attendant Spirit, as the artist who orders and watches over the tumult of the Lady's and the brothers' world, is himself free to call on other agents of freedom, to invite them (the words and rituals of the poetic world) to invite others (the Lady, the brothers) to stand up and move forward.

Even this early in Milton's developing thought the *Mask* suggests that while salvation is certainly not the product of actions not fully thought through, here represented by the brothers' routing of Comus, neither is it entirely a matter of predestination. The Lady claims an untouchable freedom of mind, derived from what the Elder Brother describes to the younger as "a hidden strength / Which if Heav'n gave it, may be termed her own: / 'Tis chastity, my brother chastity" (*Mask*, 417–19). It is easy in the twenty-first century to be amused by all the emphasis on chastity and the "sage and serious doctrine of virginity," and "glutenous heat" has been the occasion of innumerable academic jokes (and at least one very fine parodic song). But chastity was the culturally approved principal virtue appropriate to a young woman in the seventeenth century and one that could be considered (up to a point) within her power.[26] In addition, chastity, as in *Faerie Queene* book 3, is a virtue of order and restraint through which both sexes, but particularly women, can rationally manage compelling and sometimes frightening passions. It provides a foundation from which one can make rational choices in an irrational world, and in that sense, at least, offers the possibility of individual freedom. The Lady does not speak after her freedom, but she does accept the Attendant Spirit's invitation, "while Heaven lends us grace," to "fly this cursed place," and "com to holier ground" with her "faithfull guide" (*Mask*, 938–44).

The Attendant Spirit's epilogue underscores the lesson and asks the members of the audience to participate in the experience of freedom by developing their own love of virtue.

> Mortals that would follow me,
> Love vertue, she alone is free,
> She can teach ye how to clime
> Higher then the Spheary chime;
> Or if Vertue feeble were,
> Heav'n itself would stoop to her.   (1017–22)

Love of virtue is a passage to knowledge, one that participates in God's call to salvation. If virtue is the only freedom, love of virtue would seem to be a choice, whether freely made in any absolute sense or made possible by redeeming grace.

Whatever else it does, the *Mask* shows Milton moving beyond the early Reformation's dismissal of free will. It follows that the author's concluding stance, represented by Lawes in the *Mask*'s epilogue, is a posture of invitation toward right choice, which will become the core of Milton's developing rhetoric of freedom. Truth may shine clear and pure, but knowledge enters in through the unreliable world of physical sensation and appearances, an eye that may be "blear" or deceived. Further, even if Scripture is our only direct source of ultimate truth, and its stories are presumably clear to everyone, there remains disagreement about ultimate things, and no human interpreter has a final authority to tell someone else what Scripture means.[27] The *Mask* begins to raise the questions that will dominate *Areopagitica:* how do we know what we know in a fallen world, and whom can we trust? In Milton's view, we know that God invites us to knowledge through the Scriptures, and "Heav'n itself" will give us strength—virtue in the original sense of power or energy—so long as we seek to love virtue in the broader sense of following God's laws. God speaks to the individual, well-intentioned conscience engaged in thoughtful reading. God's help is available, the *Mask* seems to say, but the person in need must invite it. In strict Calvinist terms, God offers grace to whomever he chooses so that person becomes able to ask God's help. But there is more. The teacher invites the pupil to knowledge as in the *Mask* the teacher literally leads his pupils through the wood of error into the light of salvation. Or, since they are Milton's words in the *Mask* and since the Lady's release comes through song, the poet leads his audience to the love of virtue, the way of freedom. But the audience or reader must follow the lead. Milton's emphasis on unmediated salvation, along with the natural recalcitrance of any fallen soul, makes this a more complicated problem than it at first appears. How does an author who increasingly distrusts authority invite the freedom in which he believes?

One answer, as this work makes clear, is through the appeal of poetry and song. The *Mask* contrasts the excess and riotousness of Comus and his "rabble" with the elegant song of the Attendant Spirit and Sabrina, just as it contrasts Comus's bad logic with the Lady's enlightened reason. Comus uses force to attach the Lady to the things of this earth. Sabrina's "printless feet" (897) mark her of a higher order, and her incantatory sprinkling of water from her "fountain pure" (912) evokes Helicon as well as baptismal rites. In the twin impulses to imitation and harmony that Aristotle attributes to poetry we find the power to invite a reader or listener's imagination into the fictive world and to present a moment of concord in contrast to the discord of most human experience.

Milton everywhere asserts the power of poetry to reveal and represent the highest kind of knowledge, from his early pamphlets through his last poems. In the Latin poem to his father, *Ad Patrem*, Milton justifies his vocation, saying, "nothing more commends our heavenly birth and seed" (18). As he thanks his father for the opportunity to pursue his extended studies, he situates poetry at that point of learning where the scholar may choose to know, may interpret through the devices of poetry toward a direct truth:

> At end, whatever heaven holds and mother earth
> Below, and flowing between them the earth and heaven, air,
> And what the marbled sea foam hides, thanks to you,
> I may learn, thanks to you—if I but care to learn.
> Clouds part, knowledge comes to be seen. Unveiled, she bends
> Her bright face forward for my kisses—unless I want
> To run away—or unless I find her irksome to try.
>
> (*Ad Patrem*, 86–92)[28]

Poetry, for Milton, is a mode of knowing, in which the "clouds part," but choice is key; one can "care to learn" or "run away." What choice one makes defines who one is, as it does for the Lady in the *Mask*. Poetic expression, like "divine philosophy," can be both a means to and an emblem of virtue. In the last of his antiprelatical tracts, *An Apology for Smectymnuus* (1642), Milton makes the connection specific: "he who would not be frustrate of his hope to write well hereafter in laudable things, ought him selfe to be a true Poem, that is, a composition and patterne of the best and honourablest things" (YP 1:890). Milton was well aware that self-formation takes time, however, and he had a habit of defining himself as too young, not ready, waiting for a certain ripeness, when he addressed his career as a poet.[29]

The preeminent example is *Lycidas*, the pastoral elegy on Edward King that concluded a volume of eulogies by King's Cambridge schoolmates.[30] If *L'Allegro* and *Il Penseroso* set up paradigms for life choices (and then complicate them), and his two Egerton entertainments present choice as a process of being and learning in a fallen world, *Lycidas* confronts the process of choosing with the reality of death. When one cares to learn, and takes the time to become a true poem, what guarantee can there be of fruition?

One way in which *Lycidas* explores this tragic question is through a poetics of dismemberment and incompletion, at once acknowledging the poet's persistent sense of unreadiness to tackle the greatest issues, and also, again, an invitation for his "elegant" and "knowing" reader to participate in the process of knowing by choosing. In *Lycidas*, Milton associates dismemberment with a call to recognize that what we know and value is always somehow incomplete. He recalls Ovid's description of enraged maenads dismembering Orpheus,

> Whom universal nature did lament,
> When by the rout that made the hideous roar,
> His gory visage down the stream was sent,
> Down the swift Hebrus to the Lesbian shore. (60–63)

The lines allude only obliquely to the resurrection of poetry through Sappho, on "the Lesbian shore," but still manage to suggest that this violent destruction is a call to reforge what was lost, to make poetry in the face of death and out of the dismembered remains of the past. This poets do and Milton does, notably in his use of genres, stories, and topics inherited through the classical humanist tradition. *Lycidas* itself is a reconstitution from classical and biblical pastoral. Typically, though, Milton leaves room for the reader to respond to questions his rhetoric raises, to complete or interpret the gaps and ambiguities the poet creates.

So, for example, formally *Lycidas* is an incomplete version of the framed pastoral monody; it begins with the voice of the "uncouth swain" but ends with a conventional narrative frame. As the death is untimely and Lycidas's vocation incomplete, so the poem is abrupt and unframed at the beginning. The narrative frame at the end is itself a formal ambiguity. The tight ottava rime stanza can be read as an epigram that concludes and accomplishes the task of consolation that the pastoral elegy seeks, or it can be read as an epic stanza returning us to the beginning of the poem and reintroducing the cycle of life and death.[31] As an epigram the poem can lead us to rise to the next thing, like the sun, Lycidas, and the swain ("Tomorrow to fresh woods and pastures new"); as an epic stanza it can thrust us forward, or rather back to the poem's opening and the impermanence of things of this world, "yet once more." The form provides either elegant closure or a disturbing sense of things constantly shaken and disturbed, a reminder of the biblical source of the poem's beginning in Hebrews 12:26–27: "now [God] has promised, saying 'yet once more I shake not only the earth but also heaven,' Now this 'yet once more' indicates the removal of those things that are being shaken, as of things that are made, that the things that cannot be shaken may remain." Like the dismembered Orpheus, the half-framed pastoral monody asks us to reconstruct what has been shaken, or transcend it, or both. Even untimely death, a dismemberment not only of a part of what is, but of what this person or this vocation may have become, may be seen more simply as that which is incomplete and will be completed in ways we cannot understand or express—a fruition sounded in the "unexpressive nuptial Song / In the blest kingdoms meek of joy and love" (176–77).

In the meantime, the picture is clouded and ambiguities remain. As Gordon Teskey notes, "the poem's stance is one of continual, uncertain, and perilous questioning."[32] In addition, the poem's prevalent theme of sinking in order to rise (including the use of the lowly pastoral to rise to epic vision) asks the reader to discern who is risen and what it means to rise, particularly in a world of things left incomplete or dismembered. Shepherds are to

>   weep no more
> For Lycidas your sorrow is not dead
> Sunk though he be beneath the watry floar,
> So sinks the day-star in the Ocean bed,
> And yet anon repairs his drooping head

> And tricks his beams, and with new-spangled Ore,
> Flames in the forehead of the morning sky. (165–71)

Are we to weep no more for Lycidas? Is Lycidas, our sorrow, not dead? Is our sorrow not dead but we weep no more because Lycidas, like the sun, will rise again, "through the dear might of him who walk'd the waves" (173), the Son? The gist of all this is clear enough: Lycidas is "sunk low, but mounted high" (172), a vision of Christian resurrection in the face not only of death itself but of the speaker's incomplete ability to mourn (there is no recovered body on which to throw the funeral flowers).

The poem's conclusion hearkens back to this crucial passage as the "uncouth Swain" sings with "eager thought... his *Dorick* lay:"

> And now the Sun had stretch'd out all the hills,
> And now was dropt into the Western bay;
> At last he rose, and twitch'd his mantle blew:
> Tomorrow to fresh woods and pastures new. (189–93)

The ambiguous reference of the pronoun combines the sun, the Son, Lycidas, and the singer in the act of rising to confront a fresh tomorrow. As in the *Mask*, the reader is encouraged, and to some degree guided, to move forward in hope and confidence, despite the abundance of things unknown or unfinished and even in the face of death. The poem liberates the singer and invites the reader into the embrace of faith that releases from the bondage of sorrow and death.

Milton's choice to include in this essentially personal commemorative elegy an attack on what he later labeled "our corrupted clergy then in their height" shows the seriousness with which he took the poet's public responsibility. It is no surprise that the events of 1638–40, the Bishops' War and the parliamentary resistance to funding it, should bring Milton home from his Italian journey and engage his pen on behalf of reform.[33] As Milton turned to prose, his concerns about freedom attach initially to what he argues is the oppression by prelates of the free consciences of Reformed Christians. We have seen in his preface to the second book of *Reason of Church-Government* that his personal sense of incompletion and his poetic vocation are still very much on his mind. So, too, is an expanding sense of personal freedom. By 1643 Parliament and the Presbyterian Westminster Assembly were sufficiently in charge of English state and church that Milton could address other issues in what would later become his threefold construction of liberty—the ones that he describes retrospectively as "domestic or personal liberty," consisting of "the nature of marriage itself, the education of the children, and finally the existence of freedom to express myself" (YP 4.1:624). His disquisition on marriage is tied directly to the subject of divorce, an issue sparked by his own unhappy initial experience of marriage.[34] Notably, he sees not only an incomplete but, again, a dismembered society struggling to get past the "custom" that limits it: "Custome," which prevents the informed and thoughtful behavior that is true freedom, is a "meer face" that "accorporats" with "error...a blind and serpentine body without a head" (YP 2:223).

Writing the divorce tracts allowed Milton to think personally about tyranny as well as freedom, and in this and other ways prepared him for the brilliant and evocative prose of *Areopagitica*. Milton's principal argument throughout the divorce tracts is that "in Gods intention a meet and happy conversation is the chiefest and noble end of marriage," and that "love in marriage cannot live nor subsist, unlesse it be mutual" (YP 2:246, 256). Not adultery, but default in companionship should therefore be the grounds for divorce; not sex, but compatibility should be the essence of a marriage. To be yoked without recourse to someone you cannot talk to, who leaves you isolated and lonely, is a bondage worse than civil tyranny.[35] In the introduction to the second edition of *The Doctrine and Discipline of Divorce* (1644), addressed to

Parliament, he draws a parallel between the person trapped in an inappropriate marriage and the recent effort on behalf of civil liberty in England: "He who marries, intends as little to conspire his own ruine, as he that swears Allegiance: and as a whole people is in proportion to an ill government, so is one man to an ill marriage. If they against any authority, Covnant, or Statute, may by the sovereign edict of charity, save not only their lives, but honest liberties from unworthy bondage, as well may he against any private Covnant, which he never enter'd to his mischief, redeem himself from unsupportable disturbances to honest peace, and just contentment" (YP 2:229). God's "sovereign edict of charity" transcends any human law or "Covnant." Milton's contemporaries were clearly shocked by this "divorcer," often assuming that the real purpose of his arguments was to allow for unbridled lust, and labeled him a heretic.[36] What he is saying, however, is that domestic freedom depends on conversation with a compatible companion. Even here Milton was in search of a fit audience with whom to exercise a free dialogue.

More importantly for the purposes of my argument, the divorce tracts helped Milton rethink the transparency of biblical authority and begin to model interpretive strategies.[37] Biblical passages remain at the core of Milton's arguments, but in *Doctrine and Discipline* Milton is forced to contend with those passages that would seem to disallow divorce, forcing him to interpret the biblical style that in the antiprelatical tracts he had cited for its plainness and clarity (YP 1:568, 778). In addressing this newly recognized rhetorical complexity, Milton's strategy is twofold. For the first, he marshals the passages that provide evidence for his position on marriage and divorce and situates them within other biblical contexts that emphasize the foundational elements of Christianity, especially faith and charity, and sets them against those passages that would seem to make divorce impossible. At the heart of his argument is Genesis 2:18, "the

Lord God said, It is not good that the man should be alone; I will make him a help meet for him," and the provision for divorce in the Mosaic law, "when a man hath taken a wife, and married her, and it come to pass that she find no favour in his eyes, because he hath found some uncleanness in her; then let him write her a bill of divorcement, and give it in her hand, and send her out of his house" (Deut. 24:1). Early in his treatise Milton makes Genesis the basis of his view of companionate marriage and implies that adultery should not be the main consideration for divorce: "God in the first ordaining of marriage, taught us to what end he did it, in words expressly implying the apt and cheerful conversation of man with woman, to comfort and refresh him against the evil of solitary life, not mentioning the purpose of generation until afterward" (YP 2:235).

His second strategy is to reach beyond the biblical context to assert a rational argument that explains a biblical authority otherwise damaging to his case. Most particularly, he must contend with passages in Matthew (5:32, 19:3–9) in which Jesus is reported to have allowed divorce only for adultery or not at all (what "God hath joined together let not man put asunder," Matt. 19:6) To respond he must claim a tradition of noncontextual interpretation that has rigidified what should otherwise be seen as an argument meant for more thoughtful, individual interpretation: "our Saviours words touching divorce, are as it were congeal'd into a stony rigor, inconsistent both with his doctrine and his office, and that which he preacht only to the conscience, is by canonicall tyranny snatcht into the compulsive censure of a judiciall court" (YP 2:237–38). Against this he would set Christ's emphasis on the centrality of faith and love of God, which, in the right context, might actually demand divorce. So, for example, "an idolatrous Heretick ought to be divorc't after a convenient space giv'n to hope of conversion," since marriage to such a person challenges the more important love of God (YP 2:261–65).

The second book of *Doctrine and Discipline* continues to urge situational interpretations informed by contexts both evidentiary and rational, particularly in wrestling with Christ's own words against divorce in Matthew, chapter 19. Here Milton explicitly rejects strict literalism in favor of contextual analysis: "all places of Scripture wherin just reason of doubt arises from the letter, are to be expounded by considering on what occasion every thing is set down: and by comparing other Texts" (YP 2:282). Scripture may be "plain," as he had asserted in his earliest tracts, but it still requires study, comparison, reason, and decisions about contextual meaning that are enlightened by individual reason and conscience. From the contentious exercise of writing the divorce tracts, then, Milton crucially valorizes the reader's responsibility for interpretive attention to a text.

Finally, I would suggest that in *Doctrine and Discipline* Milton's metaphoric habit of mind more clearly becomes part of his invitational poetics. For example, in the work's preface he describes Truth "as impossible to be soil'd by any outward touch, as the Sun beam" (YP 2:225), a metaphor that anticipates both the stance and the invitational strategy of *Areopagitica*. As I noted in the previous chapter, metaphor is by its nature invitational, at least to some degree, requiring the reader to make the translation between the vehicle and the tenor, between the terms being used and the ideas they are meant to convey. Here the "Sun beam" that represents truth is light and enlightening, visible but intangible, originating from a powerful and (in this cosmology) immutable source, and in all these things both eminently clear and ultimately elusive. It is an image that invites the pursuit of knowledge, as one reads by light, but does not define itself. It cannot be sullied by the effort to grasp it through outward touch, but can only be apprehended by thoughtful assent. The image provokes an active mind whose response is a form of intellectual freedom.

Areopagitica was published in 1644 shortly after the first two divorce tracts were printed. Here Milton has come to a confident poetics of freedom, founded on his affirmation of contextual interpretation, a Sidneian (and Horatian) belief in the power of poetry to effect moral good, and a rhetoric of invitation. *Areopagitica* relates the new civil and religious liberties, presumed to be secured by Parliament's ascent over monarchy and episcopacy, to individual liberties made possible by and reflected in the power of choosing. Mostly ignored in its own time, it has since had a rich and influential tradition as a cultural document.[38] A prominent authority on civil liberties law describes *Areopagitica* as "in some respects the foundational essay of the free speech tradition."[39] It is also by consensus the most poetic of Milton's prose works, often through the now-familiar metaphors of dismemberment and incompletion.[40] The work's central premise is that each individual must be part of the process of re-membering truth, that virgin hewn "into a thousand peeces, and scatter'd...to the four winds" until "her Masters second coming" when "he shall bring together every joynt and member, and shall mould them into an immortall feature of loveliness and perfection" (YP 2:549). This is a process both necessarily incomplete and necessary, hence Milton's argument against prior censorship: "Suffer not these licencing prohibitions to stand at every place of opportunity forbidding and disturbing them that continue seeking, that continue to do our obsequies to the torn body of our martyr'd Saint" (YP 2:549–50). For those who would complain against the tearing apart of the church, the "schisms and sects" that might thereby get a hearing, Milton responds that repressive orthodoxy is rather the danger: "They are the troublers, they are the dividers of unity, who neglect and permit not others to unite those dissever'd peeces which are yet wanting to the body of Truth" (YP 2:550–51).

Stanley Fish argues that *Areopagitica* is not about free speech or a free press at all, but rather about struggle that reveals moral being, for which books are ultimately irrelevant. Fish claims that the moral of *Areopagitica* "is not 'Seek and ye shall find,' but 'Seek and ye shall become,'" and that both books and free speech "are subordinate to the process they make possible, the process of endless and proliferating interpretations whose goal is not the clarification of truth, but the making us into the members of her incorporate body."[41] This is a compelling argument with which I mostly agree. It is true that for Milton books are crucial to a process of becoming, but I would argue that their content is not irrelevant. What Fish sees as a rejection of books and debate *except* as a means of asserting the virtuous self, I see as *an invitation to choose* toward the virtuous self. Certainly by 1644 when he published *Areopagitica*, Milton's theology of salvation had at least an Arminian tinge,[42] making free will and the exercise of reason and choice fundamental to salvation. His experience struggling with biblical passages for his divorce arguments had made clear the need for interpretive judgment. A free press allows for the process of self-formation, but not without consideration and discernment. The purpose is not to become the truth but to know the truth sufficiently in order to be free. It is not possible to "incorporate" into the body of truth without the coming of Christ, precisely because that body is dismembered, but it is possible to make choices that free the spirit toward Christian liberty, the "filial freedom" that replaces slavery to Old Testament rules and to established dogmas of all kinds.[43] That freedom, as *Paradise Lost* will ultimately illustrate, consists not in a static completion, but in a continuous process of becoming.

Milton's image of dismembered truth invites his readers to exercise that liberty by freely searching, notwithstanding the orthodoxies of his time. In another image of dis-ease, Milton warns his Puritan reader that "we have lookt so long on the blaze that *Zuinglius* and *Calvin* hath beacon'd up to us, that we are stark blind." He would have his readers willing to look beyond received truth, that "custom," no matter how valuable, recalling in the same essay that "a man may be a heretick in the truth" if he does not seek out truth for himself (YP 2:543). Milton's language of dismemberment is intended to shock the reader into a revolutionary reconsideration of his own freedom and responsibility; if truth is scattered, our responsibility is not to seek the one truth on earth, much less rest in orthodox dogma, but to exercise our choice and judgment in beginning to put it together for ourselves. Milton's project for the individual is also a project for his nation, as the body politic takes from this exercise of free inquiry the message of rejuvenation. Such lively intellectual interaction, such lively search for truth, "betok'ns us not degenerated, nor drooping to a fatal decay, but casting off the old and wrincl'd skin of corruption to outlive these pangs and wax young again" (YP 2:557). The condition of dismembered truth is a project for recovery, both individual and political.

Areopagitica is an eloquent argument on behalf of a free press and free inquiry, and also the preeminent illustration in prose of Milton's invitational poetics. Not only is it imbued with metaphor and allusion, those "springs of Helicon," but also its syntactic structures and conditional language continually demand a reader's engagement. In a fallen world, Milton insists, the individual conscience is a better judge than an outside censor, and censorship may prevent exactly the engagement with good and evil that will lead to truth. The work is full of compelling rhetoric on behalf of the free flow of ideas, arguing that the Fall has made truth elusive and its pursuit essential, and therefore each individual must invest in the re-membering of truth.

But here we are back to the central conundrum of Milton's stance: how does the author force his readers not merely to accept his rhetoric, but choose their own truth within and beyond that rhetoric? The familiar core of Milton's case, with its focus on the fallen human condition, appears about a third of the way through:

> Good and evil we know in the field of this World grow up together almost inseparably; and the knowledge of good is so involv'd and interwoven with the knowledge of evil, and in so many cunning resemblances hardly to be discern'd, that those confused seeds which were impos'd on *Psyche* as an incessant labour to cull out and sort asunder, were not more intermixt. It was from out of the rinde of one apple tasted, that the knowledge of good and evill as two twins cleaving together leapt forth into the World. And perhaps this is that doom that *Adam* fell into of knowing good and evill, that is to say of knowing good by evil. As therefore the state of man now is, what wisdome can there be to choose, what continence to forbeare, without the knowledge of evill? He that can apprehend and consider vice with all her baits and seeming pleasures, and yet abstain, and yet distinguish, and yet prefer that which is truly better, he is the true warfaring Christian. I cannot praise a fugitive and cloister'd vertue, unexercis'd & unbreath'd, that never sallies out and sees her adversary, but slinks out of the race, where that immortall garland is to be run for, not without dust and heat. Assuredly we bring not innocence into the world, we bring impurity much rather: that which purifies us is triall, and triall is by what is contrary." (YP 2:514–15)

As he has from the beginning of his "speech to Parliament," Milton here calls on his "fit-though-few" trope, which assumes a shared set of values and a shared devotion to knowledge: the locutions "we know," and "knowing person" recall the "knowing reader" with whom he made his covenant in *Reason of Church-Government*. This common rhetorical device underlies all of *Areopagitica* as Milton feigns to assume that he is speaking to a receptive body of liberals who share his values. It both invites the listener into a conversation based on those shared values and authorizes the speaker as an insider. Here the English parliamentary tradition that presumably valorized both civic rights and free speech (as I outlined in chapter 1), comes directly into Milton's argument.

Throughout *Areopagitica* Milton assumes that parliamentary freedom is the ground on which he stands, and the members of Parliament and all like-minded readers are his natural allies.[44]

In that context Milton's rhetoric encourages dialogue, as he hedges or complicates even his most apparently direct pronouncements. He begins by asserting that "we know," but immediately undercuts what we can know, since good and evil are so intertwined, "and in so many cunning resemblances hardly to be discern'd." Indirect locutions and double negatives further complicate meaning: instead of a simple simile—good and evil are as intermixed as Psyche's famous seeds—we have those seeds "not more intermixt" than good and evil; instead of our race for truth being run with dust and heat, it is run "not without dust and heat." The effect is to invite the reader to consider the statement in the context of its opposite, hinting at contrast and choice. Similarly, Milton uses rhetorical questions: "what wisdom can there be?" "what continence to forbeare, without the knowledge of evill?" While this is a standard technique for inviting emphatic assent, it also raises the possibility of an answer that might challenge the implicit assertion. In *Paradise Lost*, Milton's Raphael encourages unfallen Adam to make his own choices, implying he can know good by good and should not think he must know good by knowing evil: "To stand or fall, / Free in thine own Arbitrement it lies. / Perfet within, no outward aid require" (8.640–42). But, of course, it is exactly Milton's point in *Areopagitica* that, since the Fall, outward aids are required, and one of them is the need/ability to test truth against falsehood. Finally, and perhaps most interestingly, Milton uses the language of surmise: "perhaps...that is to say," "it seems," "bin counted," "as they suppos'd." This language has the effect of hedging even his most assertive pronouncements, as it suggests that nothing can really be said "assuredly," or perhaps that there are those who *can* praise a fugitive and cloistered virtue.

Like Erasmus in his controversy with Luther, Milton would have "wisdome" and "continence" proved by right choice in the face of temptation and trial. Choice is not only possible, it is the core of the God-given human condition: "Many there be that complain of divin Providence for suffering *Adam* to trangresse, foolish tongues! When God gave him reason, he gave him freedom to choose, for reason is but choosing" (YP 2:527). Despite the complexity of choosing in a world where error abounds, or more to the point because of it, truth must be given a chance to contend in the war of ideas: "And though all the windes of doctrin were let loose to play upon the earth, so Truth be in the field, we do injuriously by licencing and prohibiting to misdoubt her strength. Let her and Falshood grapple; who ever knew Truth put to the wors, in a free and open encounter" (YP 2:561).

Passages such as this insist on the imperative for individual choice and the free circulation of ideas. Yet Milton is no twentieth century libertarian. His argument is against *prior* censorship, and he favors judging and even burning libelous or otherwise offensive books. Further, there seems an inconsistency between Milton's many assertions that all views should be tolerated and his exclusion of Catholic or atheist beliefs. In what sounds at first like another argument for complete toleration, Milton manages in an offhand comment to exclude "Popery" and "that...which is impious or evil": "Yet if all cannot be of one mind, as who looks they should be? This doubtless is more wholesome, more prudent, and more Christian that many be tolerated, rather than all compelled. I mean not tolerated Popery, and open superstition, which as it extirpats all religions and civil supremacies, so it self should be extirpat...that also which is impious or evil absolutely against faith or manners no law can possibly permit, that intends not to unlaw it self" (YP 2:565). By contrast, in this same period Levellers such as John Lilburne and Richard Overton would appear to allow toleration for all professed Christians, and Milton's friend Roger Williams, the founder of Rhode Island (back in London on colony business), argues in *The Bloudy Tenent, of Persecution, for the Cause of Conscience Discussed* (1644) for complete religious toleration, including for Jews and Mohammedans as well as Catholics.[45]

Some critics have found Milton's stance problematic.[46] Sirluck, however, points out that Milton's was a common contemporary argument against tolerating Catholicism (YP 2:179–81), citing Milton's concern (at base not unlike that of James I) that the pope's asserted power of excommunication could relieve subjects of their obedience to their country's government and laws, as Pius V had done in 1570 against Elizabeth in favor of Mary Stuart. If the English nation was to be sovereign and the English to enjoy the freedoms they believed their rule of law enabled, they must be vigilant to suppress those who would set them under a foreign prince. Further, the Catholic denial of the primacy of the Bible would, in Milton's view, deny one of the things we *do* know about true religion—that the Bible is the source of the word of God from which the rest of our discussion must extend. Milton's Bible-centered hermeneutics, aided by his belief in God's direct encounter with the individual conscience, is the nexus from which his free exchange of ideas extends. The argument in favor of freedom, in this reading, is an argument against tolerating Catholicism.

The freedom for which Milton argues, and which Catholicism would presumably prevent, is, on the one hand, personal, a piece of his "domestic liberty" agenda. On the other hand, Milton makes his argument not only on behalf of individual salvation, but also in the context and on behalf of a government of lawmakers, partly the inheritance of English traditions of political freedom and partly an emerging republicanism, a convergence of two fairly distinct ideas.[47] Clement Fatovic makes the interesting point that Milton's sort of anti-Catholicism is historically connected to the development of both liberal and republican views in English politics.

"In the heat of battle for the literal survival of Protestantism and a free way of life, the theoretical tension between individualistic conceptions of freedom that centered around the protection of personal rights and collective ideas of freedom that revolved around civic ideals of self-government did not seem to matter to English thinkers as much as confronting the popish menace did."[48]

Milton's understanding of freedom in *Areopagitica*, then, is a coalescence of the ideas that he later separated out for explanation in *The Second Defence*. Although he was not the only polemicist to argue for freedom, personal and civic, Milton's 1644 writings are notable for two tendencies that would have later importance for his work: he increasingly views his understanding of freedom through the myth of the Fall, and he develops increasing facility with a rhetoric and poetics that are more invitational than dogmatic. Earlier I alluded to *Of Education*, the third of his "domestic liberty" topics (written a few months before *Areopagitica*), in which Milton establishes the purpose of learning in terms of the Fall: "the end of learning...is to repair the ruins of our first parents by regaining to know God aright, and out of that knowledge to love him, to imitate him, to be like him, as we may the nearest by possessing our souls of true vertue, which being united to the heavenly grace of faith makes up the highest perfection" (YP 2:366–67).[49] His teaching method deemphasizes a focus on grammar rules and composition in favor of learning to read Latin and Greek authors for their substance, through works of graduated difficulty, and downplays learning modern languages for their own sake, "so that language is but the instrument convaying to us things usefull to be known" (YP 2:369). Unsurprisingly, then, Milton's great epic, which is about freedom and choice, centers on the biblical story of the Fall and makes divine and diabolical invitations to knowledge the principal engines of the poem's action.

Four

Knowledge, Choice, and Freedom in *Paradise Lost*

It is now commonplace to see *Paradise Lost* as "pre-eminently about knowing and choosing."[1] Its stated purpose, to "assert Eternal Providence, / And justifie the wayes of God to men," emerges from a complex portrayal of freedom as God's essential gift to humankind, and, after the Fall, of Providence as the guide to recovery (*PL* 1.25–26). Yet this commonplace has become so customary, in Milton's sense of the term, that a reader may not attend to the complexities that demand a more dislocating engagement. This chapter examines some of the ways that Milton's narrative and rhetoric challenge and encourage the reader to understand and exercise individual freedom as he defines it. For Milton, freedom is not a state of being but of developing. It is a process contingent on right choice.

Almost any passage in *Paradise Lost* will offer rich lines of inquiry into this general topic. Here, after some preliminary comments on Milton's verse, I want to focus on what *Paradise Lost* says about knowledge, freedom, and choice;

how some key scenes illustrate those ideas; and how those scenes invite a reader's interaction with the text. Milton allows his reader to participate, at some level, in paradigmatic occasions that illustrate free will and put the act of choosing at the heart of creating an individual self. These include Adam and Eve's descriptions of their coming to awareness (8.250–559 and 4.449–91) and their separate decisions to disobey God's single injunction that they not eat the fruit of the tree of knowledge of good and evil (9.733–834, 9.896–959). These scenes occur in the context of a temporal universe in which consequences are not obvious, even before the Fall, and linguistic density often signals multivalent possibilities even as it offers the reader, in turn, the possibility of multiple interpretive choices.[2]

Milton's poetics of freedom in *Paradise Lost* begins with the unfolding formal choices that anticipate the poem's thematic emphasis on knowing and choosing. *Paradise Lost* was originally published in 1667 in ten books, probably in imitation of Lucan's *Pharsalia* and perhaps suggesting a five-act structure compatible with its tragic elements and Milton's early intent to write a drama on the topic.[3] For its second edition in 1674, Milton revised it into the twelve books that emphasize its place in the epic tradition. For the fourth issue of the first edition (1668), Milton added a brief introduction on "the verse," justifying the work's lack of rhyme, along with prose summaries or "arguments," which in the second edition are placed before each book.[4] Milton's verse, as he underscores in the introductory comment, asks his reader to be receptive to a transformation of the traditions of narrative story that he inherited.[5] It is also a pervasive stylistic signal of the poem's concern with freedom and choice, as Milton calls it "an example set, the first in English, of ancient liberty recover'd to Heroic Poem from the troublesome and modern bondage of Rimeing."[6]

Although unrhymed blank verse had been the standard for the theater since Marlowe in the 1580s, narrative, on models from Chaucer through Spenser, was usually rhymed, with most Restoration narrative moving in the balanced couplets fully mastered by John Dryden and (later) Alexander Pope.[7] Against this context Milton described his medium as "*English* Heroic Verse without Rime, as that of *Homer* in *Greek*, and *Virgil* in *Latin*; Rime being no necessary Adjunct or true Ornament of a Poem or good Verse, in longer works especially, but the invention of a barbarous Age." These comments point back to experiments with classical meters and arguments over rhyme that occupied Sidney, Spenser, Thomas Campion, and Samuel Daniel, among others,[8] but instead of trying to imitate quantitative rhythms, a bad fit for English accentual verse, Milton uses his "liberty" to versify with "apt numbers," or attention to a consistent number of syllables in each line, and an undefined "fit quantity of syllables" with "the sense variously drawn out from one verse to another."[9] John Creaser notes that Milton "handles the virtual re-invention of blank verse with striking freedom," and David Norbrook sees it "breaking out of a confining frame into a wider and more universal perspective."[10] The freedom Milton claims for his verse is in service to his own choices and to the variety of lineation (along with varieties of genres and approaches to his biblical materials) that he will bring to his project. Unlike a narrative in heroic couplets, nothing in Milton's poem will feel trussed up, contained, directive. What we learn from Milton's poem will be part of an ongoing project of knowledge that evolves through time, even as the text and editorial attributes of *Paradise Lost* evolved in Milton's presenting it to the world.

The verse in *Paradise Lost*, with its sense "variously drawn out" according to the choices of the author, liberated from the demands of rhyme, is an emblem for the freedom that surrounds the poem's epistemology. What Adam and Eve know, how they know what they know, and what they desire to know are at the core of Milton's narrative. Before the Fall Adam and Eve know only good and make choices from among an abundance of good things and productive activities: enjoying the natural world and each other, tasting delicious foods, tending the garden, making love. After the Fall, to recall Milton's language in *Areopagitica*, Adam and Eve know "good by evill. As therefore the state of man now is; what wisdome can there be to choose, what continence to forbeare without the knowledge of evill?" (YP 2:514). One problem, as many readers observe, is that reason, language, and knowledge itself become perverted and ambiguous after the Fall.[11] Postlapsarian readers may find ironies in Adam and Eve's conversations before the Fall, but in general their prelapsarian language, like the language of God and the Son in book 3, may be read as direct and unambiguous. Their language immediately after the Fall is disjunctive and full of bad logic and double meanings. Their choices become confused, as their feelings, which Adam once understood as good in themselves but needing rational management, distort the process of reason. Freedom once absolute now becomes contingent in all the ways important to Milton—in personal, domestic, and political situations. Decisions are difficult and choices more obscure. In this familiar human context the poet offers a vision of the divine. Milton as Sidneian *vates* will call on biblical as well as classical models to validate the prophetic role, invoking the "Heav'nly Muse" that inspired "that Shepherd [Moses as supposed author of Genesis], who first taught the chosen Seed, / In the Beginning how the Heav'ns and Earth / Rose out of *Chaos*" (1.8–10).

While a logician, such as Hobbes, might simplify the idea of knowledge and the role of poetry into a contained set of rules, Milton complicates them into patterns of interwoven processes.[12] There are many kinds of knowledge, whole and partial, good and bad, experiential and intellectual, represented throughout *Paradise Lost*. Only God is omniscient, though his agents, the Son and the Holy Spirit, are given sweeping and transcendent knowledge (1.19, 3.116–19, 6.689). Others may know truly but not completely, as Adam knows the nature of the animals and was created to become increasingly "self-knowing" (7.493–94, 510). Since knowledge even for the unfallen is ongoing, this partial or developing knowledge is an appropriate part of the complex abundance of living in happiness. Teaching and learning are more than a way of knowing; they are ways of becoming, both the grounds for freedom and its exercise. God interrogates Adam to allow him to know his desire for a companion of his own kind (8.437–41), and Eve develops knowledge and relationship through her conversations with Adam (8.48–54).

A key question in *Paradise Lost* remains whether Adam and Eve have the knowledge to make the choices that continue them in freedom, particularly in the face of the temptations they will face. Milton's God insists that Adam and Eve are free to choose until and including their choices to disobey God's single command. The decisions of unfallen Adam and Eve in books 4–8 are not without context, complexity, and even foreboding, but they appear designed to illustrate an unfettered free will forming a conscious, happy, and integrated humanity. In a manner reminiscent of a more recent tradition of Christian existentialism, Adam and Eve become what they do, their essence deriving as much from what they choose as from the power of choice God has created them to have.[13] Prelapsarian freedom is in that sense absolute but also affected by where and how Adam and Eve come to awareness, what they see, how they reason, and what they are told. What they choose is complicated by how and what they know.

Milton's exposition of what appears to be his own understanding of knowledge, freedom, and choice comes through Adam's conversation with Raphael in book 5, which centers Eve's (in book 4) and then Adam's origin stories. Milton situates the reader to overhear these characters' origin stories from their own points of view, and therefore to understand something of how they process experience into knowledge. Adam tells his story to Raphael in book 8, in part to keep the conversation going with the "sociable Spirit" who has completed his tale of the war in heaven. Both stories, Raphael's and Adam's, come over a meal, the preparation and consumption of which suggest the continuity of human and angelic natures, leading most modern critics to see Milton's ontology as monist materialist or monist vitalist.[14] Raphael assures Adam that he will be able to enjoy the meal that Eve has carefully chosen and prepared, "for know, whatever was created needs to be sustained and fed." Heaven is a wonderful and more refined place, but even on earth God has "varied his bounty so with new delights / As may compare with Heaven; and to taste / Think not I shall be nice" (5.431–33). The angel proceeds to eat with "keen dispatch / Of real hunger" (5.436–37), affirming not only the materiality of angels but the social interaction proper to humans and angels.[15]

After dinner Raphael engages Adam in a philosophical conversation, giving the reader directly what we may presume to be something of Milton's epistemology and ontology. Through that conversation we learn the two kinds of reason by which Adam may come to knowledge: reason that apprehends through a process, either of being taught (as by Raphael's "for know"), or by observation and inference, as by watching the angel eat heartily; and that which he intuits as a result of his own nature, whether seen as reflecting the intuitive mind of his maker, or as prompted by God directly. When after this pleasant meal "a sudden mind / Arose in Adam" to use the occasion "to know / Of things above his world," particularly about heaven and the nature of its beings (5.452–56), Raphael responds first with an ontology and then an epistemology. Raphael tells Adam that earth and heaven are part of one continuum, from drosser to more refined matter, to "vital spirits" that eventually give the soul reason, "and reason is her being / Discursive, or Intuitive; discourse / Is oftest yours, the latter most is ours" (5.487–89). Knowledge comes from a compound of reason both "discursive," or logical and linear, and "intuitive," or grasped instantly, "differing but in degree, of kind the same" (5.490).

Raphael's continuum describes a monistic universe with no disjunction between matter and spirit.[16] His epistemology is similarly without disjunction. Instead of describing the traditional sharp difference between the logical reasoning attributed to humankind and the intuitive apprehension ascribed to angelic nature, he makes both to be degrees of reason. Although discursive logic is more characteristic of human beings than angels, and intuitive reason more characteristic of angels than human beings, each level of being may function with both. Adam has just displayed a moment of intuitive reason, when "a sudden mind" arose in him to ask Raphael questions about heaven. This is reasonable, since Raphael is a messenger from heaven whom one might suppose would be willing to share his knowledge, but Adam did not need to work through linear logic to get there. Conversely, Satan, originally an angelic being reliant on intuitive reason, sinks into an increasingly distorted discursive logic over the course of *Paradise Lost*.[17]

Unfallen human nature possesses unfallen reason of both kinds, although, as Raphael has said, humankind will "oftest" use discursive reason, with speech both its method and limitation. "How shall I relate / To human sense th'invisible exploits / Of warring spirits" (5.564–66) Raphael asks when he is tasked with explaining the war in heaven. And later, as he seeks to recite the instantaneous creation of Adam's world, Raphael adds:

> Immediate are the acts of God, more swift
> Then time or motion, but to human ears
> Cannot without process of speech be told,
> So told as earthly notion can receive. (8.176–79)

Adam's first memory is nonetheless of "instinctive" action. "As new awak't from soundest sleep," he tells Raphael, he found himself lying on the ground where "strait toward Heav'n my wondering Eyes I turnd" until with "quick instinctive motion up I sprung" (8.253, 257, 259). From this upright position he surveys the world around him, including "Hill, Dale, and shadie Woods, and sunnie Plaines," streams and the creatures around that "livd, and movd, and walk'd, or flew" (8.262, 264). Only then does he observe himself, beginning with his ability to walk and run: "But who I was, or where, or from what cause, / Knew not" (8.270–71). He tries to speak, and succeeds in "readily" naming "what e'er I saw" (8.272–73).

Standing, wondering, and speaking are basic to him. From these evolve discursive reasoning and a theology of creation, as Adam describes it to Raphael:

> Thou sun, said I, faire Light,
> And thou enlight'nd Earth, so fresh and gay,
> Ye Hills and Dales, ye Rivers, Woods, and Plaines,
> And ye that live and move, fair Creatures, tell,
> Tell, if ye saw, how came I thus, how here?
> Not of my self; by some great Maker then,
> In goodness and in power praeeminent;
> Tell me how I may know him, how adore,
> From whom I have that thus I move and live,
> And feel that I am happier than I know. (8.273–82)

The passage concludes with a profound recognition of both happiness felt and knowledge still sought. If this is Milton's presentation of the right original of humanity's posture toward what is unknown, he presents it, typically, as a series of questions. Yet the questions are addressed to Adam's environment, to the sun, the earth, and the mute creatures that surround him. What Adam models is not Socratic method but a meditative disposition, and one that bases its meditation not solely on what he might "feel" but also on the questions raised by what he sees around him. These meditations lead him to desire knowledge of his clearly benevolent creator, and of how such a creator may be honored.

In response, Adam is put into a drowsy slumber, which at first he thinks ("untroubl'd") is a return to oblivion. Instead a dream "gently mov'd / My fancy to believe I yet had being," and brings to this "fancy," or inner sight, a "shape Divine" who names him "Adam," calls him "First Man" and "First Father," and leads him to a garden where

> Each Tree
> Load'n with fairest Fruit, that hung to the Eye
> Tempting, stirr'd in my sudden appetite
> To pluck and eate; whereat I wak'd and found
> Before mine Eyes all real. (8.306–10)

"Here had new begun / My wandering," had not the guide of his dream appeared from "among the Trees," allowing Adam, as he had requested, to fall instinctively into adoring submission. The divine figure raises Adam and teaches him, discursively, that "Whom thou soughtst I am," the "Author" of the world he sees. This Creator gives the garden to Adam to "Till and keep," to "Eate freely with glad heart" of all the trees in the garden except the one

> whose operation brings
> Knowledg of good and ill, which I have set
> The Pledge of thy Obedience and thy faith
> Amid the Garden by the Tree of Life. (8.311–26)

If obedience would keep Adam by the Tree of Life, it follows logically that disobedience would do the opposite, a point emphasized by the "remember" locution:

> Remember what I warne thee, shun to taste,
> And shun the bitter consequence: for know
> The day thou eatst thereof, my sole command
> Trangressed, inevitably thou shalt die. (8.327–30)

God's "for know" is as direct an epistemology as any creature can receive. It is also possible that Adam's experience, anticipating possible oblivion as he falls asleep, gives him some knowledge of the idea of death. It is less clear, as I discuss later in this chapter, whether Adam and Eve can comprehend death without the experience of evil.

What the reader overhears in the story Adam tells Raphael is an elaboration of Genesis 2:7–20 from Adam's perspective. The first man reveals himself as a sentient, thoughtful, and rational being whose ability to speak and name what he sees gives him understanding up to a point, after which God, operating on the inward sense of "fancy," responds to Adam by telling him his own name and dominion and setting the conditions for the relationship with the divine that Adam had sought through both his instinctive, intuitive reason and his discursive logic. A third kind of knowledge, from an inner voice that becomes externalized as the voice of God, further empowers Adam's ability to name and understand Creation (8.349–54) and to choose to adore the Creator. Neither Raphael nor Adam names this third kind of knowledge, but it transcends the abilities of both intuitive and discursive reason and allows the divine voice to be heard directly at the core of one's being. Here in this origin story it suggests connections between conscience and the imagination, between divine inspiration and poetry, that lie behind the poet's vatic power. Like the two sorts of reasoning, it can inform choice and drive the will. Where Satan chooses to know his reality only in terms of what he desires, Adam, by contrast, learns who he is and what he desires only by recognizing first his environment and then his own nature.

Adam is prepared to make choices, and the question remains, for Adam and for the reader, whether his choices are actually free. If he is not free to eat of the tree of "Knowledg of good and ill," are all his other choices then equally bound by God's will, not his own? As Joseph Wittreich argues, the books in which Adam and Raphael converse bring together competing stories of Creation from Genesis, and competing cosmologies—Copernican and Ptolemaic—which are allowed to suspend themselves without resolution.[18] The world in which Adam finds himself and the universe in which it is situated are in this sense open ended and open for interpretation, both by Adam and Milton's reader.[19] As Wittreich notes, "contradictions and inconsistencies may effect alarming dislocation in theological but not in poetic systems where the possibilities are completely open, where an utterance may be true or false relatively."[20] In this case, I would add, the theological premise, stated unequivocally in book 3, is that obedience to the one injunction allows humankind to "stand" and to continue to make varied and valid choices.[21]

The validity of a choice for Adam or an interpretation for a reader is always situational, both before and after the Fall. Because author and reader live in the fallen state, however, there is always the danger of wrong choices and wrong interpretations ("wrong" in the sense of alienating us from God or from the author's intent to "justify [God's] ways to men"). For the prelapsarian Adam, however, obedience to the one injunction opens up myriad possible choices, and it is the very process of choosing that God both encourages and approves. This remains true even though, and because, as Barbara Lewalski points out, those choices may be "grounded on better or worse interpretations of God's pronouncements, of divine revelation."[22] Initially, Adam proves to be an excellent interpreter of God's creation, including himself.

Adam's first exercise of persistent volition, as he describes it to his angelic auditor, is to ask God to provide a companion of Adam's own kind. In arguing for a companion like himself, Adam uses the discursive reason and voice that are part of his nature and comes to recognize the freedom he has been given: "Thus I embold'nd spake, and freedom us'd / Permissive" (8.434–35). As Teresa Feroli notes, at this moment Adam "reveals his divine nature because [his "very human desire" for companionship]...is perfectly consistent with God's cosmological scheme."[23] The Creator is pleased "to find [Adam] knowing not of beasts alone, /...but of thyself / Expressing well the spirit within thee free" (8.438–40). God observes that Adam successfully reasons from what he knows, and this allows him to exercise his freedom by making choices appropriate to his own developing richness. God again puts Adam in a sleep, and again allows "Fancie, my internal sight" to see the Creator take a rib from near his heart and form it into a creature "Manlike, but different Sex, so lovely faire, / That what seemd faire in all the World, seemd now / Mean, or in her summ'd up, in her containd" (8.471–73). This vision produces a "Sweetness into my heart, unfelt before" (8.475), so precious to him than when she disappears in the dream, he wakes "To find her, or for ever to deplore / Her loss, and other pleasures all abjure" (8.479–80). He wakes to see her led toward him by the invisible presence of God, and in his joy Adam acknowledges the Creator's beneficence, names her ("Woman is her name, of Man / Extracted" [8.496–97]) and pledges himself to her. She hears him, and for reasons that Adam interprets as modesty and the need to be won of her own will, "she turn'd";

> I follow'd her, she what was Honour knew,
> And with obsequious Majestie approv'd
> My pleading reason. To the Nuptial Bowre
> I led her blushing like the Morn.   (8.506–09)

Adam concludes his tale to Raphael with a rapturous description of Eve's beauty and his own love, prompting Raphael to warn Adam not to set her above himself, but to see her as "worthy well / Thy cherishing, thy honouring, and thy love, / Not thy subjection" (8.568–70). Eve's origin, however, as Adam remembers it, begins with his power of volition to which God responds, allowing Adam to see God's work through one of those moments when the divine reveals something directly to the imagination, a vision beyond reason. At its best this imaginative vision offers the highest connection with the divine. At its worst, in the fallen state in which the author and reader live, and toward which Adam and Eve may choose or not choose to go, it turns away from the divine and displaces reason altogether.

Adam's self-description captures in story form the complexities of knowing and choosing, and outlines both the range and limits of his freedom as an unfallen being. He chooses rightly to complicate his life through love, knowing and receiving what he desires. This Eve, derived from him (both his mind's longing and his flesh) and made for him, is worth his cherishing, honoring, and love, but not his "subjection." The rebuke from Raphael contains Adam's tendency to place Eve above all else, but the tendency, arguably a self-love, is clear. Milton's Eve is not the equal female of Genesis 1:27, "male and female created He them," but the extension of Adam in Genesis 2:21–24, "bone of my bones and flesh of my flesh." To know her is at least part of how he knows himself, and a motivating fear in his fall, that "to loose thee were to loose my self" (9.959), mirrors the turn away from God and into the self symbolized by the allegory of Satan and Sin in 2.752–67.

The vitalism that infuses *Paradise Lost*—the self-organizing power implicit in a material chaos generously proffered out of his own being by a creative God—may be seen as a feature of all creatures' inherent agency.[24] Here, though, since Eve's material being emerges from Adam, it is difficult to separate that agency from Adam—her self-containment is both true and false, as her decisions are her responsibility even though her being is a product of Adam's desire for her. Hence, the literal truth of the claim, "hee for [also from] God only, shee for [from] God in [through] him" (4.299).[25] So Eve is responsible for her choices, but the Fall is not complete until Adam chooses it, their "one flesh" fully choosing what will separate them from God and therefore, ironically, from each other. Since the reader knows what is to come, Adam's self-description, and then his admiration of Eve toward the end of book 8, take on an ominous cast, a portentous narrative irony that would not exist without the reader's knowledge, thereby involving the reader directly in the creation of the poem's tone:

> when I approach
> Her loveliness, so absolute she seems
> And in her self compleat, so well to know
> Her own, that what she wills to do or say,
> Seems wisest, vertousest, discreetest, best;
> All higher knowledge in her presence falls
> Degraded, Wisdom in discourse with her
> Looses discount'nanct, and like folly shewes;
> Authority and Reason on her waite,
> As one intended first, not after made
> Occasionally; and to consummate all,
> Greatness of mind and nobleness thir seat
> Build in her loveliest, and create an awe
> About her, as guard Angelic plac't.   (8.546–59)

At the same time as it illustrates Adam's love and presages his danger, this passage showcases Milton's invitational poetics, in particular the language of surmise. "Seems" brackets the premise of the speech: Eve's excellence *seems* to trump every other. It is *as if* she were the "one intended first," the original *imago Dei*, instead of deriving her humanity secondarily, on the occasion of Adam's desire for a companion. For Adam, her beauty and virtues surround her *as if* there were a "guard Angelic plac't." The conclusion raises an implicit question: from whom or what would this (seeming) angel guard her? For the reader, the speech both reveals Adam's relationship to Eve and questions it, as Raphael does in the admonishment that follows.

Here as elsewhere, in book 9 especially, the reader's choices are an implicit part of Milton's narrative project. It is not so much that Milton "tempts" the reader into misreadings that must be corrected, as Fish claims, as that he asks the reader to see more than the characters in the narrative are able to see.[26] There is a double narrative force at play here, an interaction between what Paula Johnson calls "progressive form" and "retrospective form": we have read Genesis, and can see the shape of the emerging story retrospectively.[27] At the same time, we are watching Milton's narration unfold progressively, with story and language arranged very differently (and of course much more abundantly) than the Yahwist text of Genesis, chapters 2–3. That interaction forces interpretive choice. So, for example, I have described Adam's admiration of Eve in book 5 as "taking on an ominous cast," in part because Raphael, "with contracted brow," immediately warns Adam to be careful, assuming the pleasure of Eve's touch is becoming a problem (8.560–94). But it is also possible to argue that Raphael misunderstands Adam, as he himself claims. It is not her beauty or their lovemaking so much as

> Those graceful acts,
> Those thousand decencies that daily flow
> From all her words and actions mixt with Love
> And sweet compliance, which declare unfeign'd
> Union of Mind, or in us both one soule. (8.600–04)

One might step back and see in this higher union an appropriate valuing, a tone of delicate love and not, in the progressive unfolding of the story at this point, anything necessarily ominous at all. But this moment is further complicated by our retrospective on the earlier narrative, including Eve's own description of her coming to awareness.

Though she was the second created, Eve's origin story comes earlier than Adam's in Milton's narrative, in lover's talk with Adam in book 4. The reader overhears her along with Satan, who is spying on the couple. That context, rich with desire fulfilled and thwarted, complicates Eve's self-description even before we read some of the language about Eve's position in Eden that has disturbed modern readers.[28] It immediately offers the reader a quadruple perspective on the events Eve will describe: the narrator's creation of setting, Eve's own stated memories, Adam's presence as audience receiving and in some way sharing those memories, and Satan's hidden presence as eavesdropper.

In the reader's first view of Eden's "happy rural seat of various view" (4.247) with its "luxuriant" (4.260) bounty of all kinds, the narrator proclaims Adam and Eve "the lovliest pair / That ever since in loves imbraces met" (4.321–22). Their "wholsom thirst and appetite" are easily fulfilled by the abundant "nectarine fruits" and "brimming stream"; their desire for each other fulfilled by "youthful dalliance as beseems / Fair couple, linkt in happy nuptial League" (4.330, 332, 336, 338–39). Satan, taking in this same scene, beholds it "with grief," and his complex desire (an inchoate merging of anger, envious longing, jealousy, self-pity, and domination) twists through various rationales for what he hopes to achieve:

> League with you I seek,
> And mutual amitie so streight, so close,
> That I with you must dwell, or you with me
> Henceforth; my dwelling haply may not please
> Like this fair Paradise, your sense, yet such
> Accept your Makers work; he gave it me,
> Which I as freely give. (4.375–82)

To the conjoined happiness of Adam and Eve Satan would seek to join himself, not in the freedom of their abundance but in the "streight" confines of his own "close" and restrictive embrace. He couches his intent to destroy their freedom in terms of fate and necessary compulsion ("must dwell," "haply"), and makes an ironic parallel between the freedom God gives his obedient creation and the choice of hell Satan proposes to give "as freely" as it fell to him. It is a pivotal moment that looks back to Satan's casting down in book 1 and forward to the temptation of Eve in book 9. If Adam and Eve are to have enough knowledge to make good choices and so remain free, God must assure they know about Satan, as he does through Raphael in the next books.[29]

Yet can unfallen reason, discursive or intuitive, understand fully evil intent and the danger it poses? Until they taste of the tree of that knowledge, one classic argument goes, how can they truly know good? Satan's response to what he sees from his perch in Eden both underscores and contrasts with the anticipated human fall, since Satan typically does not know good by knowing evil, but rather, as here, knows evil by knowing good. As he observes the beauty of Eden, he sees "undelighted all delight" (4.286) and hopes for the same for Adam and Eve: "more woe, the more your taste is now of joy" (4.369). Since his fall, as his use of "accept" and "freely" suggest in the passage above, Satan's knowledge of good is perverse, including an ironic or deliberate misunderstanding of choice and therefore of freedom. Instead of offering the opportunity for choice, Satan's sense of rational justice ("public reason just,"), "compels me now / To do what else though damned I should abhor" (4.389, 391–92).

In this first view of both Adam and Eve, then, prefatory to Eve's story of coming to awareness, the fallen reader is able to contrast Satan's sense of compulsion and self-confinement with Adam and Eve's awareness, knowledge, and possibilities, but not without some sense of dread and pathos. We understand Satan's point of view in a way clearly impossible for Adam and Eve in these tableaux of innocence. While it seems clear what Adam, and then Eve, do know, it is not clear that they either are capable or can be capable of knowing the danger they confront.

Adam's first speech in book 4 picks up some time after the nuptials with Eve that he later describes in book 8, addressing her affectionately as "Sole partner and sole part of all these joyes, / Dearer thy self than all" (4.411–12). From this joy Adam reasons, as he will describe himself doing at his first view of the world in book 8, toward the goodness of God who gives these gifts to his creatures:

> Needs must the Power
> That made us, and for us this ample World
> Be infinitely good, and of his good

> As liberal and free as infinite,
> That rais'd us from the dust and plac't us here
> In all this happiness. (4.412–17)

"Needs must" is a logical conclusion based on evidence. Here the very assertiveness is consistent with Milton's invitational poetics. It invites us to follow the reasoning from the point of view of Adam's evidence and assess the logic that brings him to what he knows: that he has been created from dust, that he and Eve have "nothing merited" their happiness and cannot repay it (4.418–19), and that they are only required the one "easie charge" of not tasting from the tree of knowledge

> planted by the Tree of Life,
> So neer grows death to Life, what ere Death is,
> Som dreadful thing no doubt; for well thou knowst
> God hath pronounc't it death to taste that Tree,
> The only sign of our obedience left
> Among so many signs of power and rule
> Conferrd upon us. (4.424–30)

Adam knows that he must not trespass this injunction because it would bring "Some dreadful thing" that he does *not* know, and the "no doubt" is surely an invitation for the reader to recognize the potential for doubt, whether in Adam or the reader. Adam also asserts that both he and Eve "well" know that the tree is "the only sign" of obedience while he and Eve otherwise have complete dominion over "Earth, Aire, and Sea."

> Then let us not think hard
> One easie prohibition, who enjoy
> Free leave so large to all things else, and choice
> Unlimited of manifold delights. (4.432–35)

This short passage is rich with locutions that ask the reader to consider more negative potential than Adam's confidence suggests. "Not think hard" implies that one might, calling a prohibition "easie" suggests it may in fact go against the "free leave so large" and the "choice / Unlimited" he praises.

Adam's reasonable conclusion, however, is that he and Eve have almost complete and certainly sufficient freedom, delivered by the free liberality of God's abundant gifts. Unlike Satan who knows evil by contrasting it with good, and unlike the "doom" that they will fall into of "knowing good by evil," here before the Fall they know good by knowing and being able to choose among "manifold delights"—they know good by good. Eve concurs: "what thou hast said is just and right" (4.443). She also knows that she is formed from Adam, that he is her "Guide / And Head" (4.442–43), and she considers herself the luckier partner since she has him to enjoy while he "Like consort to thy self canst no where find" (4.448).

Knowledge of her own happiness prompts Eve to talk about her coming to awareness, one of those "how we met" stories that lovers like to repeat. In telling of "that day I oft remember" (4.449), Eve recalls that she had no understanding when she awoke into consciousness, but she had physical sensations and questions, and at least a preliminary instinct for the principle of causation, "much wondering where / And what I was, whence hither brought, and how" (4.451–52). She hears the sound of water, following it "with unexperienced thought" (4.457) to "see a shape" in the pool with which she is pleased, and pleased to see in it "answering looks / Of sympathy and love" (4.464–65).

At this moment Eve's awakening knowledge is limited to the outer image of beauty—her own, in the reflection of the pool—and her narcissistic reaction is appropriate (she is the epitome of attractive beauty) but incomplete, requiring intervention. A voice then leads her to where "no shadow staies / Thy coming" (4.470–71), bringing her to achievable union rather than "vain desire" (4.466). She does not fully understand this instruction but is compelled by the voice: "What could I do / But follow straight, invisibly thus led" (4.475–76). This is a genuine rhetorical question, suggesting that the "voice" speaking and compelling Eve is akin to Adam's dream: it is a divine intervention intended to tell Eve who she is, and comes to her beyond discursive or intuitive reason, which always involves choice. It contrasts, too, with her reaction to where she is led.

Brought to Adam, she finds him fair but not as fair as "that smooth wat'ry image" (4.480). Eve's first volitional choice is to turn back, until the voice of Adam calls her and claims her as "my other half" (4.488). Their union concludes with his touch and her compliance, as Eve recalls

> Thy gentle hand
> Seised mine, I yielded, and from that time see
> How beauty is excelld by manly grace
> And wisdom, which alone is truly fair. (4.488–91)

The juxtaposition of "gentle" and "seised" in this passage is a reminder, possibly a troubling one, that the creation of Eve complicates life for both of them. If indeed she is, as she seems to Adam, "so absolute.../ And in her self compleat" (8.547–48), his need to seize and her choice to yield set their hierarchy, if not necessarily their value. Milton has allowed Eve to learn about manly grace and wisdom, presumably part of that ongoing process of becoming that continues "from that time" forward. The reader's multiple perspectives on this scene allow for no complacent finality about its meaning.

On the simplest interpretive level, Milton's Eve is born a sentient being with questions and a longing for beauty who must be led, held, and taught the superior beauty of wisdom. Without intervention she would presumably be able to choose only in the direction of outward beauty, perfect in itself but incomplete. Her completeness depends on God's call and Adam's gift of wisdom, apparently a successful gift: she enjoys being Adam's student ("With thee conversing I forget all time" [4.639]) and Adam refers to her as "accomplished Eve" (4.660). Unlike Eve, Adam first notices his surroundings before he wonders about himself, and when he wonders, it is not simply the who, where and somewhat vague "how" of Eve's first reaction, but the logician's more technical "from what cause." He is a fully reasoning being from the beginning, untaught. Eve, formed from near Adam's heart, does not share his instinct to discursive reason, but can be taught it, can become "accomplished." In both cases, good choices depend on what they know—hence God's emphatic "know this" to Adam about the consequence of eating from the tree of knowledge of good and evil, a "rigid interdiction," as Adam tells Raphael, "which resounds / Yet dreadful in mine ear, though in my choice / Not to incur" (8.334–36). Adam knows it is his choice to make and he wills to choose correctly.

In all, Adam and Eve know a great deal from what they see around them, what they have been told, and what they experience. The happiness they enjoy is not a static, unchanging placidity but active involvement with each other and the world around them. They need to tend their garden or it will grow wild. They get hungry and thirsty. They are able to experience distress, as when Eve awakes from the troubling dream that Satan has whispered in her ear (5.28–128). By the beginning of book 9 both are able to reason discursively, as they have what turns out to be a most unfortunate disagreement over whether to work separately or together, but even that difficult conversation occurs in their unfallen condition (9.205–385).[30] Each of them understands that they face danger from Satan, even if they do not fully understand the danger they face, and it seems clear they have been sufficiently educated and warned.[31] From this knowledge Adam reasons that the two of them should stay together (9.251–69), but Eve reasons quite logically that to do so on that basis would be to restrict their freedom and their happiness:

> If this be our condition, thus to dwell
> In a narrow circuit strait'nd by a Foe,
> Suttle or violent, we not endu'd

>   Single with like defence, wherever met,
>   How are we happie, still in fear of harm?   (9.322–26)

Milton's characteristic conditional and interrogative set up a core interpretive problem for the reader. Is Eve right, that by not being free to separate from each other without fear they are less than free? Does that make their world a "narrow circuit"? Does fear itself make Satan successful in abrogating their perfect happiness? The answer will depend to a great extent on how one thinks of God's providence, which within the narrative has been largely a function of intuitive reason.

One can argue, then, that what fails them both, but Eve especially, is their intuitive reason, limiting what they can imagine, which limits their prudence. As a result, in Lewalski's terms, Eve has failed to "interpret and respond" to God's warning correctly.[32] On the one hand, even if he cannot fathom the magnitude of Satan's power to deceive, Adam can at least sense that their God-given "right" reason might be "by some faire appearing good surpris'd" and therefore dictate falsely to the will "to do what God expressly hath forbid" (9.354–55). Eve, on the other hand, cannot imagine "a Foe so proud will first the weaker seek" (9.383). They do know about evil—they do not need to eat of the tree of knowledge of good and evil to know that both exist. But on a more fundamental level they have not experienced evil in themselves, and they do not know death. Instead of reasoning between themselves, they would have been wiser, perhaps, to focus more fundamentally on their need to be obedient to God's command. That is one of several interpretive insights the "elegant and learned reader" can bring to this dangerous narrative moment, but it depends on what we already know, not on what Adam and Eve know in the progressive unfolding of their story.

Knowledge in *Paradise Lost* is a compound of reason and experience that may be turned true or false, virtuous or vicious, by choice. For all the characters of *Paradise Lost* except the omniscient God, knowledge has limits, and its validity and value depend on the use made of it. Knowledge is essential to making choices—you can only choose what you know—but at the same time it is the product of choosing; what you choose is part of the reasoning process that creates knowledge, for (as Milton insists in *Areopagitica*), "reason also is choice" (YP 3:108). Happiness derives from active, rational choosing, which enriches and is made richer by knowledge.

In their prelapsarian full potential, Adam and Eve's world appears boundless. By contrast, as Satan views unfallen earth in book 4, his insistence that the "mind is its own place" becomes ironic. Seeing earth's beauty and regretting his loss, acknowledging both the goodness of God and his own decision to choose "freely what [he] now so justly rues," Satan concludes: "Which way I flie is Hell; my self am Hell" (4.72, 75). By the end of book 4 Satan's self-enclosure and diminished glory affect not only what he knows of himself, but also what can be known about him. When the sentinels Ithuriel and Zephon discover him, transformed into a toad whispering into Eve's sleeping ear, he leaps "up in his own shape" (4.819). They demand "which of those rebel Spirits adjudg'd to Hell" he might be (4.823), and he indignantly replies:

> Know ye not then said *Satan*, fill'd with scorn,
> Know ye not mee? Ye knew me once no mate
> For you, there sitting where ye durst not soare;
> Not to know me argues your selves unknown,
> The lowest of your throng. (4.827–31)

Zephon, like Uriel earlier,[33] is able to see what the once grand Satan has now revealed himself to be and, "answering scorn with scorn," tells Satan that what he thinks he knows of himself is now delusion:

> Think not, revolted Spirit, thy shape the same,
> Or undiminisht brightness, to be known

> As when thou stoodst in Heav'n upright and pure;
> That Glorie then, when thou no more wast good,
> Departed from thee, and thou resembl'st now
> Thy sin and place of doom obscure and foul. (4.834–40)

Satan chastises those who "durst not soare," or rise up against God, as low, "unknown." Zephon responds that Satan is no longer "upright," but "obscure" and unrecognizable; his fall has diminished what he knows, making it inadequate to the reality he confronts, and his choices are equally diminished. Satan's rebellion has become a self-chosen confinement and not the uncontrolled freedom he originally sought.

Yet even this new reality appears to hang on a cusp of possibility, never realized over the course of the poem but always in interesting suspension: Satan had asked himself earlier in book 4, "Hadst thou the same free Will and Power to stand" as those angels who did not fall? "Thou hadst: whom hast thou then or what to accuse, / But Heav'ns free Love dealt equally to all?" (*PL* 4.66–68). Flirting with repentance, he concludes it is not for him and continues his destructive journey. Yet again, as he views Eve's beauty in book 9, he is momentarily "stupidly good, of enmitie disarm'd," his destructive purpose balked by the sight of her "graceful innocence" (9.465, 459). Moments such as these reveal gaps in Satan's self-knowledge even as he articulates his situation to himself privately.[34]

The choice to fall is a choice away from happiness in large part because it restricts knowledge, especially self-knowledge, and leads to delusion and confusion. With limited knowledge, choice and, therefore, freedom are limited. Milton illustrates this principle and Satan's concomitant self-delusion throughout *Paradise Lost*, but because the fallen reader's knowledge is also inevitably limited, the illustrations are never simple and the language is often richly eloquent, inviting interpretation even as it would appear to persuade. The role of language in persuasion and choice is tricky, as the Ramist streak in Milton understood and Satan's frequent eloquence illustrates, but it is nonetheless important to the poet who claimed freedom from rhyme, and who drew on the entire Western intellectual tradition for his epic similes. Eloquent language sometimes clarifies, as in Eve's love song to Adam (4.639–46), and sometimes obfuscates, as when Satan rouses the rebel angels (5.772–802). Sometimes it expands a vision of worlds beyond ordinary human ken, as in Raphael's description of the war in heaven in book 6, and sometimes it folds the mind into a Pandora's box of confusion, as in the serpent's temptation of Eve.

At the same time, plain language does not necessarily say simple things. The council of heaven in book 3, which establishes the complicated relationships among God, the Son, the angels and humankind, seems to many readers flat and static compared to the satanic passion and classically heroic journey of books 1 and 2. Yet this is where Milton's God makes the crucial theological point that both angels and humankind have free will and the ability to stand on their own, the premise (whether or not a given reader believes it) without which the rest of work makes no sense at all.[35] As God looks down at Satan's flight through hell and Chaos, and then at Adam and Eve "in the happie Garden plac't, / Reaping immortal fruits of joy and love" (3.66–67), he also sees a future in which "man will hark'n to [Satan's] glozing lies" and disobey the "one restraint," that they should not eat of the fruit of the tree of knowledge of good and evil, "Lords of the World besides" (1.32). Milton's God insists (as Saint Augustine had argued) that foreknowledge is not the same as causation.[36] "I made him just and right," God says, "sufficient to have stood, though free to fall" (3.98–99). Without that freedom, there could be no "true allegiance, constant Faith or Love" (3.104). There could be no merit for humankind, no "pleasure" for God, if love and obedience,

> Will and Reason (Reason is also choice)
> Useless and vain, of freedom both despoild,
> Made passive both, had served necessitie,
> Not mee. (3.108–11)

With this, and with the subsequent offer of the Son to sacrifice himself for humankind (3.236–51), the language is sufficient for the argument though not exciting, not titillating, the way Satan's passionate speeches are on behalf of the supremacy of the self. Arguably, however, the freedom described in this plain language opens up many more possibilities than the freedom Satan claims for himself and his followers.

Milton's God has been a problem for many critics since at least the Romantic period.[37] His injunctions seem so clear (and, to some, repressive), his test of obedience so absolute, that they find it difficult to see in him the liberating force that Milton apparently would have him be. He explains, for example, in foreseeing Adam and Eve's fall:

> So without least impulse or shadow of Fate,
> Or aught by me immutablie foreseen,
> They trespass, Authors to themselves in all
> Both what they judge and what they choose; for so
> I formd them free, and free they must remain,
> Till they enthrall themselves; else I must change
> Thir nature, and revoke the high Decree
> Unchangeable, Eternal, which ordain'd
> Thir freedom, they themselves ordain'd thir fall.
>
> (*PL* 3.120–28)

God's "high Decree / Unchangeable," which is fixed in the nature of humankind, ordains "thir freedom." The emphatic language of unrelenting rigidity actually describes a condition of infinite possibility. Only one choice—to disobey God—can "enthrall" them; their choices are otherwise limitless. Nonetheless, the tone of anger and implacability have seemed to some readers unbecoming to the God so jubilantly praised by the angelic hosts.[38]

Once Milton made the decision to cast God as one of his characters, he had to give him a rhetoric noticeably different from Satan's, and it is difficult to see how else Milton should have handled God's pronouncements. Recall that

Milton insisted on the clarity of Scripture, even as he began to argue in the divorce tracts for a greater contextualization. I do not think that Milton meant his readers to doubt the accuracy of God's statements; they contrast so starkly with the surrounding rhetoric that the choice he made to set them apart acts almost as if they were in bold print (or red letter). But I would suggest that they serve an important function beyond underscoring Milton's own basic theology of liberty, choice, and consequence: they highlight the complexity of the poem's more (and more usual) metaphoric language. By drawing attention to kinds of language, God's speeches alert the reader to the need to make interpretive choices. The poet's language, the figures and fictions that compel us in *Paradise Lost*, are objects for reflection and invitations to understanding.[39]

The danger for the reader, as it is for Eve, is that the power of satanic language and self-asserting heroism will override interpretive clarity.[40] Further, God's creation, no less than Satan's ambition, is variously proclaimed in great rhetorical beauty, as in Adam and Eve's morning hymn (*PL* 5.153–208). When Raphael reports to Adam the heavenly song with which the angels celebrated the day of rest after Creation, it contains not only a vision of the beauty and purposes of the new world and humankind's place in it, but an implicit injunction:

> Thrice happie men,
> And sons of men, whom God has thus advanc't,
> Created in his Image, there to dwell
> And worship him, and in reward to rule
> Over his Works, on Earth, in Sea, or Air,
> And multiply a Race of Worshippers
> Holy and just: thrice happie if they know
> Thir happiness, and persevere upright.   (7.625–32)

The conditional "if they know" is important here. It serves the progressive and retrospective forms of the epic, as it sends the narrative forward to the choices Adam and Eve will make, while our knowledge of Genesis overlays the angelic hymn with dramatic irony. It also centers the challenge of interpretation. To "know / Thir happiness," Adam and Eve must see and make choices toward it within the context of their obedience to God. The reader, in turn, is challenged to consider why "thrice happie." Presumably because the unfallen are in fact happy, have the added pleasure of knowing they are happy, and actively maintain that happiness by "persever[ing] upright," and remaining in control of their own circumstances, or "hap." By implication, even the fallen reader, wisely interpreting, can make choices that enrich possibilities for happiness, even if the reader cannot change the fallen condition.

Here the classic objection about Adam and Eve's free will may emerge: God and Raphael have made it very clear that Adam and Eve's choice of whether or not to eat of the fruit of the tree of knowledge of good and evil presents a right choice and a wrong choice. In this one case, Adam and Eve cannot continue to have a myriad of possible right choices if they make the wrong choice. That is, disobedience to God is a confining condition (they "enthrall themselves" [3.125]), while obedience liberates to multiple possible right choices (as Eve chooses her banquet for their angelic guest [5.332–49]). Further, when Adam and Eve, like Satan, forget or ignore their experience of God's abundance, Milton implies here and illustrates in the eventual outcome of the Fall, language that was once spontaneous song turns into bad logic, and taste once associated with infinite varieties of feasting degenerates into a dominating sensuousness that undermines the pleasure it would exploit. It is at these moments that the reader's interpretive choices become, ironically, more free. As we begin to share the human condition of those who choose to fall, our own interpretive choices are at once more rich and demanding. The choices and consequences the story will set before the reader invite application of our own theology and ontology, since how one takes the injunction not to taste of the tree of good and evil depends on how one thinks of God and what one thinks of the nature of being. In a world where there is "no more...God or Angel Guest / With man, as with his friend" (9.1–2), both discursive and intuitive knowledge of God is necessarily obscured. In that world, it is easy to make wrong choices, from the perspective of Milton's theology and ontology, but that does not mean that there remains only one right choice. Some freedoms, as the narrator makes clear in books 11 and 12, will remain.

The temptation scenes and those that immediately follow put readers directly into the decision processes of Eve and Adam. I suggest that these scenes also invite readers to consider their own responses to the temptations, necessarily multivalent given the readers' greater knowledge. If Adam and Eve know their happiness experientially through the abundance of God's gifts, as they have variously expressed earlier in the poem, the choice to disobey is a choice to forget or deny that knowledge in favor of self-centered and self-deluding logic. In conversation with Raphael, Adam shows that he knows reason must rule passion (8.607–11). In her conversations with Adam, Eve admires his intellectual force and happily learns from him (4.440–47, 657–58; 8.48–57). At the moment of her fall, however, she seeks no other logic or comfort but that of the temptation set before her, and at the moment of his fall, Adam abandons what he knows in order to stay with Eve no matter what. Her choice is usually seen as a function of Satan's temptation, his as a function of his love for Eve. Another way to see both lapses is as a choice of the self over God, the sin of pride found essentially in Satan. And yet another, related way to see each fall is as a choice toward ignorance, away from knowledge, manifested in a new way of knowing, that is, of knowing good by knowing evil. The reader adds another layer to these interpretations, simply because the reader already has the experience of knowing good by knowing evil and can measure this one absolute good or bad choice against all the surrounding choices, not necessarily either bad or good, that lead up to and later follow it.

When Satan in serpent guise surprises Eve by speaking to her—"What may this mean," she asks, "Language of Man pronounc't / By tongue of brute, and human sense exprest?" (9.553–54)—his rhetoric of worshipful praise moves easily to indignation that she should be forbidden anything, much less the wondrous fruit that has brought this dumb beast to "degree / Of reason in my inward Powers, and Speech" (9.599–600). She will not die if she eats, he insists, but have "Life / To knowledge" (9.686–87). God will surely not punish her, but admire her courage in the face of death "whatever thing Death be" (9.695), in order to achieve a "happier life, knowledge of Good and Evil," for if evil "Be real, why not known, since easier shunned? / God therefore cannot hurt ye, and be just; / Not just, not God; not feard then, nor obeyd" (9.699–701). From this Satan begins to describe a God bent on keeping Eve ignorant, and tempts her to aspire as he claims to have done, "I of brute human, yee of human Gods" (9.712), suggesting that death only means that her human nature will be displaced by a divine one. Satan's concluding peroration is full of questions that he would have Eve believe are rhetorical, their answers implicit in the questions:

> And wherein lies
> Th'offence, that Man should thus attain to know?
> What can your knowledge hurt him, or this Tree
> Impart against his will if all be his?
> Or is it envie, and can envie dwell
> In heav'nly brests? These, these and many more
> Causes import your need of this Fair Fruit.
> Goddess humane, reach then and freely taste. (9.725–32)

These are questions to be analyzed, not "causes" in the logical sense, and Milton has situated the reader to analyze as well as to react to Eve's response. Unlike the Lady in the Ludlow *Mask*, Eve's ear is deceived as her eye regards the outward beauty of the fruit, "which to behold / Might tempt alone" (9.735–36). It is noon and she is hungry. The Serpent seems to make sense. By eating, he has risen from animal to rational creature. He argues by analogy that Eve might equally expect to rise from rational creature to divine spirit. The appeal to knowledge combined with the sensuous power of carnal appetite is confusing but not necessarily catastrophic. Nonetheless, Eve's speech to herself before finally choosing to disobey God echoes first the faulty logic and then the pattern of questioning modeled by the Serpent's rhetoric. Until this moment, despite the disagreement with Adam at the beginning of book 9 over whether to work together or alone, Eve has seen everything in terms of completion and harmony, often in poetry, and her questions are part of her relationship with Adam. At the end of her elegant poem to him in book 4, she wonders why stars shine at night when the lovers are asleep and unable to see them (4.641–58). It is a real question, and she expects he will be able to answer it. After the Serpent's speech, by contrast, Eve falls into dichotomous thinking that ignores her earlier experience of happiness. God's prohibition against eating from this tree, Eve reasons disjunctively and somewhat confusedly,

> Commends thee more, while it inferrs the good
> By thee communicated, and our want:
> For good unknown, sure is not had, or had
> And yet unknown, is as not had at all.
> In plain then, what forbids he but to know,
> Forbids us good, forbids us to be wise?
> Such prohibitions bind not. (9.754–60)

Eve has abandoned her understanding and experience of God to fall into a crabbed reasoning with an illogical conclusion. The vehicle for her linguistic fall is a failure of interpretation. What she has chosen to hear in Satan's language is the "glozing," her appetite heightened in advance by his description of the "savorie odour," "the smell of sweetest Fenel, or the Teats / Of Ewe or Goat dropping with Milk at Eevn" (9.579, 581–82). In trying to situate that appetite into a logical construction, Eve argues herself into disobedience. The prohibition is not based on logic but on a relationship. The prohibition binds only if Eve chooses to be in harmony with God, chooses to "know...happiness."

In his pamphlets, Milton maintained the need for each person to choose an individually understood truth through study and conscience. His language in *Areopagitica* and elsewhere is careful to state or suggest alternatives to his own authority. His rhetorical preferences tend toward double negatives, conditional language, and rhetorical questions. In his earlier poetic works, such as the Ludlow *Mask* and *Lycidas*, he used the devices of poetry, including generic conventions, metaphor, and symbolic action, to deepen the complexity of human experience and human choice. At this crucial moment in *Paradise Lost* he illustrates the breach of faith, denial of experience, the chosen ignorance that combine to complicate all further human choosing. As in his prose, Milton invites his reader to see and choose, to be active in forming one's self through time. Eve's concluding questions, therefore, while part of the pattern of her self-deluding rhetoric, are not rhetorical to the reader. We know death, that "dreadful thing" that Adam and Eve are incapable of comprehending, and are therefore able to answer Eve's questions.

> But if Death
> Binds us with after bands, what profits then
> Our inward freedom? In the day we eate
> Of this fair Fruit, our doom is, we shall die.
> How dies the Serpent? Hee hath eat'n and lives,
> And knows, and speaks, and reasons, and discerns,
> Irrational till then. For us alone
> Was death invented? Or to us deny'd
> This intellectual food, for beasts reserv'd? (9.760–68)

There is no single moment when Eve succumbs to the temptation or loses her ability to think this may possibly be a trick. But when she decides that the Serpent "envies not" and is "farr from deceit or guile" she has moved a long way toward accepting his word (the words of a talking animal) over the word of God. Having done this, her concluding questions and decision move with increasing inevitability:

> What fear I then, rather what know to feare
> Under this ignorance of good and Evil,
> Of God or Death, of Law or Penaltie?
> Here grows the Cure of all, this Fruit Divine,
> Fair to the Eye, inviting to the Taste,
> Of vertue to make wise: what hinders then
> To reach, and feed at once both Bodie and Mind?
> So saying, her rash hand in evil hour
> Forth reaching to the Fruit, she pluck'd, she eat.   (9.773–81)

The key question is not what should she fear, but what does she know of fear (or death), since she claims to be ignorant of good and evil? It's a question that looks both ways—back to innocence and forward to the fallen experience. She does know good. I mentioned Adam and Eve's spontaneous morning hymn, which acknowledges the glory of creation and its creator; its language of rational trust provides a counterpoint to the direction Eve has chosen at this terrible moment:

> These are thy glorious works, Parent of good,
> Almightie, thine this universal Frame,
> Thus wondrous fair; thy self how wondrous then!
> Unspeakable, who sitst above these Heavens
> To us invisible or dimly seen
> In these thy lowest works, yet these declare
> Thy goodness beyond thought, and Power Divine.   (5.153–59)

If the "lowest works...declare / Thy goodness beyond thought," then even the serpent might "declare" what Eve has logically seen and praised earlier, the glory of God. Instead, the serpent declares against the word of "Power Divine," a logical contradiction within her paradisal frame of reference that Eve does not notice or chooses not to notice. It is true that she does not before this moment know the experience of evil. Yet she does know, and has experienced, God as the "Parent of good, / Almightie" and should be able to rely on that knowledge and on her "native innocence," amply forewarned (9.373). Fooled, tempted, hungry both for food and knowledge, she falls into an illusion of godhead, knowledge, and freedom, which we observe in the form of her descent into worshipping the tree and her debate over whether or not to include Adam in her trespass; she is tempted to keep this treat for herself since it might make her superior, "for inferior who is free?" (9.787–837).

On the possibility that this vague death may happen to her, and, "a death to think," that Adam would then be "wedded to another Eve" (9.826–30) Eve offers Adam the fruit. Here the cumulative emphasis on knowledge, especially self-knowledge, which the author has built up over the preceding books, quite literally meets its moment of truth, which is subject to multiple interpretations by the postlapsarian reader. One might begin by recalling the language of surmise in Adam's earlier conversation with Raphael, in which he confesses to seeing a wholeness and wisdom in Eve. Adam is aware that his doting is grounded not in the absolute nature of things, but in what "seems":

> Well I understand that in the prime end
> Of Nature her th'feriour, in the mind
> And inward faculties, which most excel
> ....
>   Yet when I approach
> Her loveliness, so absolute she *seems*
> And in her self compleat, so well to know
> Her own, that what she wills to do or say,
> *Seems* wisest, vertuousest, discreetest, best. (8.540–42, 546–50)

Raphael's response, that the more Adam knows an appropriate self-esteem, "well manag'd," the better Eve will recognize Adam's superiority and the better grounded will she be in the reality of inner truth rather than the beauty of surface appearances (8.570–75). Adam, "half abash't," insists that he has merely disclosed "what inward thence I feel, not therefore foild" when he experiences these sensations, remaining "still free [to] / Approve the best, and follow what I approve" (8.595, 607–11). In confessing his feelings, though insisting they do not rule him, Adam acknowledges their power, but he understands them as part of the "harmonie" of his life and his marriage, "which declare unfeign'd / Union of Mind, or in us both one Soule" (8.605, 603–04).

When Adam therefore takes the fruit "Against his better knowledge, not deceav'd, / But fondly overcome with Femal charm" (9.998–99), he has precisely chosen to be "foild." His internal reasoning, both like and unlike Eve's, depends on an inner interrogation. Adam's first question to himself is a real one—how did it happen? He concludes, correctly, that "some cursed fraud / Of Enemie hath beguil'd thee, yet unknown" (9.904–05). Yet he immediately chooses this "unknown," this ignorance, over what has up to this point been his knowledge of God's infinite abundance. The interlinking of question and statement in Adam's self-reflection invites the reader to respond to his questions even as we may variously react to his apparent self-sacrifice:

> And mee with thee hath ruind, for with thee
> Certain my resolution is to Die;
> How can I live without thee, how foregoe
> Thy sweet Converse and Love so dearly joyn'd,
> To live again in these wilde Woods forlorn?
> Should God create another Eve, and I
> Another Rib afford, yet loss of thee
> Would never from my heart; no, no, I feel
> The Link of Nature draw me: Flesh of Flesh,
> Bone of my Bone thou art, and from thy State
> Mine never shall be parted, bliss or woe.   (9.906–16)

Beyond the gender politics of Adam and Eve's relationship is the fundamental premise of the story: that Eve is taken from Adam, derived both from his longing and his material substance. Trapped in Adam's powerful declaration of complete love and personal sacrifice, therefore, is the "Link of Nature" that draws him back into himself; "to loose thee were to loose my self," he tells Eve (9.959). She is of him, is him. Like Satan's passion for his own rebellious thoughts, signified in the allegory of Satan, Sin, and Death (*PL* 2.727–67), Adam denies the experience he has of God's complete goodness and the *imago Dei* within him, and chooses the image of himself instead. "On my experience," Eve says, validating a move made from ignorance and deception, "freely taste" (9.988).

Since the Romantic period some readers have taken this to be a liberating moment for Adam and Eve; pain, sorrow, and death are the prices they pay for a larger knowledge, and for the freedom of their independence from a domineering deity. Michael Bryson goes so far as to claim that Milton portrays God as an "unavoidable combination of good and evil," to be displaced by the image of the Son in the author's effort to rid both temporal and spiritual worlds of kingship.[41] Bryson's complicated reading explicitly honors the interpretive opportunities Milton sets before his readers, though I find it difficult to concur that Satan is merely a secondary source of evil or that Milton's authoritarian God is directly complicit in the pain and suffering Adam and Eve have chosen. Nonetheless, while their fall clouds Adam and Eve's reason and closes off the "thrice happiness" they once could experience, it opens up interpretive choices within the fallen language of author and reader.

The point is clear from the first "Fruit" of "Man's... Disobedience" (*PL* 1.1), in which Adam models multivalent language that invites interpretation. As he descends to the rule of sensation over reason and to drunken lust, his language falls to bad puns that situate knowledge in physical experience:

> Eve, now I see thou art exact of taste,
> And elegant, of Sapience no small part,
> Since to each meaning savour we apply,
> And Palate call judicious; I the praise
> Yeild thee, so wel this day thou hast purvey'd.
> Much pleasure we have lost, while we abstain'd
> From this delightful Fruit, not known till now
> True relish, tasting. (9.1017–24)

The central pun is "Sapience," whose Latin root, *sapere*, means both to taste and to know. Reason is overthrown, the self diminished into knowing by tasting. Eve's skills as meal provider were once varied and complex, based on "what choice to chuse for delicacie best," meals "so contriv'd as not to mix / Tastes, not well joynd, inelegant" but rather to offer "Taste after taste upheld with kindliest change" (5.333–36). Hers was a rational mind ordering the best pleasure for the senses. In offering Adam the forbidden fruit "with liberal hand" (9.997) the meal is reduced to one taste, sensuously indulged and praised in ambiguous language. "Knowledge is as food," Raphael tells Adam, "and needs no less / Her Temperance over appetite, to know / In measure what the mind may well contain" (7.126–28).

What Adam and Eve come to know after the Fall, then, is like and unlike Satan's diminished knowledge and self-delusion. It is like in its narrowing of possibilities. Death will limit their lives, the expulsion from paradise will limit their pleasures, childbirth and labor will bring them pain. It is unlike because they repent, and God has assured all heaven that he will grant them a way to recover. He will hear and respond to Adam and Eve's prayers and repentance, and

> place within them as a guide
> My Umpire *Conscience,* whom if they will hear
> Light after light well us'd they shall obtain,
> And to the end persisting, safe arrive. (*PL* 3.194–97)

Now their freedom depends (as it had before) on their knowledge and choices, but in a much more fractured and duplicitous world. Where they needed to interpret their experience and the language of that experience correctly in order to remain free, now they will define their freedom through interpreting, in the light of conscience.[42] Poetic freedom—the freedom to say things otherwise ineffable, either because they are fraught or because they reach for meanings beyond denotation—is now also the freedom to interpret, and to know the world through interpretive choices.

Book 10 begins the process of enacting that redemption and revising the relation of knowledge and choice. Before the Fall Adam and Eve both know what they need to know in order to make decisions toward their own and each other's happiness. After the Fall their fate rests on the "mysterious terms" of God's pronouncement first on the serpent then on Eve and Adam (*PL* 10.164–208). The terms of the judgment are mysterious, because "more to know / Concern'd not Man (since he no further knew) / Nor alter'd his offence" (10.169–71). The freedom that comes from right knowing and choosing is now inhibited, and fallen Adam and Eve can no longer stand or understand without help. Knowledge, which came from direct instruction from God and Raphael before the Fall, now must come from study and interpretation, a process represented by the tutelage of Michael to Adam in books 11 and 12 and the dream vision that Eve reports at the end of book 12. Adam's tendency to misunderstand Michael's teaching, or not to comprehend it fully, is a paradigm for the human descent into a discursive reason that sometimes obscures intuitive reason, or intuitions that block or mislead discursive reason. Both kinds remain, but both are obscured by the Fall. In this obscurity choice becomes a difficult process of discernment. In the new human dilemma the prophetic vision that Michael offers Adam, like the biblical story the poet offers the reader, becomes the principle vehicle for knowledge.

Human freedom in that vision is limited not only by the collapse of rational self-governance but also by its reflection in the political realm. Michael describes the rise of Nimrod as the first tyrant, "who not content / With fair equalities, fraternal state" (12.26) uses war and a claim of divine right to "tyrannize." Adam is "fatherly displeas'd," calling him "an execrable Son so to aspire / Above his brethren," and asserts Milton's own republican view that God gave man dominion over the animals, "but Man over men / He made not Lord; such title to himself / Reserving, human left from human free" (12.69–71). Michael approves Adam's disapproval, but (as I noted in chapter 1) points out that external tyranny is a consequence of the internal tyranny the Fall has enabled:

> Justly thou abhorr'st
> That Son, who on the quiet state of men
> Such trouble brought, affecting to subdue
> Rational Libertie; yet know withal,
> Since thy original lapse, true Libertie
> Is lost, which always with right Reason dwells
> Twinn'd, and from her hath no dividual being:
> Reason in man obscur'd, or not obeyed,
> Immediately inordinate desires
> And upstart Passions catch the Government
> From Reason, and to servitude reduce
> Man till then free. (12.79–90)

Michael's "know withal" is a direct invitation to understand how the human condition affects the social structure. The cascade of terms "Rational Libertie," "true Libertie," "right Reason," and the "Reason" that is "in man obscur'd, or not obeyed" calls such attention to these words that they demand interpretive nuances from both Adam and the reader. The tyrant subdues "Rational liberty," but there is no rational liberty if "true Libertie" is lost and "Reason" is unclear or ignored. On the one hand, Michael is presenting a parallel between the fallen condition of the individual and the condition of "servitude" under a tyrannous political state. On the other hand, he is offering an opportunity to meditate on the very idea of liberty, which he locates (as Milton's project is) within "right Reason." Michael's direct instruction from God to Adam may perhaps be seen as a figure for God's redeeming intervention through the individual conscience, which Milton elsewhere insists is the only remaining access to right reason after the Fall.[43]

As he begins to understand over the course of books 11 and 12, Adam perfectly illustrates the overthrow of reason in his decision to fall and in his language and actions after the Fall. Michael expands on the political consequence, continuing to connect outward to inward enslavement. God's judgment subjects the unruly

> to violent Lords;
> Who oft as undeservedly enthrall
> His outward freedom: Tyrannie must be,
> Though to the Tyrant thereby no excuse.
> Yet sometimes Nations will decline so low
> From vertue, which is reason, that no wrong,
> But Justice, and some fatal curse annext
> Deprives them of their outward libertie,
> Thir inward lost. (12.93–101)

Right reason is "twinn'd" with liberty and has "no dividual being," and now "vertue" *is* "reason," whose decline demands "Justice" that may come in the form of a "fatal curse." Whatever implications this passage has for Milton's view of the Restoration, "taken as a whole," as Mary Nyquist phrases it, passages such as these organize "degrees of servitude hierarchically, with the most completely interior coming first and the most exterior [actual bondage] coming last."[44]

In sum, loss of political liberty derives from loss of internal governance, whether it comes as a by-product of internal confusion or as an act of justice against moral decline. The first is not necessarily a choice but a general consequence of the fallen condition, while moral decline is the result of particular choices that exacerbate the fall "from vertue, which is reason." The Platonic connection of individual temperance with political governance tended away from inherited aristocracy to meritocracy. Milton's meritocratic republicanism, like that of many of his contemporaries, rejected tyranny in favor of rule by the best and wisest, those educated rightly, as here Michael is educating Adam.[45] Yet right education is never simply the delivery and receipt of static truth; it remains an ongoing process, in the political as well as the personal realm. As Mary Ann Radzinowicz sums it up, "political wisdom is found through time and experience by stages of choice."[46] So, too, is personal wisdom; and freedom in both arenas is interconnected and dependent on what Milton calls "ecclesiastical" or Christian liberty—the freedom, even the mandate, to pursue the truth continually with the aid of conscience. Inevitably, as it did for Milton himself, this leads to questions about what a person should do in the world, or how one discovers vocation. The freedom toward and in that discovery is a key topic of Milton's last two great poems.

FIVE

⚜

Freedom and Vocation in *Paradise Regained* and *Samson Agonistes*

Milton chose *Paradise Regained* and *Samson Agonistes* to be published together in 1671, and to give the more ambiguous *Samson* the last word.[1] The works differ in genre (the first is a "poem" on the model of what he had earlier called a "brief epic," the second "that sort of Dramatic Poem which is call'd Tragedy"), source (both biblical, but New Testament versus Old Testament), style (relatively plain narrative versus impassioned speeches), and outcome (the beginning of one calling, the end of another). Nonetheless, both are firmly centered on what Sharon Achinstein calls "the central philosophical questions of Milton's writing life: what was it to act in the service of God? How [do we] ground human choice upon God's indeterminate means?"[2] Taken together, these two poems focus on how the individual hears and responds to a righteous vocation, and both embody an invitational poetics, represented in large part through the devices of interrogation and surmise.

Milton published these poems after the major choices of his own life and after what would turn out to be the major public events that marked his lifetime. The republican experiment into which he had thrown so much of his passionate rhetoric, and in whose service as its apologist he believed he went blind, had given way to the Restoration. Milton, highly visible as the defender of regicide and a spokesperson for the more radical elements of the Interregnum, was lucky to escape with his life.[3] Whatever his disappointments and continuing concerns after the Restoration, however, Milton in these two poems reaffirmed his belief in individual liberty as the exercise of knowledgeable choice, though with knowledge, unwinding into an unknowable future, inevitably shadowed and incomplete.

Like *Paradise Lost*, both poems are about knowing and choosing, but in a postlapsarian context in *Paradise Regained* and *Samson Agonistes*. Even more than in *Paradise Lost*, in these poems Milton creates fictions in which the reader is confronted with contradictory evidence, obscure purposes, ambivalent characters, and ambiguous signs. *Paradise Regained* offers the example of the perfect man discovering his calling, but the reader is invited into the process of that discovery from several points of view: that of Jesus, of course, but also his mother Mary, the disciples, and, especially, Satan. In this poem Milton performs the quite remarkable act of presenting the divine in time; while the introductory verses offer the cosmic overview and assurance that infused much of *Paradise Lost*, the rest of the narration deals moment by moment with the uncertainties of linear time—the world of continuous choosing. *Samson Agonistes*, on the other hand, makes immediate through drama the consequence of Samson's life choices and his struggle (*agon*) to claim or reclaim a vocation and freedom that appears initially to leave him no choices at all. In the case of each poem, whatever the difficulties or apparent contradictions, the one constant is the author's invitation to the reader: to see these choices enacted, and to liberate yourself through choosing what is true for you.

Paradise Regained seems at first a much more static work than *Paradise Lost,* its author asking for inspiration "to tell of deeds / Above Heroic, though in secret done" and its action largely confined to the debate between Jesus and Satan. It describes the Son, limited by time and without the perspective of heaven, coming to interpret his divine vocation.[4] In a fallen world he can only discover the good he is meant to accomplish by first encountering evil. The Son regains paradise by facing and rightly countering Satan's temptations.

Much of the poem's interest lies in Satan's struggle to understand who this particular "son of God" might be. He observes John's baptism of Jesus and hears "the Father's voice / From Heav'n" pronounce this man "his beloved Son" (*PR* 1.31–32). Satan's first reaction to this "exalted man" is "wonder, then with envy fraught and rage" (*PR* 1.38). He quickly gathers a council of devils and recalls to them the "mysterious terms" of God's curse pronounced after the Fall, that a man "shall bruise thy head, thou bruise his heel" (*PL* 10.181). He fears that this may be the man to strike his "fatal wound" (*PR* 1.53) and worries who, exactly, he may be facing:

> His mother then is mortal, but his Sire,
> Hee who obtains the Monarchy of Heav'n,
> And what will he not do to advance his Son?
> His first-begot we know, and sore have felt,
> When his fierce thunder drove us to the deep;
> Who this is we must learn, for man he seems
> In all his lineaments, though in his face
> The glimpses of his Father's glory shine.   (*PR* 1.85–92)

The three temptations through which Satan tests Jesus—of the senses, of worldly power, and of spiritual pride (the order from Luke 4:1–13)—become the means for both Jesus and Satan to uncover the Son's divine calling. For Jesus, knowledge comes largely through the discursive reason suitable to most human learning, "musing and much revolving in his brest, / How best the mighty work he may begin" (*PR* 1.185–86). His thoughts, like his pace into the quiet wilderness, are "step by step led on" (192), even as "a multitude of thoughts...swarm" in his meditation (196–97). By contrast, Satan, his angelic nature fallen from intuitive reason to a perverted linear ratiocination, cannot use reason to discover what he desperately wants to know. He reasons, for example, that God's paternal pride might effect some special power ("what will he not do to advance his Son?" [*PR* 1.88]), but cannot imagine that God's knowledge of the Son's virtue assures an inherent power, a "merit," that manifests God's own power without the need to enforce it externally (*PR* 1.161–79).

In the first instance the rhetorical question turns out to be a real question that invites the reader to consider, over the course of the poem, the unexpected ways in which the Father advances the Son, and perhaps to suggest the reader's own need for confidence and perseverance in the face of temptation and hardship. God's trust in the Son is based on his own omniscient choice, to present a model so that first the angels,

> and men hereafter may discern
> From what consummate vertue I have chose
> This perfect Man, by merit call'd my Son,
> To earn Salvation for the Sons of men. (*PR* 1.164–67)

Merit precedes the call, and will earn salvation; humanity in turn will "discern" the "consummate vertue" that brings praise to the Son for his actions, the Father for his choice, and will see how a perfect human being negotiates worldly temptations. The logic here is mostly linear, but the ultimate insight is intuitive: "The Father knows the Son; and therefore secure / Ventures his filial Vertue, though untri'd." God, of course, knows completely and can trust what he knows; we can know only partially, yet still must trust what we know and allow for the insights of intuitive reason to give us a confidence that complements what we can discern through discursive reason. Satan's fallen linearity prevents his connecting *this* Son back to God's "first-begot" whose "thunder drove us to the deep" (*PR* 1.89–90), but in a nice irony Satan will come to understand this earthly Son of God through a flash of intuitive knowledge directly accompanied by his own fall from power.

Jesus is a model reader both of texts and experience, observant and patient, while Satan sees everything from his self-involvement and his experience of fallen humanity. The temptation story is therefore exemplary of free as opposed to self-diminished choices. Typically, Milton does not direct but rather invites his reader to weigh the "merit" of the poem's differing perspectives. This is sometimes pushed through connotative language, as in the differing descriptions of the antagonists' motions toward their encounter: Satan's "easie steps; girded with snaky wiles" (*PR* 1.120), as opposed to Jesus' "thought following thought, and step by step led on" (1.192). It is mostly done, though, through narrative counterpoise, and most generally between Satan's temptations and the Son's responses. We are invited into the logic of their encounters, but we are also invited to come to know the Son as "the Father knows the Son," an intuitive trust based on our understanding, through the sequence of his trials, of the Son's "merit." In the conflict between Satan and Jesus we are invited to choose whose version of the human condition and human value—whose narrative—we trust.

Jeffrey Morris summarizes a tradition of finding the narrative of *Paradise Regained* unsatisfactory as fiction, particularly in its lack of clear narrative time and space.[5] Morris notes that this forces the reader to pay attention to the speeches that constitute the encounter between Jesus and Satan, and at the same time produces a disorientation in the reader that is presumably part of Milton's intent. I would add that the

Freedom and Vocation 149

purpose of this disorientation is to make the reader alert to differences in various narrative perspectives. Embedded in the larger narrative structure, and instructive for reading that larger narrative, are the multiple versions of twelve-year-old Jesus at the temple with the rabbis. The only biblical version, and indeed the only story of Jesus' boyhood, is Luke 2:41–52, here in the King James Version:

> His parents went to Jerusalem every year at the Feast of the Passover. And when He was twelve years old, they went up to Jerusalem according to the custom of the feast. When they had finished the days, as they returned, the Boy Jesus lingered behind in Jerusalem. And Joseph and His mother did not know it; but supposing Him to have been in the company, they went a day's journey, and sought Him among their relatives and acquaintances. So when they did not find him they returned to Jerusalem, seeking Him. Now so it was that after three days they found Him in the temple, sitting in the midst of the teachers, both listening to them and asking them questions. And all who heard Him were astonished at His understanding and answers. So when they saw Him they were amazed; and his mother said to Him, "Son, why have You done this to us? Look, Your father and I have sought You anxiously." And he said to them, "Why did you seek Me? Did you not know that I must be about My Father's business?" But they did not understand the statement which He spoke to them. Then He went down with them and came to Nazareth, and was subject to them, but His mother kept all these things in her heart. And Jesus increased in wisdom and stature, and in favor with God and men.

This story comes to mind as Jesus moves into the wilderness to sort out both the "swarm" of thoughts "from within" and what he has heard "from without" about his calling (1.197–200). He begins by recollecting a childhood exemplary in its Miltonic definition of learning, knowing, and choosing:

> When I was yet a child, no childish play
> To me was pleasing, all my mind was set
> Serious to learn and know, and thence to do
> What might be public good, born to that end.   (PR 1.202–05)

He further recalls how his desire to "do...public good" led him to read precociously "the Law of God," with his "delight" in it urging him

> To such perfection that, ere yet my age
> Had measur'd twice six years, at our great Feast
> I went into the Temple, there to hear
> The Teachers of our Law, and to propose
> What might improve my knowledge or their own;
> And was admired by all, yet this not all
> To which my Spirit aspir'd; victorious deeds
> Flam'd in my heart, heroic acts; one while
> To rescue Israel from the Roman yoke,
> Then to subdue and quell o'er all the earth
> Brute violence and proud Tyrannic pow'r,
> Till truth were freed and equity restor'd.   (PR 1.209–21)

While the language here is not particularly invitational in suggesting a variety of meanings to the reader, it models a way of learning that is conditional and exploratory. He goes to "hear / The Teachers," but not simply to accept their authority. He must also "propose / What might improve my knowledge or their own." Even the knowledge of the "Teachers" is not complete, and all knowledge must be obtained as part of a process and be pertinent to the individual.

For Jesus the episode in the temple is but one event in a childhood and youth of pondering Scripture, "yet this not all" to which he feels called. He anticipates a life of heroic action and first thinks in the conventional messianic terms of liberating Israel from the Romans. His mother, observing in her son "these growing thoughts," takes him aside to tell him her story, including what the angels, the magi, and the prophets Simeon and Anna predicted at her son's birth.

Reading, thinking, studying with the scholars in the temple, and hearing his mother's story combine to send Jesus back to "The Law and the Prophets, searching what was writ / Concerning the Messiah." He comes to understand that "of whom they spake / I am" (*PR* 1.260–63). This renewed reading of Scripture tells him that his calling will be no grand earthly triumph, but rather it will be

> Through many a hard assay even to the death
> Ere I the promis'd Kingdom can attain,
> Or work Redemption for mankind, whose sins'
> Full weight must be transferr'd upon my head.   (*PR* 1.264–67)

He rightly interprets the voice of God at his baptism to mean that the time has come to take up openly "the Authority which I deriv'd from Heaven" (290). He is not sure how to begin, but "some strong motion" leads this second Adam not to a rich garden but into the wilderness of man's fallen experience, "To what intent / I know not yet; perhaps I need not know; / For what concerns my knowledge God reveals" (*PR* 1.292–94).

Jesus' remarkable studiousness and precocity, the story of the boy with the learned doctors in the temple, is just one experience along the way to self-knowledge, based also on books, his mother's teaching, rereading, and the revelation at his baptism. Its purpose, along with the rest of his accumulation of knowledge through time, is not an end in itself but a means to heroic action. Jesus' humility in the face of what he does and does not know contrasts with the impulse of the Fall to know more than God reveals. Jesus now has all the discursive knowledge he needs, has ceded the greater knowledge to God, and above all trusts God to provide what he needs and to lead him, in due time, to what he must do.

Mary's version of Jesus staying behind at the temple in Jerusalem balances a mother's concern with her trust in God and in her son. She understands that she, too, will suffer as her "favor'd lot / My Exaltation to Afflictions high" (*PR* 2.91–92) and accepts it without argument as part of God's plan. Still, a mother worries when her son is long absent:

> But where delays he now? Some great intent
> Conceals him: when twelve years he scarce had seen,
> I lost him, but so found, as well I saw
> He could not lose himself; but went about
> His father's business; what he meant I mus'd,
> Since understand; much more his absence now
> Thus long to some great purpose he obscures.
> But I to wait with patience am inur'd. (*PR* 2.95–102)

Mary, too, must learn how her own and her son's experiences reveal who they are and how they must be in the world. She "mus'd" over how to interpret her son's determination to be "about / His father's business," and musing brought her understanding. Now her recollection of her son's earlier absence gives her conviction that the current one is part of God's plan for him. Though it does not eliminate her maternal anxiety, this knowledge frees her to trust God and be patient.

Satan's version, which introduces a temptation to all worldly knowledge, misreads both Jesus and his mother. Since Jesus has shown himself unmoved by Satan's offers of empire and glory, Satan decides he is

> Addicted more
> To contemplation and profound dispute,
> As by that early action may be judg'd,
> When slipping from thy Mother's eye thou went'st
> Alone into the Temple; there wast found
> Among the gravest Rabbis disputant
> On points and questions fitting Moses' Chair,
> Teaching not taught; the childhood shows the man,
> As morning shows the day. Be famous then
> By wisdom; as thy empire must extend,
> So let extend thy mind o'er all the world,
> In knowledge, all things in it comprehend. (*PR* 4.213–24)

Satan knows that this Son of God is destined, somehow, to an "empire" that "must extend" over the whole world, and he is actively trying to find the way to derail the moment. By this point in the larger narrative Jesus has responded so learnedly and brilliantly to Satan's earlier temptations that Satan decides on an appeal to all knowledge. It worked on Eve. But Satan's understanding of knowledge, like his interpretations of Scripture, are simplistic and self-involved.[6] To Satan, the precocious boy's engagement with the rabbis is a disputation over points of Mosaic law, in which the know-it-all child would be "teaching, not taught." This reduces him to an oversimplification, which, typically of Satan, is both true and untrue: "the child shows the man." He sees the studious activity and misses the call to heroic deeds. He has characterized without comprehending and does it in a clichéd simile: "As morning shows the day." Morning may not necessarily show the day, as God may lead by "some strong motion" or his creature may choose a different sort of day. No example is better than Satan himself, once the magnificent Lucifer, the morning star, by his own choice fallen to an obscurity that contrasts with Jesus living "obscure" until his time comes. The Son's rise, as in heaven, will be Satan's fall.

Jesus situates the familiar biblical story in time, among other experiences that lead him to an accumulating self-knowledge. Mary turns to her experience of losing her son briefly to the rabbis in the temple as a lesson in patience and trust, which she is able to apply in the immediate worry over his current absence. Satan sees the temple story as a willful act of disobedience ("slipping from thy Mother's eye") and a possible key to pride. The two good readings are contextual, faithful, and lead beyond the event itself. Satan's reading is self-interested and literal-minded. The story for him is not a sign of something larger, but the child showing the man, one he believes he can now label "addicted...to contemplation and profound dispute." For my purposes, what stands out here is that there are two good readings of the story and one bad one. It is not necessary that we all have the same interpretation of the same set of circumstances. People have different personal histories and temperaments, and, if they are wise, have learned that knowledge and experience, thoughtfully considered, accumulate new and revised meanings over the course of time. Satan's effort to define and determine, to render static (and eventually and truly dead) that which God has shown to be dynamic and creative, is the bad reading. It is bad, in large part, because it defines and delimits, closes off, makes no room for the continuing process of right choices that divinity encourages as the freedom for which God's creatures were made.

On the model of Jesus and Mary, a careful reading of our own knowledge and experience attunes us to God's purposes and to individual vocations. Even so, the reader is not offered access to a sure knowledge of what is, but insight into the process of becoming that characterizes both Jesus and his mother. Jesus is drawn into the desert "to what intent / I know not yet; perhaps I need not know," while Mary waits, knowing but not understanding the full import of her perfectly phrased "Some great intent / Conceals him." Neither dwells in certainty any more than we do, and what they present is not complacency but an active effort to interpret experience, set on a foundation of trust. As the "Father knows the Son," Jesus trusts the Father, and Mary trusts them both. The truth of relationship (an aspect of intuitive reason) is the platform for confronting uncertainty and discerning a right course, which is always an individual course. A valid understanding of relationship increases freedom.

On the model of Satan, on the contrary, a self-interested and self-involved reading of the world cuts off and diminishes what we know, and therefore affects the choices available to us. Satan's largest mistake rests in his inability to "know" the Father or the Son, that is, to understand relationship;

instead, he assumes that his own motives reside in others: "what will [God] not do to advance his Son?"; "how could [Jesus] hope / Long to enjoy" the throne of David without the martial powers Satan is offering him? (*PR* 3.359–60); if royal power does not appeal, "be *famous* then / By wisdom" (4.221–22; emphasis added). Tribal privilege, personal power, personal fame are Satan's values, each self-limiting. Instead of opening up possible interpretations, Satan shuts them off. Instead of seeing the development of an individual being through choices that combine discursive discernment with an openness to intuitive apprehension, Satan can only reduce everyone and everything to himself.

Satan's misreading of the temple story leads to the wiliest of his temptations, the power of all Athenian knowledge with its "Olive Grove of Academe," its "secret power / Of harmony" in music and verse, its "famous Orators," its "sage philosophy" (*PR* 4.241–72). All of this, Satan insinuates, particularly the schools of philosophy, would make Jesus the sort of ruler that Plato might admire:

> These here revolve, or, as thou lik'st, at home,
> Till time mature thee to a Kingdom's weight;
> These rules will render thee a King complete
> Within thyself, much more with Empire join'd.
>
> (*PR* 4.281–84)

Satan again misreads, in this case Plato, by emphasizing "rules" as the key to self-rule and inner harmony. In fact, Jesus has already shown his correct understanding of the principle, when he rejects Satan's model of kingship as domination and instead invokes the model of self-rule: "Yet he reigns within himself, and rules / Passions, Desires, and Fears is more a King" (*PR* 2.463–64). Satan is unable to think beyond worldly models of power and glory, so offers the life of learning and contemplation as a prelude to "Empire."

Ultimately, even if rightly read, Plato's model for inner and outer governance is insufficient for the Christian humanist for whom no good governance is possible without knowledge of and from God. All the beauty of classical learning is of no use without the knowledge that only the Bible and the individual conscience can give. Milton's Jesus, therefore, dismisses classical learning, arguing that it is incomplete and insufficient:

> Alas! What can they teach, and not mislead;
> Ignorant of themselves, of God much more,
> And how the world began, and how man fell
> Degraded by himself, on grace depending? (PR 4.309–12)

Without the counterpoise of biblical revelation and the conscience receptive to God's grace, all classical learning is "an empty cloud" (PR 4.321). Rather than dismissing the virtue of reading altogether, however, Milton's Jesus emphasizes the crucial importance of individual judgment:

> Many books
> Wise men have said are wearisome; who reads
> Incessantly, and to his reading brings not
> A spirit and judgment equal or superior
> (And what he brings, what needs he elsewhere seek)
> Uncertain and unsettled still remains,
> Deep verst in books and shallow in himself. (PR 4.321–27)

Knowledge is not found in books alone but in what one brings to reading.[7] The "spirit and judgment" one must "elsewhere seek" derive from who one is, an accumulation of those free choices made during the linear unfolding of a life. This is a mature exposition of a much earlier idea. In *Reason of Church-Government* (1642), Milton had declared that virtue proceeds from a sense of self formed in relation to the Christian God: "He that holds himself in reverence and due esteem, both for the dignity of God's image upon him, and for the price of his redemption...accounts himselfe both a fit person to do the noblest and godliest deeds, and much better worth than to deject and define, with such a debasement as sin is, himselfe so highly ransom'd and enobl'd to a new friendship and filiall relation with God" (YP 1:842). Later, in *Likeliest Means to Remove Hirelings* (1659), Milton would dispute the need for university as an asset to the ministry, in effect casting aside classical learning: "it were much better, there were not one divine in the university...and that they who intended to be ministers, were traind up in the church only, by the scripture and in the original languages therof at schoole" (YP 7:317). Self-knowledge cannot be found in books but in the "filiall relation with God," the precondition for all learning, "for what concerns my knowledge God reveals" (*PR* 1.294), primarily through the Scriptures, over which Jesus has pored, and then directly through providential guidance. All reading must therefore begin with and be based on the Bible, whose stories, songs, prophetic oratory, and law both precede and go beyond classical works (*PR* 4.332–64).

Satan is baffled: "What dost thou in this World?" (*PR* 4.372). When wild weather and ghostly visions leave Jesus nothing "worse than wet" (*PR* 4.486), Satan's frustration leads to an important consideration of what it means "to stand" in a postlapsarian world. He has tried to learn, he claims,

> In what degree or meaning thou art call'd
> The Son of God, which bears no single sense;
> The Son of God I also am, or was,
> And if I was, I am; relation stands;
> All men are Sons of God; yet thee I thought
> In some respect far higher so declar'd.   (*PR* 4.516–21)

As he seeks to probe the essence of being ("if I was, I am") and relationship ("relation stands"), Satan crucially misreads yet once more. "Son of God" may have no single sense, though here it has the special sense that so enraged Satan in *Paradise Lost*, but neither does "relationship" have the meaning Satan would give it here. Ironically, those who truly understand relationship with God will "stand," no matter how many possible senses of terms are available for inquiry, and will recognize the freedom that Satan would restrict, just as he would restrict interpretation. His vision of reality is static, two-dimensional, and, although his own language can be duplicitous, to him stories and events are literal and monovalent. Jesus understands God to be dynamic, working through the processes of his creation, including the individual calling that Jesus is seeking to discern. The world is complex, and all stories have the potential for multiple meanings, even multiple correct meanings, personalized to individual circumstances.

"Relation stands," as the "filiall relation" is the basis for that which makes a creature upright both literally and figuratively. However, this sense must be chosen, not merely assumed; it does not stand *still*. Satan again literalizes even this concept, as he whisks Jesus to the top of the temple in Jerusalem to try one last test on the "highest pinnacle" of that same Jerusalem temple where the boy Jesus first sought to decipher his calling. As Satan calls on Jesus to "stand," his mocking puns only emphasize the literalness of his meaning:

> There stand, if thou wilt stand; to stand upright
> Will ask thee skill; I to thy Father's house
> Have brought thee, and highest plac't, highest is best,
> Now show thy Progeny; if not to stand,
> Cast thyself down; safely if Son of God:
> For it is written, He will give command
> Concerning thee to his Angels, in thir hands
> They shall up lift thee, lest at any time
> Thou chance to dash thy foot against a stone.   (*PR* 4.551–59)

Satan's encouragement to "cast thyself down" is a push toward what would amount to suicide if Jesus were to fall (literally) for the temptation. But ironically for Satan, "relation [to God] stands," and in Jesus' better understanding of

God's word, he does stand, literally and figuratively: "To whom thus Jesus. Also it is written / Tempt not the Lord thy God; he said and stood. / But Satan smitten with amazement fell" (*PR* 4.560–62). As in the war in heaven in *Paradise Lost* (6.746–866), the Son prevails, not by the fiery chariot of "Paternal Deitie, / ...instinct with spirit" (*PL* 6.750, 752) but by the linear, discursive language of the biblical word of God.

Following the lead of Luke, the author has angels bring Jesus down from "his uneasy station" (*PR* 4.584) and provide him with all the food and drink he needs, while (Milton adds) "Angelic choirs / Sung Heavenly Anthems of his victory" (4.593–94). These conclude with a valediction to the "Son of the most High, heir of both worlds" and the call, "on thy glorious work / Now enter, and begin to save mankind" (4.633–35). The heroic beginning that ends the poem brackets Jesus in his role as "heir of both worlds" of heaven and earth, as the "Son of the most High" leaves the wilderness and "unobserv'd / Home to his Mother's house private return'd" (4.638–39).

In *Paradise Regained* Milton offers a picture of perfect judgment, which depends on trust in God and the right pursuit of one's calling. That judgment is unique and individual, drawing on biblical law but transcending it through "filiall relation." Each vocation is self-determined by the individual response to God's call. With no memory of his prior role in heaven, Jesus in *Paradise Regained* must make his choices based entirely on human knowledge and through the course of time, just as the reader must do.[8] In a fallen world, each moment requires interpretation of the past and present and anticipation of the future. Jesus does it perfectly, as God foreknows he will, but Jesus does not share that foreknowledge. He continues to struggle to know and to choose, confident that he will learn what he needs to know to make right judgments. In that resides his perfect freedom.

While Jesus may model a perfect performance of choosing, readers are left with many choices of their own through this narrative. Stella Revard cites the continuing debate over whether Jesus' "Thou shalt not tempt the Lord thy God" is self-referential, and points out the hints of potential repentance that flavor Satan's language in *Paradise Regained* as opposed to his rejection of repentance in *Paradise Lost*. She concludes, "*Paradise Regained* invites us to a richer range of interpretive thought than its predecessor as it re-orchestrates the meeting between the old adversaries and opens a dialogue between the two that reconfigures the relationship of Satan and the Son of God."[9] While I cannot agree with the broad statement that the later poem is "richer" in its "range of interpretive thought" than the earlier, its invitation to weigh and consider these human experiences does seem more accessible to our own. We can follow this narrative path, with direct language about the need for interpretation through time.

The principal invitation here, I believe, is for the reader to weigh and consider the attractions of "pompous Delicacies" (*PR* 2.390), glory, power, fame, and even our engagement with ideas for their own sake. The earthbound narrative structure, like all good novels, asks us to invest our selves into the scenes, our individual situations onto the questions Jesus and Satan ask themselves and each other. "Where will this end" (2.245), Jesus, and we, might wonder. Jesus in response to Satan: "Shall I seek glory then, as vain men seek / Oft not deserv'd?" How might one "seek not mine, but his / Who sent me?" (3.105–07). Satan offers the vision of Tiberian Rome and asks, "might'st thou expel this Monster from his throne / Now made a stye, and in his place ascending / A victor people free from servile yoke?" (4.100–02). As Richard DuRocher points out, many readers, like Satan, might want to ask the Son that "exquisite, existential question": "What dost thou in this World?" (4.372).[10] The same stories might have different readings that may be good for the differing individuals, as with Mary and Jesus' reading of the temple story, but in all things, in this fallen linear time, we are invited to discern among temptations and to find the paths to our personal vocations.

Samson Agonistes is also a temptation story, but the difficulties and ambiguities of this pre-Christian tale are even closer to fallen human experience than the clash of heaven and hell that underlies *Paradise Regained*. Samson's *agons* over his use and misuse of freedom and vocation, choice and election, are messier and their moral direction more difficult to fathom. Milton's question, as Achinstein phrased it (how do we "ground human choice upon God's indeterminate means?"), has a less reliably certain set of answers derivable from the model of Samson than may be derived from the model of Jesus. Yet this is the work with which Milton chose to end what would turn out to be his last major volume. Unlike the period in Jesus' life (the *pax romana*) portrayed in *Paradise Regained*, but like Milton's time (and our own), Samson's world is one of violence and oppression. Over the course of the play Milton uses violence and the threat of violence to underscore Samson's choices and to shock his reader into paying attention to the danger of wrong choices. Violence is the bread and butter of tragedy, but here I think it adds a special sense of urgency to Milton's invitation to see the necessity for and difficulty in discerning and responding to God's call.[11]

Samson's theme is bondage and freedom—Samson's and the Israelites'—but the resolution of that theme is problematic. At the end of his tragedy Samson is not only destroyed along with the Philistine aristocrats he has been asked to entertain, but there is no evidence that his Danite kin have learned any lesson of liberation, personal or political, from this destruction.[12] The violent conclusion, and to some extent Samson's whole violent calling against the Philistines, is at the heart of the controversy over whether Samson is a hero called by God to fulfill God's purposes, however inscrutable they may sometimes seem, or whether he is simply a hubristic man acting on his passions, a model of the flawed postlapsarian heroic.[13] The terrorist attacks of September 11, 2001, exacerbated this long-standing controversy by bringing out the parallels between the Allah-driven Islamic terrorists, self-destructing in their drive to attack the symbols of Western oppression, and the Samson story. John Carey used these events to reassert his position that we are meant to read Samson's final act as "morally disgusting," in spite of the praise heaped on it by the Danite chorus and Manoa, while Stanley Fish insists that Samson's final act "must be considered praiseworthy because he believes (he cannot be sure) that it is what God wants him to do."[14] Feisal Mohamed, responding to these views and others, argues that Samson's final act does not, in fact, derive from his personal confrontations with Dalila and Harapha, as Samuel Johnson complained and John Rumrich more approvingly argued. Mohamed portrays him as "a hero of faith achieving [a] saintly militarism," and he challenges the modern Western need to raise Milton above imagining such militarism as somehow virtuous.[15]

I am less interested in the question of whether Milton did or did not approve of Samson's violence, however, than I am in how Milton uses it as part of his larger challenge to involve his reader actively with his text. As John Rumrich notes, Milton's "mature writings make moral freedom, and the indeterminacy it entails, the prime element in relation to God," and in no other work is that issue more vividly set before the reader.[16] Mary Ann Radzinowicz, usually associated with an approving view of Samson's final choice, nonetheless sees in *Samson* a particularly difficult "ethical task...to elicit from [Milton's] mimesis of biblical fable" a rule for living in a postlapsarian world and "to elicit that rule in such a way as to enable man to follow it."[17] It is hard not to see that task as difficult and troubled. Michael Lieb, for example, describes Milton's drama as a "manifestation of Godhead in its most archaic form," with Samson "empowered to be triumphantly destructive in God's cause." Joseph Wittreich, the preeminent scholar of *Samson* and its critical tradition, sees the play as "less an exaltation of a hero than a problematizing of a received notion of heroism."[18] It is commonplace to note how Samson and the chorus of his kin seem to talk past each other, and Wittreich establishes the vexed nature of Samson's heroic performances on their behalf; there seems no "rule of living" evident from the Danites' response to their champion. Daniel Shore argues that Samson's sacrifice is part of Milton's effort to hold icons up to judgment, and even as he destroys the Philistine icon, the Danites create another one in the legend of Samson himself.[19] On the other hand, Margaret Thickstun argues that Samson's engagement with the Danites, as well as with Manoa, Dalila, and Harapha, leads him from shame to a repentant guilt, from hubris to a new understanding of himself as called to be part of a community: "In order to fulfill his role as Israel's 'great deliverer' (*SA* 40), Samson had to learn to care about his tribesmen not as mirrors who reflect back his glory, but as companions in his search to do God's will."[20] Shore extends that view in a violent direction by arguing that *Samson* is a "threat" designed to put fear, or terror" into the unfit audience on behalf of the fit, the community of dissenters who remained despite the Restoration.[21]

The ambiguities and difficulties of *Samson* seem to me to point to Milton's larger project: the reader or audience must make its own judgments, fill in the gaps of information, see the examples provided by the play, weigh them, and choose their significance. The play both illustrates and requires the thoughtful choices that make up the ethical task of the postlapsarian world. The drama begins with Samson in blindness and despair—a broken Samson, "dead more than half" (*SA* 79)—an unlikely place from which to model and invite some form of liberty. Yet Samson, who at first defines himself "in power of others, never in my own," comes to a renewed sense of personal agency through his encounters with the chorus of Danites, his father Manoa, Dalila, the Philistine giant Harapha, and the officer sent to bring Samson to entertain the Philistines. The efficient cause of his initial impotence is the loss of his hair and maiming of his power, leaving him "despoiled, / Shav'n, and disarmed among [his] enemies" (*SA* 539–40). Despite his successful vow to take no strong drink, his "temperance" was "not complete," his pride and uxuriousness leaving him "effeminately vanquished" (558, 562). Samson has lost his generative power along with his locks, and while the process of the poem returns Samson to his manhood, even as his hair grows out sufficiently for the Philistines to think to make a show of his returning strength, it is not clear whether the return of strength also calls him to a share of wisdom.

Despite his moral weakness and physical confinement, over the course of the play Samson does seem to be re-called toward some divine mission, whether or not the calling may be seen to derive logically from the encounters that precede it. The process of re-calling does not come through a direct line of "aha" moments, and it never strays entirely from the violent world Samson both challenges and represents. While Thickstun sees Samson slowly coming to understand his violence not as an avenue to personal fame and glory, but as a God-given gift for his community, Wittreich reads a more complicated Samson and *Samson,* where "meaning is lodged within proliferating contradictions, including a simultaneous toleration of violence and revulsion in the face of it."[22] Images of violence illustrate that simultaneous toleration and revulsion, along with what Thickstun has suggested is Samson's dialogic process of self-knowledge, even as they invite the reader to judge Samson's words and actions. When Dalila's persuasions fail and she seeks to use the erotic power of her touch to reclaim Samson ("Let me approach at least, and touch thy hand" [*SA* 951]), he warns her back: "Not for thy life, lest fierce remembrance wake / My sudden rage to tear thee joint by joint. / At distance I forgive thee, go with that" (952–54).

Samson avoids both violence and eroticism in this scene (and the link between them) in his choice to keep "distance" between himself and Dalila, a retreat from past dangers and a move to avoid future ones. The moral value of this forgiveness, and what it may or may not serve to accomplish in making Samson wiser, is left to the individual interpreter. Again, when Harapha reveals his cowardice by avoiding direct combat with an increasingly determined Samson, the blind hero sends a final challenge to the retreating giant:

> Go, baffl'd coward, lest I run upon thee,
> Though in these chains, bulk without spirit vast,
> And with one buffet lay thy structure low,
> Or swing thee in the Air, then dash thee down
> To the hazard of thy brains and shatter'd sides.
>
> (*SA* 11237–41)

Here Samson taunts with a variety of possibilities dependent upon Harapha's own choices: "Go...lest I run upon thee /...Or swing thee...then dash thee." The vividness of "brains and shatter'd sides" has the dramatic effect of frightening Harapha as well as claiming the attention of the audience. This encounter, derived entirely from Milton's imagination and not from his biblical sources, has no logical relation to the previous encounter with Dalila; combined, they comprise the famous absence of a logical, Aristotelian "middle" of which Samuel Johnson complained.[23] The impulses to violence in both instances come in the context of much larger arguments that frame a nuanced picture of Samson's motives and weaknesses, and of his call to be God's and the Israelites' hero. They go well beyond simple rage or the desperate longing for self-annihilation that begins the play. Samson's self-understanding may be muddied, but we are asked to measure it in terms of what he does as much as what he says. He would dismember Dalila, but warns her away, pushing her with his certainty that she will be remembered as the model for "Matrimoniall treason" (*SA* 959). Words rather than actions end his encounter. The impulse to fight Harapha and his certainty that he would shatter the brains and break the body of the Philistine champion move away from words and back to action, but only after answering the verbal challenge of his adversary. These reversed responses, toward words with Dalila and toward action with Harapha, both suggest some increasing "share of wisdom." Samson recognizes past mistakes and looks forward, however hazily, to being God's champion again. Both images may shock, but they also show that he is making choices that liberate his mind.

As I suggested in chapter 3, Milton's images of maimed or incomplete figures represent opportunities to heal and complete, to reconstruct what has been deconstructed. As a torn Orpheus in *Lycidas* may reinvigorate Greek and then ultimately Milton's English poetry, and dismembered Truth in *Areopagitica* may demand active inquiry by the energetic faithful, so a blind and deformed Samson may struggle toward a new exercise of freedom. He begins to understand his renewed ability to make choices, at first in defiance of the Philistines ("If I obey them, / I do it freely" [*SA* 1372–73]), and then through "some rousing motions in me which dispose / To something extraordinary my thoughts" (1382–83). He concludes that he will freely go with the Philistine officer to Dagon's feast, and although he will do nothing to dishonor himself or God, "This day will be remarkable in my life / By some great act, or of my days the last" (1388–89). The reader knows to convert the "or" to "and" in this famous passage, and that this "great act" will complete both Samson's mission and his life. The rest of the story is familiar to a reader of the Bible, though complicated by Milton's framing: soon after Samson leaves, his father returns with hope of buying his son's freedom, and imagines a sentimental picture of blind Samson by the household hearth, perhaps with God restoring his sight with his strength for yet more great deeds. Sounds of violence break through this hope, as a "hideous noise" and "universal groan" interrupt Manoa's conversation with the Danites. Soon a messenger lets all know that Samson has literally pulled the roof down on the Philistines and "inevitably / Pulled down the same destruction on himself" (1657–58). Samson's sense of agency and vocation, recast over the course of his encounters in the drama, exercises its freedom in an act of spectacular violence.

The chorus, in praising this "dearly-bought revenge, yet glorious" (*SA* 1660) attributes Samson's self-destruction not to his own will, but to his being "tangled in the fold / Of dire Necessity" (1665–66). Whether one interprets Samson as heroic or merely violent, God's chosen avenger or a deluded strongman, his act of self-chosen liberation is not "dire Necessity" but a way of changing his own story. When he first meets with the Danite chorus, he asks, "Am I not sung and proverbd for a fool / In every street?" (204–205).[24] Samson will, like the earth shaken "yet once more," find himself reformed and translated like the phoenix who, "though her body die, her fame survives" (1706). His act of violence may change the way he is remembered, from a "proverbd...fool" into, as Manoa hopes, the subject of "copious legend, or sweet lyric song" (*SA* 1737). Yet Milton embodies his story in neither of these, but rather in tragedy, "the gravest, moralest, and most profitable of all other Poems."[25] It is up to the audience to see this spectacle with the eyes of imagination, replacing Samson's blindness and Manoa's sentimentality with their own various understandings of what this story means. Unlike the maxim-spouting Danite chorus, there is no settled assurance that Samson, they, or we can confront such a violent calling with "calm of mind, all passion spent." We may, however, "temper and reduce...to just measure" the "pity and fear, or terror" that the violence of this poem arouses.[26]

In addition to taxing the reader's judgment (and exciting the action) with the play's violent elements, Milton's invitational poetics, here most certainly what I have called elsewhere "elective poetics," are particularly integral to Samson.[27] Through literary techniques that tend to invite the reader into the process of Samson's choices, election as Samson's choice of action and election as God's choice of Samson at last come together. Among these techniques are disjunction ("Acknowledged not, or not at all consider'd / Deliverance offered" [*SA* 245–46]), interrogation ("Can this be hee, / That Heroic, that Renown'd, / Irresistable *Samson!*" [124–26]), qualification ("a living death / And buried.... / Buried, yet not exempt / By privilege of death and burial / From worst of other evils" [1001–01, 103–05]), the conditional ("had I sight, confus'd with shame, / How could I once look up" [196–97]), and Milton's ubiquitous litotes, or double negatives. They abound in Milton's preface to *Samson,* as they tend to do in much of his prose: "Nor is nature wanting in her own effects to make good on [Aristotle's] assertion"; "The Apostle *Paul* himself thought it not unworthy to insert a verse of *Euripides* into the Text of Holy Scripture"; "Heretofore Men in highest dignity have labour'd not a little to be thought able to compose a Tragedy" (*Complete Shorter Poems,* 461). In the play itself, Dalila's approach to Samson is an interesting example, its ambiguity anticipating the various turns in her argument:

> With doubtful feet and wavering resolution
> I come, still dreading thy displeasure, *Samson,*
> Which to have merited, without excuse,
> I cannot but acknowledge. (732–35)

"Doubtful," "wavering," and "dreading" set the tone of uncertainty even as they are part of Dalila's artful approach to the betrayed Samson. She "cannot but acknowledge" meriting his displeasure, the syntax suggesting more "wavering." It is not difficult to see this as part of Dalila's deceitfulness, although a case can be made for her complexity.[28] Yet even the chorus, who perhaps comes closest to offering a mirror to the audience, is prone to speaking in disjunctions and rhetorical questions, revealing the ambiguous confusion of its roles as friend to Samson and slightly misguided community voice. After the encounter between Manoa and Samson, for example, the chorus leads itself to an essentially classical vision of a God who throws down the hubris of his heroes:

> God of our Fathers, what is man!
> That thou towards him with hand so various,
> Or might I say contrarious,
> Temperst thy providence through his short course,
> Not evenly.
> ....
> Nor do I name of men the common rout,
> ....
> But such as thou hast solemnly elected
> With gifts and graces eminently adorn'd
> To some great work.
> ....
> Yet toward these thus dignifi'd, thou oft
> Amidst their height of noon,
> Changest thy countenance.
> ....
> Not only dost degrade them,
> ....
> But throw'st them lower then thou didst exalt them high.
> (SA 667–71, 674, 678–80, 682–84, 686, 689)

"Various" or "contrarious"? "Degrade" or the more extreme "lower than thou didst exalt them high"? It is a wavering tribute, if such it can even be called, to a changeable God. Like Job's friends, the chorus keeps trying to define the situation, get it right, showing not only its own limitations but also the limits on human knowledge and reason.

In the cognitive and emotional space in which alternatives or gradations are allowed free play, the audience engages its own judgment.

Drama is the genre in which the authorial voice is least directive. Milton early thought his story of the Fall might be a tragedy, "Adam Unparadiz'd,"[29] and at the beginning of book 9 of *Paradise Lost* the narrator shifts from the pastoral song of Adam's encounter with Raphael to the "tragic" dialogue and actions of Adam and Eve's fateful choices (*PL* 9.6). Yet *Samson* is his only drama, beyond the early entertainments. It may be that he needed to extract the authorial voice entirely from this very human story that had so many contiguities with this own life—marriage problems, blindness, possibly a sense of failed or incomplete mission in the world.[30] *Samson* also seems a fitting way for Milton to invite his reader to participate directly in the imaginative world he proffers, as he recasts a familiar biblical story to emphasize its ambiguities and uncertainties. Tragedy most explicitly sets individual characters, and individual audience responses, within and against the array of events that the plot unfolds, and in that sense the play asks its audience to weigh not only individual choices but also community values.

From earliest times, as Aristotle's *Poetics* affirms, the experience of tragedy was both communal and individual. The values of a community (and of a cosmology) hold the flawed human hero accountable. At the same time, the hero's stature combined with his flaws, which made him both greater than and similar to the audience, evoking communal and individual pity and fear.[31] Milton in *Samson* steps back from the narrative voice in order to let "the gravest, moralest and most profitable" of poetic types perform their combined individual and communal function, "said by *Aristotle* to be of power by raising pity and fear, or terror, to purge the mind of those and such like passions, that is to temper and reduce them to just measure with a kind of delight, stirr'd up by reading or seeing those passions well imitated."[32] The "just measure" will depend on how each reader reacts to the challenges and ambiguities of *Samson*, and their common response will affirm whether they are frightened and reluctant Danites or God's people ready to seize their personal and political freedoms. In *Samson*, Milton sets the possibilities within the drama, but absents himself from the decisions. It is in that sense his most invitational poem, his freest poetic.

Six

Areopagitica's Reception History and Modern Contestations of Freedom

Over the course of the seventeenth century "freedom" went from meaning primarily a social condition (not under the control of another) and a set of privileged exemptions from certain jurisdictions (the "liberties" of the universities or the guilds) to describing a personal condition of self-determination characterized by making one's own choices. Personal agency, implicit in medieval and early modern uses of "free" to mean generous, was to remain a core meaning of freedom, with free expression both the means and the vehicle for exercising self-determination. Milton is centrally implicated in this change, which he helped to effect not only by active redefinition through his own usage, but also by making room for his readers to exercise freedom as he presented it in his poetry and prose: a process of knowledgeable choosing that, through time, allows the conscious self to follow God's vocational call, what a secular age might label mindful self-fulfillment, though not without political and social implications.

Thomas Hobbes and John Locke, not Milton nor his midcentury controversialist colleagues, are generally acknowledged as the major English political thinkers of the seventeenth century. Yet Milton has had an equally substantial impact on English and American ideas of freedom, a point illustrated through some highlights of *Areopagitica's* reception history. As its nineteenth century editor, Thomas Holt White, was to insist, Milton "was more fortunate in his subject" than Locke and other early Whig theorists who rejected the Stuart case for divine right monarchy, in part because Milton's eloquent rhetoric (though no longer fashionable) lifted him beyond the specifics of his occasion.[1] *Areopagitica* has had continuing resonance for quite different views of what constitutes individual freedom, in large part because of Milton's invitational poetics of freedom. His eloquence is both inspiring and indeterminate.

Hobbes, Locke, and Milton share beliefs, with some differences, in the inherent liberty of the individual, the authority of the social contract, and the separation of church and state. The first right of nature, Hobbes insists in *Leviathan*, "is the Liberty each man hath, to use his own power, as he will himselfe, for the preservation of his own Nature," defining "Liberty" as "the absence of externall Impediments."[2] Milton has many versions of the claim he makes most emphatically in *Tenure of Kings and Magistrates*, that "no man who knows ought, can be so stupid as to deny that all men naturally were borne free, being the image and resemblance of God himself" (YP 3:198). In his *Second Treatise*, Locke sets out his view that "all Men are naturally in...a *State of perfect Freedom* to order their actions, and dispose of their Possessions, and Persons, as they think fit, within the bounds of the Law of Nature, without asking leave, or depending upon the Will of any other Man."[3] Hobbes has a more pessimistic view of human nature than Milton or Locke, on which he bases his theory of social contract: our right reason leads us to make social covenants and contracts so that we do not kill each other; otherwise, we would be always at war. As a consequence, his social contract is not republicanism, neo-Roman, or otherwise, but a means to an orderly, absolutist state, preferably a monarchy, from which the people have no recourse once the contract is made.[4] Milton, by contrast, insists that "the power of Kings and Magistrates is nothing else, but what is only derivative, transferr'd and committed to them in trust from the People, to the common good of them all, in whom the power yet remains fundamentally, and cannot be taken from them, without a violation of thir natural birthright" (YP 3:202). Locke similarly insists that "the *Liberty of Man, in Society,* is to be under no Legislative Power, but that established, by consent, in the Common-wealth, nor under any Dominion of any Will, or restraint of Law, but what the Legislative shall enact, according to the Trust put in it" (*Two Treatises,* 283). In contrast to Hobbes, both Milton and Locke insist that the power to remake the social contract, to change governing structures and governors, remains with the people.

Milton and Hobbes, then, have little in common beyond the fundamentals of the social contract, and this applies even to their apparent shared vision of a separate church and state. Hobbes's focus is against the intrusion of religious authority on civil power more generally. Echoing arguments we may recall from James I, Hobbes asks,

> who is there that does not see, to whose benefit it conduceth, to have it believed, that a King hath not his Authority from Christ, unlesse a Bishop crown him?... That Subjects may be freed from their Allegeance, if by the Court of *Rome,* the King may be judged an Heretique? That a King...may be deposed by a Pope...for no cause.... So that I may attribute all the changes of religion in the world, to one and the same cause; and that is, unpleasing Priests; and those not onely amongst Catholiques, but even in that Church that hath presumed most of the Reformation. (*Leviathan,* 86)[5]

This language fits the definition of "rhetorical questions" as Virginia Tufte describes, "formed strictly for effect and therefore making any answer at all superfluous," used for emphasis and with little or no invitation toward what else they may imply.[6] (Contrast Hobbes's "who is there that does not see" with Milton's "wherefor did God creat passions within us" [*Areopagitica*, YP 2:257].) More directly, in his chapter on "Power Ecclesiasticall," Hobbes argues that "in every Christian Common-wealth, the Civill Sovereign is the Supreme Pastor, to whose charge the whole flock of his Subjects is committed, and consequently...it is by his authority that all other Pastors are made....in the same manner as the Magistrates of Towns, Judges in Courts of Justice, and Commanders of Armies, are all but Ministers of him that is the Magistrate of the Whole Commonwealth" (*Leviathan*, 373). While Hobbes insists on public conformity, he does imply considerable leeway in private worship (252–53).[7] Nonetheless, this is not separation of church and state in Milton's terms; Milton rejects civil authority over religion, and his religious freedom would tolerate multiple public expressions.[8] Hobbes's vision is subordination of the church to the state, and his acceptance of multiple private beliefs, which he views as passive rather than volitional activities, anticipates the increasing diminution of established religion as a political force. For Hobbes, and even more for Locke (who scarcely mentions it), church as a power in competition with civil authority simply ceases to exist.[9]

In its place, and importantly for the subsequent history of arguments about freedom, Locke brings to the theory of freedom a well-developed view of a natural right to private property, a key argument of his *Second Treatise*. That right, according to Locke, begins with ownership of one's self and extends first and foremost to ownership of one's own labor. By adding the value of his labor to tilling the land, a man justifies the use and possession of what he has tilled: "though the things of Nature are given in common, yet Man (by being Master of himself, and *Proprietor of his own Person, and the Actions of Labour of it*) has still in himself *the great Foundation of Property;* and that which made up the great part of what he applied to the Support or Comfort of his being, when Invention and Arts had improved the conveniences of Life, was perfectly his own, and did not belong in common to others." As a direct result, individual freedom leads to "*a Right of Property*," which communities then must regulate when land becomes scarce (*Second Treatise*, 298–99). Money is a means of extending the value of labor that would otherwise have no immediate use, as when a farmer produces more grain than he and his family can eat, such things as silver and gold offering "some lasting thing that Men might keep without spoiling, and that by mutual consent Men would take in exchange for the truly useful, but perishable Supports of Life" (300–01). Instead of individual freedom as a function of God-given right, it becomes increasingly a function of individual effort, signified by the right to one's property.

Milton is closer to Locke than Hobbes on the fundamental and inalienable freedom of individuals and on the pliability of governance by social contract, and in a minor way anticipates Locke's arguments on private property.[10] Like Hobbes, Milton sees social issues within a divine framework, but his is closer to Locke's view of knowledge. Hobbes is systematic about knowledge,[11] but does not see it as individually verified. Locke rephrases Milton's main point in *Areopagitica* when he asserts in his *Essay concerning Human Understanding* (1694) that "so much as we ourselves consider and comprehend of Truth and Reason, so much we possess of real and true Knowledge. The floating of other Mens Opinions in our brains can make us not one jot the more knowing, though they happen to be true." From this parallel with Milton's "heretick in the Truth," Locke goes on to explain: "what in them was Science, is in us Opiniatrity [sic], whilst we give up our Assent only to reverend Names, and do not, as they did, employ our own *Reason* to understand those *Truths* which gave them reputation."[12] Milton and Locke share a vision of individual autonomy based on individual effort, with Milton's views based on his reading of God's call to the individual conscience, and Locke's views based on the principles of right reason.

Although Locke argues for a secular version of Milton's central premise in *Areopagitica*—that individual effort and comprehension are at the heart of the search for knowledge and truth—his rhetorical method is completely different. Locke is not only a master and advocate of clear, plain prose, he has a rationalist's suspicion of poets and poetry, as in *Some Thoughts concerning Education* (1693): "I know not what reason a Father can have, to wish his son a Poet, who does not desire to have him bid defiance to all other Callings, and Business, which is not yet the worst of the case; for if he proves a successful Rhymer, and get once the reputation of a Wit, I desire it may be consider'd what Company and Places he is Like to spend his Time in, nay, and Estate too, For it is very seldom seen, that any one discovers Mines of Gold or Silver in *Parnassus*. 'Tis a pleasant Air, but a barren soil."[13] This is in part the same suspicion of poetry shared by Stephen Gosson and others in the sixteenth century, but it is newly tied to a vision of the free individual freely pursuing a prosperity that has more to do with "gold and silver" than the life of the mind. This places him beyond the tradition that Milton inherited, of finding in imaginative writing and figures of speech channels for subversive thought. By Locke's time, one might say that a tradition of free speech was strong enough that visions of constitutional republicanism could be freely argued. But it is well to remember that Locke published his *Two Treatises* anonymously, and Sir Philip Sidney's great-nephew Algernon was executed for his republican views in 1683, just seven years before the *Treatises* were published.[14]

Hobbes also differs from Milton on the subject of poetic liberty, which for Milton, as *Paradise Lost* amply illustrates, may be boundlessly imaginative and continuously invitational. Hobbes, in fact a generation older than Milton and trained in the same tradition of humanist eloquence (though at Oxford, not Cambridge), does not appear to have a metaphoric cast of mind, despite his metaphoric "leviathan," and, to the extent he might, he would be suspicious of it. Using words "metaphorically" is, according to Hobbes, an abuse of the purposes of speech (*Leviathan*, 25–26). In his "Answer" to William Davenant's "Preface" to his "heroick" poem *Gondibert*, Hobbes dismisses "bold" fictions that "not onely...exceed the *work*, but also the *possibility* of Nature: they would have impenetrable Armours, Inchanted Castles, Invulnerable Bodies, Iron Men, Flying Horses, and a thousand other such things, which are easily feigned by them that dare." He resists "those that think the Beauty of a Poem consisteth in the exorbitancy of the fiction. For as truth is the bound of Historical, so the resemblance of truth is the utmost limit of Poetic Liberty." Hobbes gives his perspective on poetic knowledge and authority in terms that would seem almost a rebuke of Sidney's "second nature": "That which giveth a Poem the true and natural Colour," Hobbes says, "consisteth in two things, which are: *To know well*, that is, to have images of Nature in the memory distinct and clear; and *To know much*. A sign of the first is perspicuity, property, and decency, which delight all sorts of men, either by instructing the ignorant, or soothing the learned in their knowledge. A sign of the latter is novelty of expression, and pleaseth by excitation of the mind; for novelty causeth admiration, and admiration curiosity, which is a delightfull appetite of knowledge."[15]

In Hobbes's view, the reader will either be instructed or soothed, though novelty might excite the mind. This perhaps comes closest within either Hobbes or Locke to Milton's invitational poetics: novelty leads to "admiration," which leads to "curiosity," which leads to an "appetite" for knowledge. Yet the gist of Hobbes's "Answer" is that good literature should be a logical exposition of the world of human activity, anticipating not only Locke's rationalism but also the balance of the Popean couplet and the distaste with which Samuel Johnson approached the pastoral.[16]

Hobbes and Locke are more systematic philosophical thinkers than Milton. It is Milton's rhetoric that explains his continuing influence. Few people read Locke or Hobbes for pleasure. Compared with *Areopagitica,* the works of neither great thinker offer the thrill of discovery that Milton's rhythmic progressions and overlapping metaphors provide. Milton's invitational poetics, his eloquence carefully honed to incite individual thought, are what have carried this seventeenth century mind through the interests and adaptations of subsequent generations.

Notwithstanding its theological and perhaps arcane ontological elements, Milton's expressions of radical individualism continue to stand behind modern contestations of freedom. Milton remains important to how we continue to think about various meanings of freedom and liberty because he remains an eloquent polemicist we enjoy reading, and also because his inspiring invitational rhetoric was sufficiently indeterminate to help found both (what we now call) conservative and progressive definitions of individual freedom. His works and words have been used so variously that it is difficult to separate what he actually affirmed from what succeeding interpretations have assumed.[17] The reception history of *Areopagitica* is an illustrative case in point. As I noted in chapter 3, critics have pointed out that in some respects Milton's protest against prepublication licensing remains inadequate to the high claims often made about it. Not only does Milton's case for a free press exclude Catholics and atheists and allow that authors may be rightly punished for offensive writing, but its immediate impetus likely included a self-serving frustration over the licensing system's impact on his divorce tracts. Further, during 1649–51, as secretary for foreign tongues in Cromwell's government, Milton performed inspection and censorship duties, although apparently without much enthusiasm, under a licensing act only slightly less stringent than the one he had attacked in 1644.[18] Why, then, has this essay come to symbolize a tradition of freedom in the English-speaking culture?

Areopagitica, as I have been suggesting, has taken its role as Milton's great exhortation on behalf of free thought, a free press, and even freedom of religion, with its contradictions and difficulties intact, because it defines individual self-determination in passages of astonishing eloquence and in terms that invite interpretation. As a result, it could be used politically to give the impression of a tradition of English free speech on which later polemicists might build, adapting Milton's rhetoric to their particular visions of freedom. The reference to "Wicklef," which I cited in the introduction, insists on such a tradition, prefacing what could be interpreted as a rousing patriotism for this "City of refuge, the mansion house of liberty, encompast and surrounded with [God's] protection.... What could a man require more from a Nation so pliant and so prone to seek after knowledge. What wants there to such a towardly and pregnant soile, but wise and faithfull labourers, to make a knowing people, a Nation of Prophets, of Sages, and of Worthies" (YP 2:553–54). Progressive and optimistic, Milton's invitational and incantatory rhetoric explains why the reform wing of the Whig party especially embraced this essay as their own and used it to argue for secular purposes sometimes alien to Milton's apparent intent.[19] *Areopagitica* was turned into a foundational advocacy—even an authority—on behalf of a free press, free speech, and even free trade. It was, as Lewalski notes, "the first Milton book published in America (1774)."[20] The reception history of *Areopagitica*, nonetheless, is not a Hegelian story of ever-more-progressive views interacting with hegemonies to create new syntheses, but of Milton's eloquence providing the seed for various definitions of freedom that pulled away from or at least changed the early modern view of freedom as a function of social order, and also set the stage for the split between "liberty" and "liberalism" that Skinner describes.[21]

In its own time, as far as we can tell, *Areopagitica* was ignored, but by the twentieth century it had become an iconic cultural document on both sides of the Atlantic. Oxford's Clarendon Press produced an edition in 1875 that went through numerous printings until after World War II, while a beautifully printed Grolier Club edition in 1890, with an introduction by influential poet and critic James Russell Lowell, shows the status it had reached in the United States.[22] Although Milton's ideas were variously cited (if not necessarily acknowledged) even in the late seventeenth century, the two editions most responsible for the work's enhanced reputation, signaling the two directions later taken by proponents of this new kind of freedom, appeared in 1738 and 1819. The first argued for self-determination as an element of British nationalism and economic freedom, while the second situated Milton in the forefront of the nineteenth century social and parliamentary reform movement. The 1819 edition also included Le Comte de Mirabeau's imitation/translation of *Areopagitica*, "Sur la liberté de la presse, imité de l'Anglois, de Milton," originally published in 1788 on the eve of the French Revolution.

In 1738 the poet James Thomson (1700–48) introduced the first separate edition of *Areopagitica* since the original of 1644.[23] Thomson was an important propagandist for the Whig view of the "progress of European civilization and the triumphs of British freedom," although his most explicit poem on this topic, "Liberty," is widely considered "one of his greatest aesthetic failures."[24] Best known as the poet of *The Seasons*, a work that both states and reflects his admiration of Milton (and a poem that Wordsworth was to admire), Thomson was a Scot who came to London in his twenties to seek his literary fortune. He became associated with the particular Whig faction attached to Frederick, Prince of Wales, in opposition to the policies of the prime minister, Sir Robert Walpole. At issue was Walpole's pursuit of peace with Spain by agreeing not to allow British trade in the Spanish colonies. "Liberty," for Thomson and his friends, included resistance to Spanish "tyranny" over the freedom of English trade.[25]

In 1737 Walpole led the passage of an act to license theatrical productions. Thomson's own play, *Agamemnon,* was held up briefly in the process, but it seems likely that an accumulated irritation led him to use Milton's essay as a response and an occasion for his own preface locating the future of England's greatness with liberty of the press. "Thomson's preface," his biographer notes, "sharpened what was already provocative; for, though Milton's towering literary reputation had now achieved sufficient respectability in the seats of authority for a monument to be raised to him in the Poets' corner of Westminster Abbey in 1737, his forthright political views could still serve a purpose in current controversy, particularly if the subject at issue was freedom or Spain."[26] The moment combined current controversy with Milton's heightened reputation to bring this essay forward and for Thomson and his partisans to see in it a muscular affirmation of free trade. Thomson's definition of freedom focuses on "independent life," a form of Miltonic self-determination, along with independence from foreign rule and trade regulation, and while it becomes part of the backdrop of British colonialism it also asserts an honorable and cohesive society for which a free press remains essential:

> By those three Virtues be the Frame sustain'd,
> Of British Freedom: Independent life;
> Integrity in office; and, o'er all
> Supreme, A Passion for the Common-weal.
>
> (*Liberty* 5.120–24)

While at first Thomson's definition of "British Freedom" seems to follow the republican view of liberty as a function of a free people in a free state, the emphasis on "Independent life" and unimpeded trade (here implicit in the "Passion for the Common-weal") reflects Locke's emphasis on private property and pushes toward the liberalism that fellow Scotsman Adam Smith's work will come to embody a generation later.[27] Smith's classic *Wealth of Nations* is the foundational work for laissez-faire capitalism and offers a major theoretical basis for modern conservative "liberalism," as expressed, for example, by the Cato Institute and the American Enterprise Institute, both private organizations located in Washington, DC: "The mission of the Cato Institute is to increase the understanding of public policies based on the principles of limited government, *free markets*, individual liberty, and peace"; "The American Enterprise Institute is a community of scholars and supporters committed to expanding liberty, increasing individual opportunity, and *strengthening free enterprise*" (emphasis mine).[28] Locke's theory of property as a function of individual freedom is the principle behind these modern equations, but in Thomson's preface to *Areopagitica* we can see Milton's individualism, as well as his praise of a free press, used to advance a line of thinking about freedom that will increasingly center on private property. At the same time, we see increasing suspicion of government, no matter how representative, as Thomson's negative rhetoric admonishes (in Milton's name) on behalf of a free press: "I hope it will never be in this Nation's Misfortune to fall into the Hands of an Administration, that do not from their souls abhor any thing that has but the remotest Tendency towards the Erection of a new and arbitrary Jurisdiction over the Press" (A3v).

This sentiment, in favor of a free press as part of individual liberty in an entrepreneurial system, would eventually extend into the fight for copyright. Two generations later, the

Whig historian Catharine Macauley produced *A Modest Plea for the Property of Copyright* (1774), a pamphlet with some rhetorical homage to Milton's form of address to Parliament in *Areopagitica*. In Macauley's "plea," Milton (though not *Areopagitica* explicitly) becomes the figure for the brave, independent author faced with loss of property rights in the face of a hostile government. The lesson she takes: "If some positive law does not lend its aid to the support of the tottering state of literature in this country, this decision will be a more mortal stab to the freedom, virtue, religion, and morals of the people of England, than the unthinking multitude in general at present apprehend."[29]

Areopagitica's publication in 1819 comes in a different time and adds another dimension to its role as a document of English cultural self-definition. Its editor, Thomas Holt White (1763–1841) was of a generation of university-educated men, mainly lawyers and clergymen, who helped establish and professionalize modern bibliographic and editorial principles. These included Sir Egerton Brydges (1762–1837), one of the founding members of The Roxburghe Club (1812), from whose members would derive at the end of the century the *Early English Text Society* and the *Oxford English Dictionary*; George Frederick Nott (1767–1841), who produced in this same period what is widely recognized as the "first adequate edition" of Wyatt's poetry in his *Works of Henry Howard, Earl of Surrey and Sir Thomas Wyatt* (1815–16); and Henry John Todd (1763–1845), a clergyman with an "erudite philological and historical flair" whose *Poetical Works of John Milton* (London, 1801) remained the standard edition for at least 50 years.[30]

Holt White likely knew Todd's edition of Milton's poetry. It includes earlier commentary, some of it incorporated in Todd's biographical essay, "Some Account of the Life and Writings of John Milton." This Milton is "the proud boast of his own country, and the admiration of the world." He is also a "a lover of liberty...as little disposed to submission and conformity in college as in a state," as Todd chooses to explain the poet's brief rustication from Cambridge.[31] A good episcopal churchman himself, Todd finds in Milton's antiprelatical tracts "too many expressions which we must lament," but still follows Milton's earlier editor, Thomas Newton, in judging *Areopagitica* "perhaps the best vindication...that has been published at any time, or in any language, of that liberty which is the basis and support of all other liberties, the liberty of the press."[32]

What Todd appears both to admire and deplore in Milton is an idiosyncratic uniqueness that he associates with Milton's concept of liberty. The patriotic spirit that expressed itself in seeing freedom as unfettered trade in Thomson's time has been reforged as a combined appreciation and fear of romantic individual genius. To place it in context, Todd's Milton appeared when the French and American Revolutions were in most Britons' living memories, and the Napoleonic wars were only two years away. It was also just three years after the first edition of Wordsworth and Coleridge's *Lyrical Ballads* and shortly before Wordsworth would exclaim "Milton! Thou shouldst be living at this hour." Wordsworth's sonnet was a screed against a wealthy and thoughtless complacency that one could, in a double retrospect, attribute to the social and entrepreneurial "liberty" of Thomson's time. Wordsworth laments the forfeiting of the "ancient English dower / Of inward happiness," and calls for the spirit of Milton to "give us manners, virtue, freedom, power."[33] Wordsworth associates Milton's "freedom" with a particularly English expression of inner virtue and personal agency.[34]

Holt White takes Todd's picture of Milton a step further, and somewhat reflects Wordsworth's reading, as he describes in impassioned prose a broadly imaginative and generous-spirited genius set against the pinched Puritanism of his own time. This separate edition of *Areopagitica,* appearing less than a generation later than Todd's *Poetical Works*, is already in a different era of British Romanticism. By 1819 Byron had published *Childe Harold's Pilgrimage*, Shelley *Queen Mab*, and Keats *Endymion*; Britain had decisively won the Napoleonic wars; and in 1819 George III, as Shelley famously exclaimed, was "an old, mad, blind, despised and dying king."[35]

Holt White, the nephew of the popular naturalist and writer Gilbert White, was active in reform politics from at least 1796, when he published *Letters to William Paley, M.A. ... on His Objections to a Reform in the Representation of the Commons*. The "Prefatory Advertisement" to the *Letters* accuses Paley's "seventh Chapter of the sixth Book of the *Principles of Moral and Political Philosophy*" of "following the example of the writers employed by The Stuarts" to use the patriarchal scheme of government against John Locke's social contract.[36] Holt White assumes that the reform Whig view of social contract accurately describes both the history and aspirations of England's parliamentary form of government, and that Paley, the archdeacon of Carlisle, was in league with the king's party to take the country back to the tyrannical days of the Stuarts.

Holt White's edition of *Areopagitica*, with its introduction, Thomson's preface, various "Commendatory Testimonies" from 1712 forward, "Illustrations" (endnotes and appendices), and publication of Mirabeau, is an impressive collection, and the editor was well situated to define Milton's work as a rhetoric of freedom congenial to later romantic sensibility and reform politics. Letters and papers at Harvard and in the Hampshire Public Record Office show him to have corresponded with leading reformers of his day, including Major John Cartwright (1740–1824), Sir Francis Burdett (1770–1834), and Charles Cowden Clarke (1787–1877).[37] Major Cartwright is notable for refusing to fight against the colonists in the American Revolution and later, in 1812, for founding the Hampden Society, a radical group named in honor of civil war parliamentary hero John Hampden (1596–1643). Sir Francis Burdett, along with Cartwright and others, anticipated the chartist movement by proposing a bill in Parliament that called for universal "manhood suffrage, annual parliaments, equal electoral districts, and the ballot."[38] It was "soundly defeated" in June 1818, but he tried once more the next year, about the time of Holt White's publication of *Areopagitica*. Charles Cowden Clarke, critic and literary scholar, was a friend of Charles and Mary Lamb, Leigh Hunt, and especially of John Keats, who had been a pupil of Clarke's father.

With connections such as these, and early participation in the organization "Friends of Parliamentary Reform," Holt White unsurprisingly celebrates Milton as a great genius in the ongoing progress of English history. It is also interesting to note that Holt White's appreciation for British political liberties lauds a tradition that produced the balance of powers structure in the United States Constitution:

> It might perhaps be received as a fundamental axiom in this science [of "free Government"], that no well-policied State can tolerate the confusion of the legislative with the judicial and executive functions. With our illustrious line of countrymen, to whose Wisdom, Firmness, and Virtue we are indebted for the Liberties of England, the praise lies of being the first who held out to other Nations the pattern of a political organization, which for the most part kept these authorities asunder, and which they distributed and adjusted so happily in a Constitution of three Estates, as to render them wholesome restraints to moderate or over-rule the exorbitancies of each other.

The free press that Milton advocates is presumably part of the overall balance of "wholesome restraints" on potential government "exorbitancies." Further, Milton's arguments are to be admired because they are foundational: whatever objections there may be to Milton's prose style or the restrictions on liberty his essay would continue to condone, Holt White insists, are attributable to the relative ignorance of

Milton's time and the need to persuade those not far along in their understanding of freedom. "The informed class of the community was at that time much less numerous than it is at present," the nineteenth century barrister opines, "and...the Liberty of the Press was to Milton and to his contemporaries a topic of discussion altogether new.... In regard to their political Education, the Public, we should remember, were still in their infancy, and it was indispensable to initiate them in the rudiments."[39]

Explicit everywhere is a utilitarian theory of progress and the patriotic assumption that a specifically English tradition of civil liberty and free expression is to be modeled and exported.[40] By the time Holt White is finished with his project, Milton is fully implicated in this vision of English history, identity, and purpose. Good barrister that he is, Holt White ignores elements of Milton's case less congenial to his own, notably the role of religion, but credits him with an ongoing relevance that other writers on similar subjects do not have: "Milton's defence of unrestricted Publication may confidently lay claim to a duration of practical utility far more extended [than even the political theory of Locke, for example]. It can never cease to have its value on political considerations, till this natural and constitutional Right ceases to be an object of jealousy or hatred with those who may bear rule over us."[41] Free expression has entered English cultural self-definition as a "natural and constitutional Right," in perceived opposition to the preferences of "those who may bear rule over us." As he had from his publication against the Tory views of William Paley, Holt White continues to see freedom necessarily expanding to more fair and general suffrage and to include other elements of parliamentary and political reform that would make for a more valid representative government. This view of freedom as a function of representative statecraft that can improve the conditions of its citizens we now find in another Washington-based private think tank, the Center for

American Progress: "we believe America is a land of boundless opportunity, where people can better themselves, their children, their families, and their communities through education, hard work, and the freedom to climb the ladder of economic mobility. We believe an open and effective *government can champion the common good over narrow self-interest*, harness the strength of our diversity, and secure the rights and safety of its people."[42] While "freedom to climb the ladder of economic mobility" remains important, in this vision an "open and effective government," the transatlantic heritage of Holt White's parliamentary efforts, has the potential to secure the "rights" of all citizens.

The key point of difference between Holt White and Thomson lies in their views of government's role in the construction of liberty, and the rhetoric of modern think tanks shows how these differences continue to fuel disparate ideas of liberty. Each of Milton's editors implicates *Areopagitica* in his own view of liberty, as Milton's invitational poetics has allowed him to do. Thomson is suspicious of government, and (although he did not yet have Adam Smith's language to say it) would have his independent British subject rely more on the invisible hand of a self-interested market than on magistrates, however chosen, whose control might mean censorship or trade restrictions. Holt White, by contrast, is a barrister actively engaged in a project to assure a more representative parliament, one that might both express and continue individual liberties and support the free exchange of ideas that is part of a checks and balances system. Like the Roman and neo-Roman republicans before him, Holt White, a product of the enlightenment, believes that rational men can contract for a rational state, although his preface to *Areopagitica* shows that he sees it as an ongoing and incomplete project. With less emphasis on reason, Thomson, the poet, would have "o'er all / Supreme, A Passion for the Common-Weal." Milton's hope for the liberating power of republican values in statements favoring republican principles, notably in *Eikonoklastes* and *The Second Defence*, makes him one of the fathers of Holt White's urge toward parliamentary reform, but he is equally a father of Thomson's praise of "independent life."

Following Holt White's edition, the nineteenth century in England saw Edward Arber's "reprint" of *Areopagitica* in 1868, with minimum apparatus. R. C. Jebb's *Commentary* (1872) annotated the Arber edition and offered a summary of licensing issues from the founding of the Stationer's Register in 1557 to the expiration of the 1637 licensing act in 1694. Interestingly, it was originally meant as an aide to young women, as Jebb later wrote, when "the movement for the higher education of women was just beginning at Cambridge,—that movement which is now [1905] represented by the Colleges of Girton and Newnham."[43] Neither of these offered anything new about the essay or its influence, but both show *Areopagitica*'s continuing vitality in English culture. In 1875, however, John Hales produced the authoritative Clarendon Press volume that I mentioned earlier, one remaining in print, over several editions, until 1949.[44] His introduction portrays Milton as an individual genius and a constitutional libertarian.

Hales sees Milton through the romantic lens, comparing him favorably with Wordsworth and emphasizing his individuality, but he also sees the poet as a force for constitutional law: "Perhaps there was never incarnate a spirit so impatient of all petty regulation and control as was that of Milton. Not that he meant 'license' when he cried 'liberty,' for his sense of law was as deep as his nature; and, bold thinker as he was, he was ever ready and eager to acknowledge all just and eternal restrictions upon human thought. But for any meaner limitings, they moved in him disdain and indignation."[45] This love of (anything other than divine) law might have surprised Milton, but Hales's reading both hearkens back to the parliamentary origins of free speech endemic to English self-conception even before Milton's time (recall the *Myrrour for Magistrates*' "Tresilian"), and concludes the Whig tradition, with its emphasis on general suffrage and the primacy of Parliament, into which Milton had been placed. Further, although he sees Milton's eloquent prose as sometimes overwhelming Milton's ideas, Hales makes the explicit case that Milton should be situated among the great theoreticians of free thought because of the power of his rhetoric. *Areopagitica* "is indeed not only a magnificent protest in behalf of unlicensed books, but an immortal defence of Free Thought. Jeremy Taylor's *Liberty of Prophesying*, Locke's *Letters on Toleration*, John Stuart Mill's *Liberty*—these are works of no temporary or transient value, however they may have been called forth by passing circumstances; and amongst these, and not the least amongst them, is to be ranked the *Areopagitica*. It is inspired by the very spirit of freedom."[46]

It remains to say something about the descent of Milton's ideas, or rather the interpretations of freedom based on interpretations of his ideas, toward the differing directions I mentioned early in this chapter. John Stuart Mill, who grew up in the atmosphere of parliamentary reform and who may well have known Holt White's edition of *Areopagitica*, is still arguably the foremost theorist of libertarianism in English-speaking culture, and it is in his work that Milton's radical individualism comes to fruition.[47] In *On Liberty* (1859), Mill claims from the outset *not* to address "the so-called Liberty of the Will, so unfortunately opposed to the misnamed doctrine of Philosophical Necessity," but rather "Civil, or Social Liberty: the nature and limits of the power which can be legitimately exercised by society over the individual." Mill's insistence on "individuality, as one of the elements of well-being," however, with an "imperative that human beings should be free to form opinions, and to express their opinions without reserve," assumes free will. Sounding much like a secular version of Milton, Mill takes his belief in the individual one step further: "The initiation of all wise or noble things comes and must come from individuals; generally at first from some one individual. The honour and glory of the average man is that he is capable of following that initiative; that he can respond internally to wise and noble things, and be led to them with his eyes open."[48] For Mill, individual liberty should be limited only by physical safety and respect for the liberties of others.

Like Locke, Mill also offers a secular echo of Milton's rejection of the man who may be a "heretick in the truth," insisting that each individual must choose his own knowledge: "no one can be a great thinker," Mill proclaims, "who does not recognize, that as a thinker it is his first duty to follow his intellect to whatever conclusions it may lead. Truth gains more even by the errors of one who, with due study and preparation, thinks for himself, than by the true opinions of those who only hold them because they do not suffer themselves to think." Mill's nineteenth century reformist bent takes him a step beyond Milton's fellow feeling for a "great thinker" (in Milton's terms, that "knowing" or "learned" reader): "not that it is solely, or chiefly, to form great thinkers that freedom of thinking is required. On the contrary, it is as much, and even more indispensable, to enable average human beings to attain the mental stature which they are capable of."[49] In this, for Mill as for Milton, resides their freedom.

Milton, along with his descendent Mill, advocates what cognitive linguist George Lakoff calls "simple freedom" and describes as the ability "to achieve purposes either because nothing is stopping you or because you have the requisite capacities, or both." "Simple freedom" includes free will, which Lakoff defines in the Platonic (and Miltonic) tradition as "government of the self by the self."[50] Lakoff's project is to try to redeem the use of "freedom" from what he sees as its redirection from progressive causes, such as work for social equality, toward conservative notions of freedom based on private property and free markets, yet he argues that both sides would agree on the definition of "simple freedom." In a less polemical and more systematic work, political theorist Philip Pettit notes that "there are many languages of legitimation in the world of democratic politics today," and they all share "a common idiom of freedom or liberty." There is a kind of slippage in how this language is used, allowing "shared assumptions that are abstract enough to leave room for differences and germane enough to act as constraints on debate about those differences; they make conversation possible without predetermining its direction." So we find freedom and liberty in "the language of economics...the language of rights...the language of welfare and fairness.... And the language of democratic legitimation harps on the legitimacy of what a free people freely decide, and on the way in which individual persons share in that collective freedom."[51] Milton's invitational poetics modeled and allowed for this slippage, sending a reconfigured and individualized idea of freedom into the broader community of ideas.

Controversies continue about what we mean by freedom and what supports and inhibits it. I noted that modern conservative and progressive think tanks reflect an earlier divide between "liberty" as free markets, unimpeded by government, and "liberty" as social opportunity, aided by just governance. Philosopher Isaiah Berlin described what he called "negative freedom," or the absence of authoritarian control or restraint against the individual, and "positive freedom," or those conditions that allowed for personal agency and assume free will. In desiring positive freedom, Berlin asserts, "I wish, above all, to be conscious of myself as a thinking, willing, active being, bearing responsibility for my choices and able to explain them by my own ideas and purposes. I feel free to the degree that I believe this to be true, and enslaved to the degree that I am made to realize that it is not." Berlin's views remain controversial, not least because he resisted associating even "positive" freedom with equal rights. In a distant echo of Hobbes, Berlin argues that although we may give up freedom to achieve other moral purposes, we should not delude ourselves that such choices enhance freedom: "To avoid glaring inequality or widespread misery I am ready to sacrifice some, or all, of my freedom; I may do so willingly and freely; but it is freedom that I am giving up for the sake of justice or equality or the love of my fellow men....[this] sacrifice is not an increase in what is being sacrificed, namely freedom, however great the moral need or the compensation for it. Everything is what it is: liberty is liberty, not equality or fairness or injustice or culture, or human happiness or a quiet conscience."[52] Lakoff, on the other hand, is closer to Skinner's neo-Roman tradition, seeing laws within a system of representative government as potentially enabling rather than repressing liberty. The push for social equality and the suffrage movement from the seventeenth to twentieth century reflects the neo-Roman impulse as Skinner defines it. But as Michael Sandel points out, this leaves those who see freedom within the context of community in a quandary: "Liberal freedom developed as an antidote to political theories that consigned persons to destinies fixed by caste or class, station or rank, custom, tradition or inherited status. So how is it possible to acknowledge the moral weight of community while still giving scope to human freedom?"[53]

Along with what Pettit calls the republican "Commonwealthmen" of the late seventeenth and eighteenth centuries (including Algernon Sidney and Locke), Milton was concerned (in Pettit's terms) with a "freedom of non-domination which requires that no one is able to interfere on an arbitrary basis—at their pleasure—in the choices of a free person";[54] Milton's assaults on tyranny, in *Tenure* and *Eikonoklastes* for example, make him one of the theorists of "non-domination." And although Milton was less interested in the free market elements of "negative freedom," characterized by "non-interference" in an individual's liberty (as defined and praised by Berlin), he deplored the dictates of a state church, as in *Treatise on Civil Power* and *Likeliest Means to Remove Hirelings*, and may be seen in that sense as one of Berlin's forebears. More pertinently, at its core Milton's freedom is Berlin's "positive liberty" of "self-mastery," which for Milton has its origins in classical texts and the Reform Protestant belief in the primacy of conscience, and best expresses itself in the invitational poetics of *Areopagitica* and his later poems. In this broad sense, Milton's project has been successful: his words, feeding both Thomson's "Passion" for liberty and Holt White's rational construction of the "rudiments" of civil rights, with echoes in the examples of Berlin and Pettit, have found force in the individual time and place of their interpreters, while remaining "germane enough to act as constraints on debate" over possible meanings of liberty and the role of a free press in its pursuit.

It is interesting to contemplate what Milton might have thought about modern science's contribution to the discussion of freedom. Steven Pinker, Roger Penrose, Richard Dawkins, and Michael Gazzingana have complicated the conversation by arguing for mind inseparable from the brain, innate knowledge inherent in the brain's computational structures, and behavior shaped by evolutionary psychological adaptations. At its most reductive level, their argument might go something like this: if I am genetically handed a certain brain structure and if my brain chemistry runs on complex algorithmic systems and if my encounter with my environment is further programmed to try to maximize my evolutionary prospects, then how do I think freely about my personal freedom, much less enact it?[55] Issues of brain function were not precisely in Milton's ken, but the composition of matter and spirit concerned him. As I noted in chapter 4, Milton was a monist who saw matter and spirit as gradations rather than distinctions, but he was by no means a determinist, material or otherwise, and indeed may have developed his view of monism in response to what he saw as materialist determinism in Hobbes.[56]

To conclude: Milton's definition of freedom emerges as an individualistic and meritocratic challenge to the dominant Tudor and Stuart view of freedom as a function of hierarchy and social order. For Milton, freedom resides in the ability to make knowledgeable choices, an expanded version of a classical idea set within the framework of a longstanding English tradition that took pride in being a free country of free people, a tradition that Milton manipulated to serve his expanded definition. Milton's poetics of freedom, which resists making an authoritarian case for a liberal idea, takes advantage of interpretive spaces in metaphor and in varieties of indirect syntax to offer opportunities for each reader to become active in deriving individually relevant meaning.

Contestations about freedom continue in the twenty-first century, obviously in the political arena, but also in more basic discussions of how the mind works, and whether there is free will. Questions of agency and volition continue to be subject to debate among philosophers of the mind, though, as E. J. Lowe argues, there is some consensus that "the concept of agency...[is] primitive and irreducible...if we are to retain our familiar self-conception as autonomous and rational subjects of experience. And without that self-conception, it seems, rational inquiry itself becomes impossible for us and with it all philosophical argument."[57] If there is agency, there is choice and therefore the opportunity for freedom on Milton's fundamental level. Even neuroscience, which describes the human brain as mechanistic, finds room for something like human choice. As Gazzinaga puts it, when we think we are exercising free will, "what is going on is the match between ever-present multiple mental states and the impinging contextual force in which it functions. Our interpreter [another function of the brain] then claims we freely made a choice." At the same time, Gazzinaga argues, there remains a level of social interaction in which one must respond to the rules of community, and the principle of choice remains a characteristic of human interaction.[58] Milton's poetic richness continues to reflect the mental richness of what it means to be human even in these twenty-first century terms, employing (in Lowe's description of human mental complexity) both "quasi-linguistic" (or abstract) and "analogue" or "imagistic" representations in ways that encourage a freedom "to roam over all the vast stretches of space and time and thus to reflect on past happenings and contemplate future possibilities."[59]

Milton would have been quite at home with the complex and sometimes apparently self-contradictory analyses of the neuroscientists, as well as with the more familiar arguments of philosophers and political theorists. Milton had a mind capacious enough to create *Paradise Lost* even while he was blind. The work's interweaving patterns are emblematic of the algorithmic complexity that Pinker, for example, attributes to the human brain, though he would separate Milton's morality of freedom from his own pursuit of neuroscience.[60] Milton's mental capaciousness, expressed through Milton's invitational poetics of freedom, in turn makes room for a variety of individual responses, as the reception history of *Paradise Lost*, like that of *Areopagitica*, amply proves. Milton's fictive characters display the identifiers that draw on familiar patterns of what Elizabeth Fowler (in a vein similar to Gazzinaga's) calls "social persons," and yet those characters also emerge and change through what Marshall Grossman (in a vein similar to Lowe's) describes as "the narrative of the self authored as a subject, moving through time, capable of change [i.e., free to change], yet recognizably self identical."[61] Narrative complexities through which Milton's characters emerge, along with the constellation of techniques

I have been noting (double negatives, rhetorical questions, the language of surmise, images of violence and dismemberment) all demand hermeneutics, inevitably individual. We are free to interpret, and, in interpreting, create a community of free persons.

Notes

Notes to Introduction

1. The terms "freedom" and "liberty," with their related words (free, freely, liberal), come from Germanic and Latin origins, respectively, and were essentially cognates by the seventeenth century, with a slight preference for "freedom" to refer to a personal condition and "liberty" to a political one. The *Oxford English Dictionary*'s first two definitions for each are parallel: "Freedom 1. Exemption or release from slavery or imprisonment; personal liberty...b. *fig.* liberation from the bondage of sin....2. Exemption from arbitrary, despotic or autocratic control; independence; civil liberty"; "Liberty 1. Exemption or release from captivity, bondage, or slavery...b. In religious use, freedom from the bondage of sin, or of the law.... 2. Exemption or freedom from arbitrary, despotic, or autocratic rule or control." For a summary history of both terms, along with their tendency to conflate in seventeenth century England, see David Hackett Fisher, *Liberty and Freedom: A Visual History of America's Founding Ideas* (New York: Oxford University Press, 2005), 4–12.

2. Quentin Skinner, *Liberty before Liberalism* (Cambridge: Cambridge University Press, 1998), 17–19, 66–67; and see A summary of the mid-seventeenth century advocates (including Milton) in Johann P. Sommerville, "English and Roman Liberty in the Monarchical Republic of Early Stuart England," in *The Monarchical Republic of Early Modern England*, ed. John F. McDiarmid (Aldershot: Ashgate, 2007), 205. Benjamin Myers, *Milton's Theology of Freedom* (Berlin: Walter De Gruyter, 2006), argues for a radical theology in *Paradise Lost* through which God "ordains and affirms the reality and decisiveness of human choice" (91).

3. John Milton, *Areopagitica,* in *Complete Prose Works of John Milton,* 8 vols., ed. Don M. Wolfe et al. (New Haven: Yale University Press, 1953–82), 2:527. All references to Milton's prose are from this edition, hereafter cited in the text as YP, followed by volume and page number. Milton extends his affirmation to the political arena in *Tenure of Kings and Magistrates* (1648): "No man who knows ought, can be so stupid to deny that all men were naturally born free, being the image and resemblance of God himself" (YP 3:198).

4. Harry F. Smallburg, "Prose Style," in *A Milton Encyclopedia,* ed. William B. Hunter et al. (Lewisburg, PA: Bucknell University Press, 1978–81), 7:42.

5. As when he famously complains in Sonnet 12 that the people "bawl for freedom in their senseless mood, / And still revolt when truth would set them free. / License they mean when they cry liberty; / For who loves that, must first be wise and good." *John Milton: Complete Shorter Poems,* ed. Stella Revard (Oxford: Wiley-Blackwell, 2009), 299. Unless otherwise noted, all references to Milton's poems, except *Paradise Lost,* are from this edition, hereafter cited in the text.

6. Daniel Shore, "'Fit though Few': *Eikonoklastes* and the Rhetoric of Audience," in *Milton Studies,* vol. 45, ed. Albert C. Labriola, 129–48 (Pittsburgh: University of Pittsburgh Press, 2006). The trope makes reference to the prologue to book 7 of *Paradise Lost,* as the bard encourages his muse to find "fit audience...though few"; see John Milton, *Paradise Lost,* 7.31. All citations from *Paradise Lost* will be taken from *John Milton: Paradise Lost,* ed. Barbara K. Lewalski (Oxford: Blackwell, 2007); hereafter cited in the text. Shore shows that this habit of inviting a sympathetic audience appears as early as Milton's college work, in his "Prolusions." In his earliest autobiographical statements, in *The Reason of Church-Government,* Milton asks to be "heard only...by the elegant & learned reader," a "knowing reader," to whom he promises a later poetic work "not to be rays'd from the heat of youth...but by devout prayer to that eternall Spirit who can enrich with all utterance and knowledge" (YP 1:807, 820–21).

7. Susanne Woods, "Elective Poetics and Milton's Prose: *A Treatise of Civil Power* and *Considerations Touching the Likeliest Means to Remove Hirelings Out of the Church,*" in *Politics, Poetics and Hermeneutics in Milton's Prose,* ed. David Loewenstein and James Grantham Turner (Cambridge: Cambridge University Press, 1990), 193–211.

8. Double negatives and related indirect rhetorical constructions were known as "litotes": "*Litotes*...Denial of the contrary; understatement that intensifies....in litotes 'more is understood than is said,' as in 'He is not the wisest man in the world; when we mean 'he is a fool' (Peacham).... Sister Miriam Joseph remarks

[in *Shakespeare's Use of the Arts of Language* (New York: Hafner, 1947)]: 'Litotes is related to what the logicians call equipolence or obversion, which consists of expressing a thought by denying a contrary.'" See Richard Lanham, *A Handlist of Rhetorical Terms* (Berkeley and Los Angeles: University of California Press, 1991), 95. As will be clear throughout this book, I see Milton's use of these devices as not merely for tonal nuance, but as a way to open up space for individual interpretation.

9. Susanne Woods, "Inviting Rival Hermeneutics: Milton's Language of Violence and the Invitation to Freedom," in *Milton's Rival Hermeneutics: "Reason Is But Choosing,"* ed. Richard J. DuRocher and Margaret Olofsun Thickstun (Pittsburgh: Duquesne University Press, 2012), 3–16.

10. The "serious" with which it ends is Milton's claim of personal chastity, deriving from his reasoning that if it is important for women, it is even more important to men, since the dishonor of unchastity "sins both against his owne body which is the perfeter sex, and in his own glory which is in the woman, and that which is worst, against the image and glory of God which is in himselfe" (YP 1:892).

11. In *Apology* he praises the long parliament for hearing "the meanest artisans and labourers, at other times also women, and often the younger sort of servants assembling with their complaints," with "neither their meannesse...rejected. nor their simplicity contemn'd, nor yet their urgency distasted" (YP 1:926). Don Wolfe, editor of the *Apology,* describes Milton as "an unconscious leader" of a "gathering of social forces that made dynamite of spiritual equality," though he would "retreat" from this democratic position after *Areopagitica* (YP 1:205).

12. Daniel Shore, *Milton and the Art of Rhetoric* (Cambridge: Cambridge University Press, 2012), 6–9.

13. Virginia Tufte, *Artful Sentences: Syntax as Style* (Cheshire, CT: Graphics Press, 2006), 208. Lanham defines these and other interrogative kinds, drawing his terminology from Renaissance rhetorical handbooks, for example: "Erotesis...[or] Interrogatio.... A 'rhetorical question,' one which implies an answer but does not give or lead us to expect one," and "Racionation.... Asking ourselves reasons for our own statements" (*Handlist of Rhetorical Terms,* 71, 129).

14. Tufte, *Artful Sentences,* 208–09.

15. C. S. Lewis, "The New Learning and the New Ignorance, " *Sixteenth-Century English Literature* (Oxford: Oxford University Press, 1954), 1–65.

16. Milton's belief that choices are part of God's plan to enable humankind to understand and to become resembles some aspects of twentieth century Christian existentialism. See, e.g., the Thomist

philosopher Jacques Maritain, *Existence and the Existent: An Essay on Christian Existentialism*, trans. Lewis Galantière and Gerald B. Phelan (New York: Pantheon, 1948): "[God's] existent universe, set firmly upon primary facts,... we are required to discover, not deduce; that universe traversed by all the influxes productive of being which vivify it, unify it, cause it to push onward towards the unforeseeable future; that universe, also, which is wounded by all those deficiencies of being that constitute the reality of evil and in which we must see the price paid for the interaction of beings, the price paid for created liberty, capable of evading the influx of the First Being" (20).

17. From the editors' introduction to *Milton's Rival Hermeneutics*, ed. Richard J. DuRocher and Margaret Olofson Thickstun (Pittsburgh: Duquesne University Press, 2012), xvi.

18. Peter S. Herman and Elizabeth Sauer, eds., introduction to *The New Milton Criticism* (Cambridge: Cambridge University Press, 2012), 3, 9.

19. Among work that has examined some of those heterodoxies and contexts: essays in *Milton and Heresy*, ed. Stephen B. Dobranski and John P. Rumrich (Cambridge: Cambridge University Press, 1998), beginning with Janel Mueller's "Milton on Heresy" (21–38); Kristen Poole, *Radical Religion from Shakespeare to Milton* (Cambridge: Cambridge University Press, 2000), which situates Milton's prose and *Paradise Lost* in a line from the Marprelate tracts to the Adamites; essays in *Milton and the Grounds of Contention*, ed. Mark R. Kelley, Michael Lieb, and John T. Shawcross (Pittsburgh: Duquesne University Press, 2003), especially David Norbrook, "John Milton, Lucy Hutchinson, and the Republican Biblical Epic" (37–63), and Michael Lieb, "Milton and the Socinian Heresy" (234–83); Juliet Cummins, ed., *Milton and the Ends of Time* (Cambridge: Cambridge University Press, 2003), a collection of essays that examines Milton's views on the millennium and the apocalypse; Michael Lieb, *Theological Milton: Deity, Discourse, and Heresy in the Miltonic Canon* (Pittsburgh: Duquesne University Press, 2006), an examination of Milton's confrontation with biblical depictions of God; and David Loewenstein and John Marshall, eds., *Heresy, Literature and Politics in Early Modern English Culture* (Cambridge: Cambridge University Press, 2006), in which John Rogers's "Milton and the Heretical Priesthood of Christ" (203–20), is set among essays on predecessors and contemporaries from Anne Askew to John Locke.

20. Shore, *Milton's Art of Rhetoric*, 2. Shore refers specifically to Stanley Fish, *How Milton Works* (Cambridge, MA: Harvard University Press, 2001), as an example of an approach that sets Milton mostly outside his historical context.

21. See, for example, his introduction to the second book of *The Reason of Church-Government* (1641), in which he lays out his personal literary intentions (YP 1:801–23), many of which he does, in fact, accomplish. For a response to attacks on the idea of the author by Roland Barthes, Michel Foucault, and others, see Stephen M. Fallon, *Milton's Peculiar Grace: Self-Representation and Authority* (Ithaca, NY: Cornell University Press, 2007), 5–13. Thomas Fulton places Milton in relation to the complicated and often interweaving pressures on authorship and publication, in *Historical Milton: Manuscript, Print, and Political Culture in Revolutionary England* (Amherst: University of Massachusetts Press, 2010), esp. chap. 1, "A Material History of Texts in Milton's England" (15–37).

Notes to Chapter One

1. John Milton, *A Second Defence of the English People*, trans. Helen North (YP 4.1:624).

2. Milton's arguments are, of course, not entirely new, although they remained radical; see, for example, the Protestant resistance tracts, such as Christopher Goodman's *How Superior Powers Ought to Be Obeyed by Their Subjects; and Wherein They May Lawfully by Gods Word Be Disobeyed and Resisted* (Geneva, 1558), which is an early argument for governance by social contract, and the antiepiscopal Marprelate tracts of 1588–89, online at www.anglicanlibrary.org/marprelate. As Poole, *Radical Religion*, observes, the Marprelate tracts were not only subversive of social degree and the episcopacy, but of polemical style as well.

3. John Milton, *The Tenure of Kings and Magistrates: Proving, That it is Lawfull, and hathe been held so through all Ages, for any, who have the Power, to call to account a Tyrant, or wicked King, and after due conviction, to depose, and put him to death* (1649), Bv–B2v (YP 3:198–200).

4. See Merritt Y. Hughes's introduction to *Tenure* (YP 3:101–02).

5. Thomas Fulton, *Historical Milton: Manuscript, Print, and Political Culture in Revolutionary England* (Amherst: University of Massachusetts Press, 2010), 145. For Milton as a neo-Roman republican, see Quentin Skinner, "John Milton and the Politics of Slavery," in *Milton and the Terms of Liberty*, ed. Graham Parry and Joad Raymond, 1–22 (Cambridge: D. S. Brewer, 2002); and Martin Dzelzainis, "Milton's Classical Republicanism," in *Milton and Republicanism*, ed. David Armitage, Armand Himy, and Quentin Skinner (Cambridge: Cambridge University Press, 1995). Many essays in both of these collections assume that Milton followed the line of humanist neo-Roman republicans outlined by Skinner

in *Liberty before Liberalism*, a position supported by reference to Roman authors cited in Milton's Commonplace Book (YP 1:362–513) as well as to Milton's own work. Fulton argues for a larger view of Milton's sources.

6. Hughes, introduction (YP 3:101–25), and see his earlier contextual chapters (YP 3:39–100); Stephen M. Fallon, "'The Strangest Piece of Reason': Milton's *Tenure of Kings and Magistrates*," in *The Oxford Handbook of Milton*, ed. Nicholas McDowell and Nigel Smith, 241–51 (Oxford: Oxford University Press, 2009). See also Barbara K. Lewalski, *The Life of John Milton: A Critical Biography* (Oxford: Blackwell, 2000), 229–35; and Christopher Hill, *Milton and the English Revolution* (London: Macmillan, 1977).

7. Blair Worden, *Literature and Politics in Cromwellian England: John Milton, Andrew Marvell, Marchamont Nedham* (Oxford: Oxford University Press, 2007), 228.

8. A. M. Chambers, *A Constitutional History of England* (London: Methuen, 1909), outlines the history of English institutions and the rights they presumably secured; for a more theorized study culminating in the Glorious Revolution of 1688, see J. G. A. Pocock, *The Ancient Constitution and the Feudal Law: A Study of English Historical Thought in the Seventeenth Century* (1957; rev. ed., Cambridge: Cambridge University Press, 1987). Milton also had an immediate context for the *Second Defence*, supporting the actions of the army against the protestations of the Presbyterian magistrates and parliamentarians. In that context, Milton's argument for the people's right to rebel against a tyrant when magistrates fail to act is probably his most radical. See Martin Dzelzainis, introduction to his edition of *Milton: Political Writings* (Cambridge: Cambridge University Press, 1991), ix–xxv.

9. Chambers, *Constitutional History of England*, 72: "By the beginning of the fourteenth century the unfree classes were gradually drifting towards emancipation." The last case of villeinage was tried in 1618, formally ending a practice that was already long in disuse. See also Conrad Russell, *The Crisis of Parliaments: English History, 1509–1660* (Oxford: Oxford University Press, 1971), 13.

10. How the English understood their freedom and whether it would resemble anything we would recognize today as political liberty has been the subject of debate among historians. For example, to what extent was obedience to the royal will a matter of genuine consent or mere acquiescence, and what was the relation of the monarch to the law? Joel Hurstfield, *Freedom, Corruption and Government in Tudor England* (London: Jonathan Cape, 1973), argues that freedom in any modern sense could not exist in Tudor England because "in place of equality there existed hierarchy" (59), and "power of consent was vested in a much smaller segment of

society than today and the representatives owed their powers to their wealth, their social standing and their birth" (56). Further, Hurstfield argues that the ability of the Tudor monarchy to rule by proclamation effectively put it above the law (38). G. R. Elton, by contrast, sees the Elizabethan Parliament as an important representative force, more akin to how the English themselves described it, in *The Parliament of England, 1559–1581* (Cambridge: Cambridge University Press, 1986), and "The Rule of Law in Sixteenth-Century England," *Studies in Tudor and Stuart Politics* (Cambridge: Cambridge University Press, 1974), 1:260–84: "Lawmaking was the province of Parliament, and the King alone could give to nothing the force of statute" (270). Quentin Skinner identifies a humanist "commonwealth movement" associated with English Protestantism in the mid-sixteenth century, a precursor to new theories of liberty in the mid-seventeenth century, in *The Foundations of Modern Political Thought*, 2 vols. (Cambridge: Cambridge University Press, 1978), 1:215–28, and *Liberty before Liberalism*, 11–21. Whatever the reality, by the mid-seventeenth century English, along with continental, observers saw "liberty" as a defining characteristic of the English. See Paul Langford, "Liberty," *Englishness Identified: Manners and Character, 1650–1850* (Oxford: Oxford University Press, 2000), 267–75.

11. Unless otherwise noted, citations from Sir Thomas Smith will be from *De republica Anglorum, The maner of Governement or policie of the Realme of England, compiled by the honorable man Thomas Smyth* (London, 1583); hereafter cited in the text. Entries in Milton's Commonplace Book show that Smith was one of Milton's principal sources on kingship and tyranny (see, e.g., YP 1:440, 442, 453). Fulton suggests that since the entries are so thorough, Milton may not have owned his own copy of this popular work (*Historical Milton*, 49); it is also possible that he anticipated precise use of the citations he selected—as he did, in fact, use them in *Tenure*.

12. Sir Thomas Smith (1513–77) was at Cambridge from 1526, when he matriculated, to at least 1540, when he was made the first Regius Professor of Law. Among his achievements was work (with Sir John Cheke) on Greek pronunciation based on an Erasmian approach. Smith's earlier humanist contemporaries included Erasmus and Sir Thomas More. For a biographical summary on Smith, see F. W. Maitland's preface to Thomas Smith's *De republica Anglorum*, ed. L. Alston (Cambridge: Cambridge University Press, 1906), viii–x. See also *De republica Anglorum*, ed. Mary Dewar (Cambridge: Cambridge University Press, 1983), 1–36, for a complete account of the printed text compared with the extant manuscripts. Though Smith's definitions of kinds of government

and his distinction between king and tyrant owe much to Aristotle, his description of specific English practice, including his outline of the roles of king and parliament, have no classical model.

Milton's familiarity with this whole tradition may be assumed from his Cambridge experience and is reflected specifically not only in the Commonplace Book but also in his reference to Cheke in *Tetrachordon* (YP 2:716) and Sonnet 11, about *Tetrachordon's* reception: "Thy age, like ours, O Soul of Sire *John Cheke*, / Hated not Learning wors than Toad or Asp; / When thou taught'st *Cambridge*, and King *Edward* Greek" (Sonnet 11, 12–14, *Complete Shorter Poems*).

13. Smith, *De republica Anglorum*, ed. Dewar, 1.

14. Smith, *De republica Anglorum* (1583), Fv–F2r.

15. "Sir Thomas Smith also a Protestant and Statesman, in his Commonwelth of *England*, putting the question of whether it be lawfull to rise against a Tyrant, answers that the vulgar judge of it according to the event, and the learned according to the purpose of them that do it" (YP 3:221).

16. Smith, *De republica Anglorum* (1583), chap. 7, "The Definition of a King and of a Tyrant" (B3v–B4).

17. Thomas More's "The History of King Richard the Thirde" was said to be written around 1513; it was published by Richard Rastell in 1557. Shakespeare's version (ca. 1592, one of his earliest plays) borrows heavily from More.

18. See also Ruth Mohl, *John Milton and His Commonplace Book* (New York: Frederick Ungar, 1969), 206–11. In *Eikonoklastes*: "From Stories...both Ancient and Modern which abound, the Poets also, and som English, have bin in this point so mindfull of *Decorum*, as to put never more pious words in the mouth of any person, then of a Tyrant. I shall not instance an abstruse Author, wherein the King might be less conversant, but one whom we well know was the Closet Companion of these his solitudes, *William Shakespeare*; who introduces the Person of *Richard* the third, speaking in as high a strain of pietie, and mortification, as is utterd in any passage of [Charles's] book" (YP 3:361). Ironically, King Charles I and Queen Henrietta Maria were reported to have watched *Richard III* on November 17, 1633, on the occasion of her birthday.

19. See Pocock, *Ancient Constitution*, esp. 30–55. Glenn Burgess, *The Politics of the Ancient Constitution: An Introduction to British Political Thought, 1603–1642* (University Park: Pennsylvania State University Press, 1993), argues that the idea of an ancient common law balancing rights of king and parliament preceded the Normans and was made explicit by Chancellor John Fortescue.

20. *A Learned Commendation of the politique Lawes of England: wherein, by most pithie reasons and evident demon-*

strations, they are plainely proved farre to excel, as well the Civil Lawes of the Empire, as also all other Lawes of the world, with a large discourse of the difference betweene the two governments of kingdoms, whereof the one is onely regall, and the other consisteth of regall and politique administration conjoyned. Written in Latin by the learned and Right Honorable master Fortescue Knight, Lord Chauncellor of England, in the time of King Henrie the sixt. And translated into English by Robert Mulcaster [headmaster of the Merchant Taylor's School and author of a renowned Latin grammar] (London, 1599). F. Ellis Sandoz, "Fortescue, Coke, and the Anglo-American Constitution," in *The Roots of Liberty: Magna Carta, Ancient Constitution, and the Anglo-American Rule of Law*, ed. Ellis Sandoz, 1–21 (Columbia: University of Missouri Press, 1993), argues for Fortescue's central importance and notes that Sir Edward Coke revered him in the seventeenth century as disputes over divine right heated up. The volume contains a series of essays that illustrates how foundational was the English sense of rule of law as the primary source and expression of their liberty.

21. Chambers, *Constitutional History of England*, 171, 177–80. "The years which saw the acquisition of political power by the Lower House, contain but one record of a burgess who took a prominent part in the constitutional battle which king and Parliament were fighting for the control of the machinery of government. In 1455, Thomas Yonge of Bristol claimed for members of Parliament the right to freedom of speech" (197).

22. *The Myrrour for Magistrates*, ed. Lily B. Campbell (Cambridge: Cambridge University Press, 1938), collates the versions originally developed by William Baldwin and George Ferrers. Campbell's introduction provides a history of the work and its authors (3–59). Citations are from this edition, hereafter cited in the text.

23. Scott Lucas has set this story into a larger political context in "'Let none such office take, save he that can for right his prince forsake': *A Myrrour for Magistrates*, Resistance Theory and the Elizabethan Monarchical Republic," in *The Monarchical Republic of Early Modern England*, ed. John F. McDiarmid, 91–108 (Aldershot: Ashgate, 2007).

24. Pocock, *Ancient Constitution*, 30–55.

25. Richard II was Milton's preferred example of a tyrant since he was legally on the throne (presumably unlike Richard III) and exemplified the king who becomes tyrannous by not fulfilling his oath or obeying the country's laws. See also *Articles of Peace* and *Eikonoklastes* (YP 3:306, 407).

26. Letter from John Young to William Cecil, January 17, 1569, cited in Alexander Corbin Judson, *A Biographical Sketch of John Young, Bishop of Rochester, with Emphasis on His Relations with*

Edmund Spenser (Bloomington: Indiana University Studies 103:21, March 1934), 7.

27. E.g., John Calvin, *Institutes of the Christian Religion*, trans. Henry Beveridge (Grand Rapids, MI: Eerdmans, 1989): "in man government is twofold: the one spiritual, by which the conscience is trained to piety and divine worship; the other civil, by which the individual is instructed in those duties which, as men and citizens, we are bound to perform" (140).

28. James Simpson, *Reform and Cultural Revolution*, vol. 2, 1350–1547 (Oxford: Oxford University Press, 2002), 1–2.

29. These tastes may have been reinforced through the Protestant resistance tracts of the mid-sixteenth century. See, e.g., Goodman, *How Superior Powers Ought to Be Obeyed*, chap. 5: "To obey man in anything aganst God, is unlawful and plain disobedience."

30. I will be quoting from the Huntington Library copies of the original publications (as Milton might have experienced the texts), but for a modern edition, see J. P. Sommerville, ed., *James VI and I, Political Writings* (Cambridge: Cambridge University Press, 1994); his introduction contextualizes James's work, distinguishing, for example, between James's apparent theoretical absolutism and his attendance to practical matters when speaking to Parliament (xxiv). Glenn Burgess, in *British Political Thought, 1500–1660: The Politics of the Post-Reformation* (New York: Palgrave Macmillan, 2009), goes even further by placing James within an English constitutional tradition, emphasizing the coronation oath and the distinction between good and bad kings: "James was not a theorist...of 'arbitrary' monarchy. His writing always seemed to presuppose a binary opposition between good and bad kingship, between law-abiding kings and arbitrary tyrants" (147). James will nonetheless argue that it is better for a people to serve a bad king than to rebel. For a survey of the political and ideological context of pre–civil war Stuart England, see J. P. Sommerville, *Royalists and Patriots: Politics and Ideology in England, 1603–1640* 2nd ed. (London: Longman, 1999).

31. *The Lawe of Free Monarchies; or, The Reciprock and mutuall dutie betwixt a free King, and his naturall Subjectes* (London: Printed by [Thomas Creede for] Robert Waldengrave, Printer to the Kings most excellent Majestie, 1603). Waldengrave was the actual printer of the 1598 edition. Folio pages are hereafter cited in the text.

32. James is hardly the first to deny any right to rebel, even against a tyrant. Admonitions against rebellion were an important feature of the official homiletic tradition under Elizabeth.

33. Thomas Hobbes, *Leviathan; or, The Matter, Forme, and Power of a Common-Wealth Ecclesiasticall and Civil* (London:

Printed for Andrew Crooke, 1651). The famous frontispiece of this book vividly depicts the head of a king (specifically of the putative Charles II), his body (upper torso) made up of hundreds of little figures, all looking up toward the head. Published two years after Milton's *Tenure of Kings and Magistrates*, at the height of the commonwealth, it is a daring and seminal reactivation of absolute kingship, but with arguments built from an essentially secular base.

34. The last passage was an addition to the second edition of *Tenure*.

35. This definition is at core Aristotelian (see *Politics*, 4.10 and 5.11, ideas repeated by Thomas Smith, among others). Aristotle, *The Politics*, trans. T. A. Sinclair (New York: Penguin, 1981), 263–64, 343–51.

36. *Basilikon Doron; or, His Majesties Instructions to his Dearest Sonne, Henry the Prince* (Edinburgh: Printed by Robert Walde-grave, Printer to the Kings Majestie, 1603). First publication 1599, in a very limited edition. Hereafter cited in the text, by folio.

37. Self-rule is a commonplace beginning with Plato. See Plato, *Republic*, book 4, rev. ed., ed. and trans. Desmond Lee (New York: Penguin, 1974), 218–22); humanist treatises on the education of rulers important to the English humanist tradition include Erasmus's *Education of a Christian Prince* (1516) and Thomas Elyot's *Boke Named the Governor* (1531). Elyot's arguments for monarchy in part 2 of his book are similar to those James uses, but book 1 has already posited a meritocratic, hierarchic "publick weal," interestingly connecting it with the "Latin *respublica*."

38. G. E. Hadow, introduction to *Sir Walter Raleigh: Selections from His Historie of the World, his Letters, etc.*, edited with introduction and notes by G. E. Hadow (Oxford: Clarendon Press, 1917), 20–22, summarizes the relationship with Prince Henry and James's antagonism.

39. These admonitions, not by Ralegh, were published as *The Cabinet Councill*, 1658. See Lewalski, *Life of John Milton*, 351. Ralegh was put in the Tower of London in 1603 on trumped-up treason charges, released in 1617 to try to recapture some of his old flair for exploring the New World on behalf of the English monarch, but only succeeded in irritating the newly established Spanish with whom James was bent on keeping peace. Ralegh was executed in 1618 on the old charges, but became legendary, principally to the parliamentarians. His *Prerogative of Parliaments in England*, dedicated (saucily, it would seem) to James in manuscript form, was published in 1628 at a time when Parliament was having its first serious conflict with Charles.

40. John H. Baker, *The Legal Profession and the Common Law* (London: Hambledon Press, 1986), 205–29. At issue was the

authority of the king's Chancery Court to override judgments in the common law courts for purposes of equity, a prerogative finally overturned in 1873.

41. *A remonstrance of the most gratious King Iames I. King of Great Brittaine, France, and Ireland, defender of the faith, &c. For the right of kings, and the independance of their crownes. Against an oration of the most illustrious Card. of Perron, pronounced in the chamber of the third estate. Ian. 15. 1615.Translated out of his Maiesties French copie* (Cambridge: Printed by Cantrell Legge, printer to the Universitie of Cambridge, 1616). This was an English translation of the French original, *Declaration du serenissime Roy Iaques I. Roy de la Grand' Bretaigne France et Irlande, defenseur de la foy. Pour le droit des rois & independance de leurs couronnes, contre la harangue de líillustrissime Cardinal du Perron prononcée en la chambre du tiers Estat le XV. de Janvier 1615 [n.d.1616]*, A Londres: par Jehan Bill imprimeur du Roy, M. DC. XV. [1615] Avec priuilege de sa Majesté. Hereafter cited in the text by folio.

42. The First Estate is the clergy, the Second the nobility.

43. The argument from legitimate inheritance was crucial to Elizabeth's own claim to the throne in the face of resistance to female rule. Bishop John Aylmer's *An Harborowe for Faithfull and Trewe Subjects* (Strasburg, 1559), in response to John Knox's ill-timed *First Blast of the Trumpet against the Monstruous Regiment of Women* (Geneva, 1558), makes the case for inheritance as evidence of divine election: "if it were unlawfull (as [Knox] will have it) that that Sexe should governe: yet is it not unlawfull that they should enherit.... And in this point their enheritaunce is so lynked with the empire: that you cannot pluck from them thone without robbing them of thither.... Why should we repine at that which is Gods wyl and order?... **Per me reges regunt** saith wisdom in the person of God, by him reigned they and not by us" (B2r–B2v; boldface type in original).

44. John Milton, "In quintum Novembris," *Complete Shorter Poems*, 210–23: "Peaceful, happy, and rich, he sat on his new throne" (line 5), trans. Lawrence Revard. All Latin translations, unless otherwise noted, are by Revard.

45. Conrad Russell, *The Fall of the British Monarchies, 1637–1642* (Oxford: Oxford University Press, 1991), contrasts James, who could at least put together a "cosmetic" English-Scots confessional agreement (37), with Charles, who could not comprehend what he was up against, and tended toward intransigence (51, 56–57). David Cressy, *England on Edge: Crisis and Revolution, 1640–1642* (Oxford: Oxford University Press, 2006), 3–6, summarizes the stresses Charles faced and suggests he was not entirely up to them. Kevin Sharpe, *The Personal Rule of Charles I* (New Haven: Yale

University Press, 1992), is more sympathetic to Charles, but notes that Charles's distaste for the style of his father's court may have contributed to his inability to maintain the fragile English-Scots alliance (772–74). See also works by Christopher Hill, including *The Century of Revolution, 1603–1714*, rev. ed. (London: Routledge, 1980), and *Liberty against the Law* (London: Allen Lane, 1996).

46. See the note above, and also Christopher Hill, *The World Turned Upside Down* (London: Penguin, 1984).

47. Myers, *Milton's Theology of Freedom*, provides a useful description of the theology of freedom and a reading of *Paradise Lost* that examines Milton's use of ideas he inherited. The reading of *Paradise Lost* is valuable but somewhat limited by his literal understanding of Milton as a didactic poet.

48. See also, e.g., "What have you that you did not receive [from God]? If then you received it, why do you boast as if it were not a gift?" (1 Cor. 4:7); "no man is justified before God by the law.... For through the spirit, by faith, we wait in hope of righteousness" (Gal. 3:11, 5:5).

49. See also, "What does it profit, my brethren, if a man says he has faith and has not works?" (James 2:24); God "will render to every man according to his works" (Rom. 2:6); "If any one purifies himself from what is ignoble, then he will be a vessel for noble use, consecrated and useful to the master of the house, ready for any good work" (2 Tim. 2:21).

50. *Erasmus-Luther Discourse on Free Will*, trans. and ed. Ernst F. Winter (1961; repr., London: Continuum 1999), 129, 127.

51. Ibid., 59, 78.

52. On Christian liberty, "the conscience, freed from the yoke of the law, voluntarily obeys the will of God" (Calvin, *Institutes*, 3.19.4).

53. *Sermons of John Calvin upon the Epistle to the Ephesians*, trans. Arthur Golding (London, 1577), B2v. Interestingly, in the Huntington Library copy this passage is underlined in what appears be contemporary (i.e., Elizabethan) ink. Calvin did not originate these ideas, which predate him by a generation, but he was the most famous of a group of Swiss reformers who have since, for convenience, come to be called "Calvinists." For a full accounting of the doctrine of grace (and works) in this period, see Wallace, *Puritans and Predestination*.

54. Calvin, *Cathechisme* (London, 1582), C2–C3. It was a Christian commonplace to observe that service to God was perfect freedom, but how one defined that service and that freedom might vary considerably.

55. Cardinal Robert Bellarmine, *Catechism*, trans. Richard Haydock (1602), C2.

56. William Perkins, *A Reformed Catholike* (1597), in *Works* (London, 1605), Mmm2v–Mmmm3r. Milton notably cites Perkins in the divorce tracts, important works in the development of his own thinking about freedom (see YP 2:317, 319, 320, 341).

57. Perkins, *A Golden Chaine*, in *Works*, B1r. See also Perkins's description of Christian liberty, the freedom from the old law that is the special gift of God's grace, in *A Treatise of God's Free Grace and Man's Free-Will:* "Will hath his propertie, and that is *Liberty of the will*, which is a freedom from compulsion or constraint, but not from all necessitie.... When the creature is in that estate, that it willingly serves God, and cannot but serve God, then is our perfect libertie" (*Works*, Gggg4v). Perkins, like Calvin, argues for predestination as a function of the nature of God, and nonsalvific free will as the way God chose to make the nature of humanity. For his role in the theology of his time, see Wallace, *Puritans and Predestination*, 59–60.

58. Though Milton's tutor from ages of about 10 to 12, Thomas Young, was a Puritan Milton continued to admire and support (he was the "Y" in "Smectymnuus" in *Apology for Smectymnuus*) and from whom Milton presumably received the ideas of Calvin and Knox, the high master of St. Paul's School, which he attended after studying with Young, was Alexander Gil, a humanist scholar of great distinction. As Lewalski notes, "If Young helped form Milton as a Puritan, Gil pointed him toward the tradition of Protestant rationalism from Hooker to the Cambridge Platonists" (*Life of John Milton*, 8). Lewalski also observes Milton's views evolving in the 1640s, with his Arminianism established by 1647 (*Life of John Milton*, 155, 214–15). Arminianism was generally considered a heresy by traditional Puritans; Arminius's rejection of unconditional election and irresistible grace had provoked the Synod of Dort (1618–19), which reaffirmed Calvinist doctrine.

59. *A Defence of the People of England, by John Milton: In Answer to Salmasius's Defence of the King* (London, 1692), a5v (first English translation). Interestingly, in its most recent translation (1999), it sounds even more secular: "Men first gathered to form a state so they might live safely and freely without suffering violence or injuries; to form a church so as to live piously and religiously. The former institution has its laws, the latter its teaching, quite separate: hence throughout the whole Christian world over so many years, war is sown from the seeds of war—because the magistracy and the church confuse each other's duties" (John Alvis, ed., *Areopagitica and other Political Writings of John Milton* [Chicago: Liberty Fund, 1999]).

60. J. B. Bury, *A History of the Freedom of Thought* (Cambridge: Cambridge University Press, 1913), 7–8.

61. George Orwell, *Why I Write* (1946; repr., New York: Penguin, 2005), 1–10. "Using the word 'political' in the widest possible sense. Desire to push the world in a certain direction, to alter other people's idea of the kind of society they should strive after.... No book is genuinely free from political bias. The opinion that art should have nothing to do with politics is itself a political attitude" (5).

62. Historians use the expression "politics of popularity" to refer to the use of media—e.g., sermons, pamphlets, pageants—in effecting change, perhaps even change the monarch might oppose. It is clear, however, that "popularity" tended to be manipulated by those in power, and overt use of public arenas to seriously oppose hegemonic power was dangerous. See, e.g., Peter Lake, "'The Monarchical Republic of Queen Elizabeth I' (and the Fall of Archbishop Grindal) Revisited," in *The Monarchical Republic of Early Modern England*, ed. John F. McDiarmid, 129–47 (Aldershot: Ashgate, 2007).

Notes to Chapter Two

1. N. F. Blake, *A History of the English Language* (New York: New York University Press, 1996), 228.

2. Earl R. MacCormac, *A Cognitive Theory of Metaphor* (Cambridge, MA: MIT Press, 1988), 2.2. See also Stanley R. Levin, *The Semantics of Metaphor* (Baltimore: Johns Hopkins University Press, 1977): metaphor is a "linguistically deviant" expression that changes how the reader sees the world: "Instead of attempting to construe the expression, i.e. make it conform to a sentence that has a truth value in this world, we as it were construe the world—into one in which the deviant position is no longer deviant" (127).

3. Edmund Spenser's exclamation about his experiments with classical prosody for English verse is a famous sixteenth century example: "why a Gods name may not we, as else the Greeks, have the kingdome of oure owne Language?" See Edmund Spenser, *Three Proper, and wittie, familiar Letters* (1580), in *The Poetical Works of Edmund Spenser*, ed. J. C. Smith and Ernest De Selincourt (London: Oxford University Press, 1912), 611.

4. Brian Cummings, "Metalepsis: The Boundaries of Metaphor," in *Renaissance Figures of Speech*, ed. Sylvia Adamson et al. (Cambridge: Cambridge University Press, 2007), 217–33.

5. Winifred Nowottny, *The Language Poets Use* (London: University of London Athlone Press, 1962), 49, 53. She adds: "one reason why metaphor is common in poetry is that metaphor vastly extends the language at the poet's disposal. Since metaphor uses terms in a transferred sense, this means that, subject to some not

very serious limitations, a poet who wants to write about object X but finds its terminology defective or resistant to manipulation, can simply move over to the terminology of Y" (67). Nowottny's analysis of Milton's Latinate syntax in *Paradise Lost* is also of interest: "Latinate syntax is important to Milton because it provides him with more ways than a normal English syntax could muster of devising contrasts and correspondences and of marshalling individual words into exactly those places that will set off the meaning each bears in relation to another" (22–23).

6. Cummings, "Metalepsis," 227.

7. Lanham, *A Handlist of Rhetorical Terms*, 101.

8. Victoria Kahn, "The Metaphorical Contract in Milton's *Tenure of Kings and Magistrates*," in *Milton and Republicanism*, ed. D. Armitage, A. Himy, and Q. Skinner, 82–105 (Cambridge: Cambridge University Press, 1995): "Reading is a prophetic and ethical activity precisely because meaning is not simply or literally given but must be spiritually construed. The work of prophecy or interpretation is thus inseparable from attention to the figurative dimension of Scripture. Conversely, the figurative dimension of Scripture functions...as a conditional covenant which demands the reader's interpretive and ethical response.... Thinking tropologically serves to place the ethical burden where it belongs: not on the sacrament alone but on the individual agent and believer" (93).

9. A. M. Chambers, *A Constitutional History of England* (London: Methuen, 1909), 234–38.

10. John Stubbs, *The Discoverie of a Gaping Gulf whereunto England Is Likely to Be Swallowed* (London, 1579). For a modern edition, see Lloyd E. Berry, *John Stubbs's Gaping Gulf, with Letters and Other Relevant Documents* (Charlottesville: University of Virginia Press for the Folger Shakespeare Library, 1968).

11. And language study in particular, which for the humanists tended to define what it means to be human. As Thomas Wilson proclaimed in his *Art of Rhetorique* (London, 1553), "whereas menne are in manye things weake by Nature, and subjecte to moche informitye: I thinke in this one poincte they passe all other Creatures living, that they have the gifte of speache and reason" (A7v). Earlier, in his landmark educational treatise, *The Boke Named the Governour* (London, 1531), Sir Thomas Elyot made poetry the foundational study for all learning (1.10).

12. George Puttenham, *Arte of English Poesie* (London, 1589; facsimile repr., Kent, OH: Kent State University Press, 1970), 24 (book 1, chap. 3); subsequent citations are from this facsimile edition. For a modern edition, see Frank Whigham and Wayne Rebhorn, eds., *The Art of English Poesy, by George Puttenham* (Ithaca, NY: Cornell University Press, 2007). Whigham and Rebhorn's introduction makes a case for Puttenham as an ambitious opportunist,

which is perhaps why he dedicated the edition to Lord Burghley (17, 49–71).

13. Puttenham, *Arte of English Poesie*, 166 (book 3, chap. 7).

14. Ibid, 188–89 (book 3, chap. 17).

15. *Faerie Queene* 6.12.41, *The Poetical Works of Edmund Spenser*, ed. J. C. Smith and E. De Selincourt (London: Oxford University Press, 1913). All Spenser citations are from this volume, hereafter cited in the text. For a summary of the Spenser-Burghley relationship, see the Mark Eccles article on "Burghley" in *The Spenser Encyclopedia*, ed. A. C. Hamilton et al., 121–22 (Toronto: University of Toronto Press, 1990); see also the judicious analysis by William Nelson, *The Poetry of Edmund Spenser* (New York: Columbia University Press, 1963), 13–16.

16. John Skelton early in the sixteenth century modeled the indirect and satiric mode for speaking freely against the powerful (Cardinal Wolsey in this case); see Jane Griffiths, *John Skelton and Poetic Authority: Defining the Liberty to Speak* (Oxford: Oxford University Press, 2006), 73–78, 96–100, and throughout. Early modern writers understood Horace and Juvenal in the first and second centuries CE to be the pattern for work critical of those in power. Juvenal's first satire explicitly claims the right of the satirist to expose vices in public figures; see *The Sixteen Satires of Juvenal*, trans. Peter Green (London: Penguin, 1982).

17. He continues, interestingly, to affirm the people rather than the monarch as the voice of God: "*Vox populi, vox dei,* in this case not so famous a proverb as true" (*Myrrour*, 359). Sentiments such as this make it more difficult for monarchs to argue their divine right, separate from a contractual obligation to their subjects. James had tried to skirt this by focusing on the coronation oath as a kind of substitute for popular approval or social contract.

18. "An Exhortation concerning good Order and obedience, to rulers and Magistrates" was one of the standard sermons in the official book of Tudor sermons and homilies, originating in 1547 and added to in 1563 as *Certain Sermons appoynted by the Quenes Majesty, to be declared and read, by al Parsons, Vicars, and Curates, everi Sunday and holiday, in their Churches*, bound with *The seconde Tome of homelyes*. This quarto double volume was often reprinted until well into James I's reign, when it was published in folio as *Certaine Sermons or Homilies* (1623). Most versions of *The second Tome* conclude with "An Homilie Against disobedience and wilfull rebellion," in five parts, first published separately around 1571. The first two parts of this extensive sermon show "the doctrine of the holye scriptures, as concerning obedience of true subjects to their princes, even as well to such as be evill, as unto the good." Parts 3 and 4 illustrate punishments rebels may expect from God, and part 5 warns against ambition and ignorance as the causes of rebellion.

19. See, e.g., Elyot's *Boke Named the Governour*, where those with "understandynge" and "knowlege" "oughte to be set in a more highe place than the residue" (A4–A4v). Milton would assume the primacy of merit. See the sections on "Gentleness" and "Nobility" from his Commonplace Book (YP 1:450, 471–73).

20. See, e.g., Elyot, *Boke Named the Governour*; Wilson, *Art of Rhetorique*; and, though it is more a book of manners than of rhetoric, Thomas Hoby's translation of Castiglione's *Courtier, The Courtyer of Count Baldessar Castilio* (London, 1561); specific works on the art of poetry include, along with Puttenham's *Arte of English Poesie*, William Webbe's *Discourse of English Poetrie* (London, 1586), Abraham Fraunce's *The Arcadian Rhetoricke* (London, 1588), and Sir John Harrington's more theoretical "Preface or rather a Brief Apology of Poetry" to his translation of Ariosto's *Orlando Furioso* (London, 1591). For a discussion of the relation of rhetoric and liberty in popular as well as aristocratic rhetorical treatises, see Markku Peltonen, "Rhetoric and Citizenship in the Monarchical Republic of Queen Elizabeth I," in *The Monarchical Republic of Early Modern England: Essays in Response to Patrick Collinson*, ed. John F. McDiarmid, 109–27 (Aldershot, Hamps: Ashgate, 2007).

21. These included Sir John Cheke, with whom Thomas Smith had translated Greek, and Thomas Wilson, who wrote a *Rule of Reason* (London, 1551), an Aristotelian art of logic, in addition to his *Art of Rhetorique*.

22. Roger Ascham, *The scholemaster or plaine and perfite way of teaching children, to vnderstand, write, and speake, the Latin tong, but specially purposed for the priuate bringing vp of youth in jentlemen and noble mens houses, and commodious also for all such, as haue forgot the Latin tonge* (London, 1570), C4v; citations are from this edition. By contrast to English liberties, Ascham notes approvingly, among "the old noble Persians...a yong jentleman was never free, to go where he would, and do what he liste him self, but under the kepe, and by the counsel, of some grave governour, until he was either maryed, or cald to beare some office in the common wealth" (E4v) For a modern edition, see Roger Ascham, *The Scholemaster*, ed. Lawrence V. Ryan (Ithaca, NY: Cornell University Press for the Folger Shakespeare Library, 1967).

23. The reform Protestant emphasis on preaching, along with the power of the printing press, also made free speech in the general population a complex and sometimes dangerous issue; see Lake, "Monarchical Republic," 129–48. These issues were compounded in the controversies surrounding the English civil wars, as chronicled by David Norbrook, *Writing the English Republic: Poetry, Rhetoric and Politics, 1627–1660* (Cambridge: Cambridge University Press,

1999). See esp. the introduction, "Acts of Oblivion and Republican Speech Acts": "The aspiration to a politics of open speech and dialogue was always potentially in conflict with more rigid forms of social exclusion" (20). See also Worden, *Literature and Politics*, especially on the career of Milton's friend Marchmont Nedham, "the serial turncoat of the Puritan Revolution" (1).

24. Wallace T. MacCaffrey, *The Shaping of the Elizabethan Regime* (Princeton, NJ: Princeton University Press, 1968), 42–44; and *Elizabeth I* (London: Edward Arnold, 1993): "Not unlike a modern elected ruler, the Queen had to cultivate all the arts of a politician in order to secure her right to be obeyed" (viii). On Elizabeth's claim through inheritance, see the response to John Knox's screed against women rulers by John Aylmer, *An Harborowe for Faithfull and Trewe Subjects:* "For if it were unlawfull (as [Knox] will have it) that that Sexe should governe: yet [in England] is it not unlawfull that they should enherit.... And in this point their enheritaunce is so lynked with the empire: that you cannot pluck from them thone without robbing them of the other" (B2). Stephen Orgel, *The Illusion of Power: Political Theater in the English Renaissance* (Berkeley and Los Angeles: University of California Press, 1975), establishes the case for Elizabeth's progresses and other displays as part of her imaging of power.

25. Ascham, *The scholemaster*, H1. Elizabeth's gender complicates the praise, but Ascham uses it to support his exhortation on behalf of education: "It is your shame (I speake to you all, you yong Jentlemen of England) that one mayd should go beyond you all, in excellencie of learning."

26. MacCaffrey, *Elizabeth I*, 39.

27. See *Elizabeth I: Autograph Compositions and Foreign Language Originals*, ed. Janel Mueller and Leah S. Marcus (Chicago: University of Chicago Press, 2003); and Steven May, ed., *Queen Elizabeth I: Selected Works* (New York: Washington Square Press, 2004). For an analysis of Elizabeth as a poet, see Peter Herman, *Royal Poetrie: Monarchic Verse and the Political Imaginary of Early Modern England* (Ithaca, NY: Cornell University Press, 2010), 99–156.

28. For a description of the entertainment and its publication history, see William A. Ringler, *The Poems of Sir Philip Sidney* (Oxford: Clarendon Press, 1962), 361–63. Ringler notes, "Sidney differed from the majority of his fellow courtiers who made flattery of the Queen the main business of their pens, for [he wrote only one] poem in praise of Elizabeth" (362).

29. Richard McCoy, *Rebellion in Arcadia* (New Brunswick, NJ: Rutgers University Press, 1979), 1. McCoy cites Sidney's friend and

biographer, Fulke Greville, to the effect that the queen believed Sidney did not have a proper sense of hierarchy, nor (in her words) understand "the respect inferiors ought to their superiors" (3).

30. Blair Worden, *The Sound of Virtue: Sir Philip Sidney's "Arcadia" and Elizabethan Politics* (New Haven: Yale University Press, 1996), xxiii: "The queen did recognise merits in Sidney, but ardent loyalty was not among them."

31. Katherine Duncan-Jones, *Sir Philip Sidney, Courtier Poet* (New Haven: Yale University Press, 1991), 164–65. Elizabeth's response to the quarrel was to offer Sidney a lesson in social hierarchy, insisting on "the difference of degree between earls and gentlemen; the respect inferiors owed their superiors; and the necessity in princes to maintain their own creations, as degrees descending between the people's licentiousness and the anointed sovereignty of crowns" (165). See also James M. Osborn, *Young Philip Sidney* (New Haven: Yale University Press, 1972), 496–504; A. C. Hamilton, *Sir Philip Sidney: A Study of His Life and Works* (Cambridge: Cambridge University Press, 1977), 28–32; Andrew D. Wiener, *Sir Philip Sidney and the Poetics of Protestantism* (Minneapolis: University of Minnesota Press, 1978), 19–26.

32. The text of *Arcadia* is complicated by its existence in three posthumous versions: an incomplete version published in 1590, probably through Fulke Greville (for this version, see *The Countess of Pembroke's Arcadia [The New Arcadia]*, ed. Victor Stretkowicz [Oxford: Clarendon Press, 1987]; a "complete" version of 1593 somewhat revised in 1598, under the supervision of his sister, the Countess of Pembroke, for whom it was written; and an earlier, complete, but simpler, manuscript version printed for the first time in the twentieth century, the version now called *Old Arcadia*, for which the countess in 1593 supplied the ending to the revised but incomplete material published in 1590. The *Arcadia* that Milton read would have been the 1593 or 1598 combined version, so all citations will be to the traditional Cambridge edition (see the following note).

33. *The Prose Works of Sir Philip Sidney*, ed. Albert Feuillerat (1912; repr., Cambridge: Cambridge University Press, 1963), 1:125. Subsequent references to *Arcadia* are to this text of the so-called *New Arcadia*, the revision with the end of the *Old Arcadia* rather clumsily tacked on to give the illusion of completeness. My references in this chapter will be confined to text from the revised portion of the work.

34. Worden, *The Sound of Virtue*, 128–29, in reviewing the history surrounding Sidney's *Arcadia*, sees Philanax as a stand-in for Sidney, the good servant giving good advice not necessarily heeded.

35. Hamilton, *Sir Philip Sidney*, 14.

36. See chapter 1 above, note 58.

37. Wendy Olmsted, *The Imperfect Friend: Emotion and Rhetoric in Sidney, Milton and Their Contexts* (Toronto: University of Toronto Press, 2008), compares Sidney and Milton, particularly in their use of the conundrum of rhetorical power: "How can rhetoric that moves emotion be trustworthy and capable of leading to whole-hearted consent? Clearly it must engage emotion without compelling or seducing it" (5). Although she does not see this problem as a vehicle for inviting a reader's own freedom, she nicely outlines the complications that come from stories that show characters facing conflicting values (see, e.g., 12–15).

38. Skinner, *Foundations*, esp. 1:213–62, and *Liberty before Liberalism*, 11–12. See also Patrick Collinson, "The Monarchical Republic of Queen Elizabeth I," *Bulletin of the John Rylands University Library of Manchester* 69 (1987): 394–424; Worden, *Sound of Virtue*, esp. 266–80; Andrew Hadfield, *Shakespeare and Republicanism* (Cambridge: Cambridge University Press, 2005), summarizes Worden's argument for Sidney's Languet-inspired republicanism in the Ister Bank eclogue (97–89).

39. The right to rebel is an extremely sensitive subject in this period, but Sidney's experience of the St. Bartholomew's Day massacre (he was present in Paris on August 24, 1572, and saw it directly) and his sympathy for and friendship with French Huguenots, complicate the issue. His good friends, Hubert Languet and Philippe de Mornay, supported William of Orange in his rebellion against Spain (Skinner, *Foundations*, 2:337–38), and of course Sidney himself died fighting for the Netherlands in its rebellion against Spanish rule. Like many Protestants (including Milton some three generations later), Sidney saw Catholicism as tyrannical governance that threatened political as well as religious freedom.

40. See, e.g., Martin Raitiere, *Faire Bitts: Sir Philip Sidney and Renaissance Political Theory* (Pittsburgh: Duquesne University Press, 1984); McCoy, *Rebellion in Arcadia*; and Susanne Woods, "Freedom and Tyranny in Sidney's *Arcadia*," in *Sir Philip Sidney's Achievements*, ed. M. J. B. Allen et al. (New York: AMS Press, 1990), 165–75.

41. Pyrocles and Musidorus, as most commentators on *Arcadia* have noted, are flawed heroes, particularly in their own passions and deceits of love; here and further on in this chapter, I focus on their heroic features in order to suggest something of Sidney's poetic as well as social values. I do not mean to deny, however, the tensions between reason and passion that pervade especially the *Old Arcadia* (not to mention Astrophil and Stella), and that seem inevitable to the noble youth. That tension illustrates both the young

man's struggle toward the classical ethic of the balanced nature and the Calvinist doctrine of original sin.

42. Kenneth Myrick, *Sir Philip Sidney as a Literary Craftsman*, 2nd ed. (Lincoln: University of Nebraska Press, 1965), 110–50.

43. McCoy, *Rebellion in Arcadia*, 138–41.

44. The poem among the third set of eclogues that begins "As I my little flock on Ister Bank," in which "Philisides" ("Phili-Sid") tells a parable of the Fall that he attributes to Sidney's friend, the Huguenot and international Protestant diplomat, Hubert Languet. Worden, *Sound of Virtue*, 266–80, provides a compelling reading of this eclogue, tying it to a range of themes in and Worden's own political-allegorical reading of the *Arcadia*.

45. Alan Sinfield, "Power and Ideology: An Outline Theory and Sidney's *Arcadia*," *ELH* 52 (1985): 271.

46. Skinner (*Liberty before Liberalism*, 12) finds neo-Roman republican elements in the *Arcadia*. Norbrook notes the limits of Sidney's republicanism in the *Arcadia*, however, seeing it emerge "as an easy academic indulgence," appealing to the imagination, but not practical (*Writing the English Republic*, 12).

47. *Eikonoklastes*, YP 3:362; from the Commonplace Book, e.g., "See also an excellent description of such an Oligarchy of nobles abusing the countnance to the ruin of royal sovranty Arcad. Sidney. Book 2. P 119. &c." (YP 1:463).

48. Algernon Sidney (1623–83), who initially resisted the regicide and commonwealth, was not a particular friend of Milton's, but they had friends (notably Sir Henry Vane) and ideas in common. Algernon was executed in 1683, essentially for the antimonarchical elements in his *Discourses concerning Government* (London, 1680), one of many responses to Robert Filmer's *Patriarcha* (1678). His *Discourses* advocated explicitly for Roman republicanism and for social contract and mixed government, with sections titled, for example, "The Glory, Virtue, and Power of the Romans, began and ended with their liberty" (2.12); "The Mischiefs and Cruelties proceeding from Tyranny are greater than any that can come from popular or mixed Governments" (2.27); "Our own Laws confirm to us the enjoyment of our native Rights" (3.9); "Laws are not made by Kings...because Nations will be governed by Rule, and not Arbitrarily" (3.14); "The English Nation has always been governed by itself or its Representatives" (3.28). For Algernon Sidney's similarities to Milton, see Jonathan Scott, *Algernon Sidney and the English Republic, 1623–1677* (Cambridge: Cambridge University Press, 1988), 14–30; Worden, *Literature and Politics*, 362; and Norbrook, *Writing the English Republic*, 116–17.

49. Steven N. Zwicker, *Lines of Authority: Politics and English Literary Culture, 1649–1689* (Ithaca, NY: Cornell University Press,

1993): "Sidney and his peers elevated the station of the poet, but it was the political crisis of the mid seventeenth century that transformed the role of poetry and its position among the culture's modes of discourse. All the major writers at mid-century—Milton, Marvell, Dryden, Rochester, Davenant, Cowley, Waller—were both political actors and writers.... Not only did poetry take on a full range of political and partisan issues, but it did so in forms that stood fully within the lines of public discourse" (15).

50. Robert E. Stillman, "The Truth of a Slippery World: Poetry and Tyranny in Sidney's *Defence*," *Renaissance Quarterly* 55 (2002): 1287–1319.

51. The *Defence* was published by William Ponsonby, Spenser's publisher, and the *Apologie* by Henry Olney; the latter contains laudatory sonnets by Henry Constable. Geoffrey Shepherd, the work's most thorough editor, speculates "an amicable rivalry between two parties of Sidney's friends, each in possession of a MS of the *Apology*," and chooses Olney's text as his base; see Sir Philip Sidney, *An Apology for Poetry; or, The Defence of Poesy*, ed. Geoffrey Shepherd (London: Nelson, 1965). Citations will be from this text, despite its modernized spelling, which seems unobjectionable. The Ponsonby-based text is readily available elsewhere, e.g., in *Sir Philip Sidney*, ed. Katherine Duncan-Jones (Oxford: Oxford University Press, 1989), 212–50. Duncan-Jones also summarizes the speculation about the date for the *Defence* (371).

52. Wilson, *Art of Rhetorique*; George Gascoigne, *Certayne Notes of Instruction* (London, 1575); Elyot, *Boke Named the Governour*; Ascham, *The scholemaster* (1570); Webbe, *Discourse of English Poetry*; Fraunce, *Arcadian Rhetoric*; and Puttenham, *Arte of English Poesie*.

53. One of Sidney's main sources, according to Shepherd, ed., *Apology for Poetry*, 121, 129, 131, 141.

54. See Shepherd's introduction to Sidney's *Apology* (9).

55. Sidney's contradictions in the *Defence* have been carefully examined by Peter C. Herman, "When Is a Defense Not a Defense? Sidney's Paradoxical *Apology for Poetry*," in *Squitter-wits and Muse-haters: Sidney, Spenser, Milton, and Renaissance Antipoetic Sentiment* (Detroit: Wayne State University Press, 1996), 61–93. Herman reads Sidney's tone more seriously than I do, however, as, for example, his accusation that Sidney "misreads" Plato (87), while to me it appears Sidney takes on Plato as a piece of his humanist-educated *sprezzaturra*. In another example, Herman reads the Pugliano praise of horsemanship episode that constitutes the *Defence*'s exordium as embodying contradictions that both praise and dispraise poetry, while I believe Sidney's witty disingenuousness to be part of a larger project of directly engaging his reader. As

will become clear, I do agree that Sidney's rhetoric about poetry and poets becomes unsettled, in part because he does not want to define poetry in terms of biblical poetics.

56. In a somewhat different articulation of this point, Paul Stevens, *Imagination and the Presence of Shakespeare in "Paradise Lost"* (Madison: University of Wisconsin Press, 1985), finds Sidney's "eikastike" fancy to be both a reflective Platonism and an innovative creativity: "For Sidney purely creative fancy is in fact reflective, and it is for this reason, not because they lose themselves in a divine madness, that poets are prophets" (48).

57. Barbara K. Lewalski, *Protestant Poetics* (Princeton, NJ: Princeton University Press, 1979), 39–53.

58. Sidney likes the posture of originality. See, e.g., *Astrophil and Stella*, sonnets 1, 2, 6, 15, 28, and esp. 74: "I never drank of Aganippe well, / Nor ever did in shade of Tempe sit / And Muses scorn with other brains do dwell: ...And this I swear by blackest book of hell, / I am no pickpurse of another's wit" (lines 1–3, 7–8). *The Poems of Sir Philip Sidney*, ed. William A. Ringler Jr. (Oxford: Clarendon Press, 1962), 203–04. The theme of Stella's image in his heart as source of his inspiration, though, corresponds to the "Idea or fore-conceit of the work" that underlies the poet's art in the *Defence*.

59. Stillman, "Truth of a Slippery World," 1287.

60. Sidney himself was, of course, engaged in free poetic renderings of the Psalms, based largely on Clement Marot and Theodore de Beze's French Huguenot Psalter, which he and his sister (Mary, Countess of Pembroke, who completed what Philip had left unfinished at his death) may have known from the time they were children. See Margaret P. Hannay, *Philip's Phoenix* (New York: Oxford University Press, 1990), 84–86.

61. See Herman, "When Is a Defense," 61–94; Lewalski, *Protestant Poetics*, esp. chap. 2, emphasizes the importance of biblical genres to Protestant thinking about mimesis. Sidney's outline of biblical poets and genres anticipates some of the seventeenth century enactments of an English biblical poetics as Lewalski describes them. By contrast, Ronald Levao, *Renaissance Minds and Their Fictions: Cusanus, Sidney, Shakespeare* (Berkeley and Los Angeles: University of California Press, 1985), secularizes Sidney's contradictions, seeing them as an escape into a metapoetics that can act out "the tensions of the most adventurous Renaissance thought" (96).

62. Stevens, *Imagination and Presence*, and Olmsted, *Imperfect Friend*, however, both invite a more thorough study of the connection.

63. Lewalski, *Life of John Milton*, 141.

64. For some standard approaches, see Don Wolfe, YP 1:201–03; Ralph A. Haug, YP 1:741–43; James Grantham Turner, "The Poetics of Engagement," in *Politics, Poetics, and Hermeneutics in Milton's Prose*, ed. David Loewenstein and James Grantham Turner, 257–75 (Cambridge: Cambridge University Press, 1990); the essays in *Achievements of the Left Hand: Essays on the Prose of John Milton*, ed. Michael Lieb and John Shawcross (Amherst: University of Massachusetts Press, 1974); and Lewalski, *Life of John Milton*, 150–52.

65. By focusing here on Sidney I do not mean to slight Spenser's long-recognized importance to Milton. I have, in fact, argued in "Making Free with Poetry: Spenser and the Rhetoric of Choice," *Spenser Studies* 15 (2001): 1–16, that Spenser precedes Milton in some of the rhetorical feints that make room for political freedom; but while Spenser's importance to Milton is a commonplace, Sidney's has not been properly recognized.

66. Woods, "Elective Poetics," 193–212.

Notes to Chapter Three

1. John Milton, *Ad Patrem*, Ad Thomam Juniam," *Complete Shorter Poems*, 240–47, 158–67. Latin epitaphs on the bishop of Winchester (the eloquent preacher Lancelot Andrewes) (154–57); the Cambridge vice chancellor, John Gostlin (204–09); the bishop of Ely, Nicholas Felton (224–29); and Milton's major effort on the fifth of November praising James I as a potential Protestant martyr (210–23) point toward conventional patronage. The poem to Torquato Tasso's patron, Giovanni Baptista Manso (256–65), comes closest to traditional praise of a living patron.

2. Milton's first publication consisted of commendatory verses for the second edition of Shakespeare's *Folio* (1632), where he joined Jonson in the prefatory matter. The restrained and balanced couplets of "An Epitaph on the Marchioness of *Winchester*" (ca. 1631; *Complete Shorter Poems*, 40n1) may have been intended for a volume of tributes in which Jonson might also appear. While Milton was far from being among the "Sons of Ben," Jonson's experimentation with lyric forms (as in *A Celebration of Charis*, the Cary-Morison ode, and in his songs) was a principal model for any poet learning to write English verse in the 1620s.

3. Ian Spink, *Henry Lawes: Cavalier Songwriter* (Oxford: Oxford University Press, 2000). At the same time as he was working with Milton, Lawes was involved in court masques as well (51–52). Milton's association with Lawes may have come through his father's circle of musician friends. See Cedric Brown, *Milton's*

Aristocratic Entertainments (Cambridge: Cambridge University Press, 1985), 181n1.

4. The title page of Milton's 1645 *Poems* acknowledges that "the Songs were set in Musick by Mr. Henry Lawes Gentleman of the Kings Chappel, and one of His Majesties Private Musick," and a dedicatory poem to Lawes appears among the many very Protestant sonnets Milton published in *Poems, &c. upon Several Occasions* (1573). At least to the mid-1640s the friendship transcended politics. See Lewalski, *Life of John Milton*, 200–01. Richard Helgerson, *Self-Crowned Laureates: Spenser, Jonson, Milton, and the Literary System* (Berkeley: University of California Press, 1983), outlines the complexity of becoming a professional poet in this period; Milton's *Ad Patrem* (56–66) appeals to his father's musicianship to commend the son's vocation.

5. See, e.g., *Of Reformation* (1641), YP 1:527–29, where Milton aligns English bishops with an anti-English papacy and its advocates. In 527n59 the editors unravel Milton's reference to one of the queen's Catholic chaplains.

6. Lewalski, *Life of John Milton*, 59, 76–77. Lewalski also summarizes Milton's struggle in his post-Cambridge years to come to some decision about his career, especially as holy orders became a more remote option in the Laudian environment (53–56).

7. This is consistent with his comments and list of possible topics in *Reason of Church-Government* (YP 1:812–18).

8. Casey Finch and Peter Bowen summarize the tradition in "The Solitary Companionship of *L'Allegro* and *Il Penseroso*," in *Milton Studies*, vol. 26, ed. James D. Simmonds (Pittsburgh: University of Pittsburgh Press, 1990), 3–24. They make the point that the poems are complex but not indeterminate: "If the larger meanings of *L'Allegro* and *Il Penseroso* are finally inexhaustible, there is at the same time no moment within them that resists interpretation, that sets up deliberate barriers to reading" (11). For a review of the standard parallels, see Lewalski, *Life of John Milton*, 48–52. For a sample of influential discussions over the years, see Stella Revard, "*L'Allegro* and *Il Penseroso*: Classical Tradition and Renaissance Mythography," *PMLA* 101 (1986): 338–50; Rosamund Tuve, *Images and Themes in Five Poems by Milton* (Cambridge, MA: Harvard University Press, 1957); and J. B. Leishman, *Milton's Minor Poems* (Pittsburgh: University of Pittsburgh Press, 1969).

9. See, e.g., "Song: On May Morning" and his Latin Elegies 5 and 7 (*Complete Shorter Poems*, 43, 168–77, 186–91). Elegy 6, to Charles Diodati (179–85), in which Milton appears to contrast his own studious sobriety with his friend's cheerful Apollonianism, is particular to the occasion and certainly shows no disapproval of *L'Allegro*-like play. Milton's Latin poems (first published in 1645 along with

the English *Poems*) are prefaced by six commendatory poems from distinguished Italians, including Giovanni Battista Manso. The Catholic Manso praised Milton's "mind, figure, grace, appearance, manners," but not his "piety" (*Complete Shorter Poems*, 133). For references to Milton's later sociability, see Lewalski, *Life of John Milton*, 489, 508, 536.

10. Eric C. Brown, "'The Melting Voice through Mazes Running': The Dissolution of Borders in *L'Allegro* and *Il Penseroso*," in *Milton Studies*, vol. 40, ed. Albert C. Labriola, 1–18 (Pittsburgh: University of Pittsburgh Press, 2001), 1. In a similar argument, although it does see boundaries between the poems, Finch and Bowen in "Solitary Companionship" read each poem as implying the other.

11. Milton frequently cites conscience as the basis for interpreting experience. For example, "against the rancor of an evill tongue...I must be forc't to proceed from the unfained and diligent inquiry of mine owne conscience at home (for better way I know not, Readers)" (*An Apology*, YP 1:869); "the statute and judgements of the Lord, which without exception are often told us to be such, as doing we may live by them, are doutbles to be counted the rule of knowledge and of conscience" (*Tetrachordon*, YP 2:654); the Protestant "preferrs the scripture before the church, and acknowledges none but the Scripture sole interpreter of it self to the conscience.... But if any man shall pretend, that the scripture judges to his conscience for other men, he makes himself greater not only then the church, but also then the scripture, then the consciences of other men; a presumption too high for any mortal" (*Civil Power*, YP 7:243–44).

12. Milton, *Of Christian Doctrine (De doctrina Christiana)*, YP 6:187.

13. This is the continuous theme of Milton's earliest, antiprelatical tracts; for example, from *Prelatical Episcopacy* (1641):
> the plaine truth is that when any of our men of those who are wedded to antiquity [i.e., who believe that the traditions of the early church fathers carry weight beyond their biblical foundations] come to dispute with a Papist, and leaving the Scriptures put themselves without appeale to the sentence of *Synods*, and Councells, ...where they give the *Romanist* one buffe, they receive two counterbuffs. Were it therefore but in this regard, every true Bishop should be afraid to conquer in his cause by such authorities as these, which if we admit for the authorities sake, we open up a broad passage for a multitude of Doctrines that have no ground in Scripture, to break in upon us. (YP 1:651)

14. Olmsted, *Imperfect Friend*, 12–15, sees this as a central strategic problem for Milton as well as Sidney.

15. Lewalski, *Life of John Milton*, 63, posits Lawes as the speaker in *Arcades*, as does Ann Baynes Coiro, "'A Thousand Fantasies': The Lady and the *Maske*," in McDowell and Smith, *Oxford Handbook of Milton*, 100. Coiro also points out that "the Genius of the Woods," rather than the celebrated Countess Dowager, is the "imaginative center" of the entertainment.

16. The postlapsarian inadequacy of human song is also a theme of one of Milton's loveliest early poems, "At a Solemn Musick." In it he invokes heavenly poetry and song to inspire those on earth, that they

> May rightly answer that melodious noise;
> As once we did, till disproportion'd sin
> Jarr'd against natures chime, and with harsh din
> Broke the fair musick that all creatures made
> To their great Lord, whose love their motion sway'd
> In perfect Diapason, whilst they stood
> In first obedience, and their state of good.   (18–24)

17. YP 2:366–67. "But because our understanding cannot in this body found it selfe but on sensible things, nor arrive so clearly to the knowledge of God and things invisable, as by orderly conning over the visible and inferior creature, the same method is necessarily to be follow'd in all discreet teaching" (YP 2:367–69).

18. Three of the Egerton children (Lady Alice, 15; John, Lord Brackley, 11; and Thomas, 9) enacted these roles, feigning to be on their way to their father's installation as lord president of the Council of Wales. It is commonplace to note how unlikely their speeches were; the probable acting copy, the Bridgewater manuscript, was substantially shorter. See *Complete Shorter Poems*, 88n10. *A Mask Presented at Ludlow Castle* is from *Complete Shorter Poems*.

19. The competition between the two is gracefully and wittily summarized in Ben Jonson's reply to the painter Sir William Burlase, "My Answer: The Poet to the Painter," which includes the lines: "But you are he can paint; I can but write: / A poet hath no more but black and white, / Ne knows he flattering colors, or false light." From "Underwood," in *Ben Jonson*, ed. Ian Donaldson (Oxford: Oxford University Press, 1985), 382. Milton's Lady learns here to see past "flattering colors" and "false light." See Stanley Fish, "Problem Solving in *Comus*," in *Illustrious Evidence: Approaches to English Literature of the Earlier Seventeenth Century*, ed. Earl Miner, (Berkeley and Los Angeles: University of California Press, 1975).

20. See, e.g., the language of heavenly approval in "At a Solemn Music," and in the poem's introduction: "Blest pair of *Sirens*, pledges of Heav'ns joy, / Sphere-born harmonious Sisters, Voice

and Verse" (1–2). Music is an essential part of Milton's plan in *Of Education.* After exercise, "convenient rest before meat may both with profit and delight be taken up in recreating and composing their travail'd spirits with the solemn and divine harmonies of musick heard, or learnt" (YP 2:409). See also Donald Friedman, "Comus and the Truth of the Ear," in *The Muses Common-Weale,* ed. Claude Summers and Ted-Larry Pebworth, 119–32 (Columbia: University of Missouri Press, 1989).

21. In the invocation to *Paradise Lost,* book 3, he bemoans the loss of the "Book of knowledge fair," with "wisdom at one entrance quite shut out" (47, 50). His (rare) poems to women praise their learning (Margaret Ley), their piety (the anonymous lady of Sonnet 9, and Margaret Thomason), and most notably their song (Leonore Baroni). Even the conventional Italian sonnets of his youth have a tendency to praise a beautiful voice more than an attractive appearance (*Complete Shorter Poems,* 69, 68, 199–201, 60, 62).

22. Coiro, "'A Thousand Fantasies,'" 89–98, successfully modifies a tradition that has read Milton's *Mask* retrospectively in terms of his later career, but she also acknowledges that he is trying to do something different with the form. William Shullenberger, *Lady in the Labyrinth: Milton's "Comus" as Initiation* (Madison, NJ: Fairleigh Dickinson University Press, 2008), sees the mask as an initiation ritual for Alice Egerton and makes the point that by focusing on the Lady and her emergence into virtuous womanhood, its rituals counter the praise of monarchic power that is usual in masks. See also Maryann Cale McGuire, *Milton's Puritan Masque* (Athens: University of Georgia Press, 1983). For a summary of some political implications of the *Mask,* including Milton's tendency to decentralize his vision of nationhood, see Cedric Brown, "Milton's Ludlow Mask," in *The Cambridge Companion to Milton,* ed. Dennis Danielson (Cambridge: Cambridge University Press, 1999), 25–28, 32–34.

23. In the actual performance, Lawes apparently gave the brothers a role in conjuring assistance; see the Bridgewater manuscript version (*Complete Shorter Poems,* 535). At the end of book 3 of Spenser's *Faerie Queene,* Britomart frees Amoret from the wicked enchanter Busirane, but is warned not to kill him, as only he can undo the terrible spell he had cast over his captive (3.12.34–36). Compare the Attendant Spirit's admonition to the brothers:

> Ye should have snatcht his wand
> And bound [Comus] fast; without his rod revers't,
> And backward mutters of dissevering power.
> We cannot free the Lady that sits here
> In stony fetters fixt and motionless   (*Mask,* 815–19)

with Amoret preventing Britomart from slaying Busirane:
> Dernely unto her called to abstaine,
> From doing him to dy. For else her paine
> Should be remedilesse, sith none but hee,
> Which wrought it, could the same recure againe.

(*Faerie Queene*, 3.12.34, in Spenser, *Poetical Works*). Both stories have submerged but easily recognizable sexual implications, and both involve the problem of appearances and judgment (as in Britomart's choice to enter the door that says "Be Not Too Bold" [*FQ* 3.11.54]).

24. Lewalski, *Life of John Milton*, 81.

25. Coiro, "'A Thousand Fantasies,'" 102, 103.

26. As in line 418, even if it is a gift from heaven, the virtue of chastity "may be termed her own." There is good scholarship reviewing contemporary conditions for women and the limitations on their choices and to some extent on the virtue they could claim; see, e.g., James Grantham Turner, *One Flesh: Paradisal Marriage and Sexual Relations in the Age of Milton* (Oxford: Oxford University Press, 1987), and Anthony Fletcher, *Gender, Sex and Subordination in England, 1500–1800* (New Haven: Yale University Press, 1995). Recall that Milton thought chastity even more important for a man than a woman (YP 1:892), though at the same time he acknowledged it as a virtue particularly expected of womanhood.

27. "To inferre a generall obscurity over the text [of Scripture], is a meer suggestion of the Devil to disswade men from reading it, and casts an aspersion of dishonour both upon the *mercy, truth*, and *wisedome* of *God*" (*Of Reformation*, YP 1:566). This is a polemical insistence on the clarity of Scripture. As I note later in this chapter, when Milton interprets the Bible on divorce (1643–44), he will be less sanguine about its transparency.

28. *Ad Patrem* was very probably written during the 1630s; see *Complete Shorter Poems*, 240n1.

29. And his career more generally; see Ralph Haug's summary of this tendency, YP 1:806n37. The most famous early poetic expression is Sonnet 7, "How soon hath time," probably written around his twenty-fourth birthday and in part addressing his achieving an age in which he would be eligible for holy orders. See Lewalski, *Life of John Milton*, 62–64.

30. *Justa Edouardo King Naufrago* (1638). The work contained poems in Latin and Greek, with the English section titled *Obsequies to the Memorie of Mr. Edward King*; Milton's concluding poem, the only pastoral elegy, is signed "J. M." When he republished the work in the 1645 *Poems of Mr. John Milton*, Milton added the descriptive headnote emphasizing the prophetic vision by which he foretold "the ruine of our corrupted Clergy then in their height."

Lycidas has received a great deal of critical attention beginning with Samuel Johnson's blistering dismissal in 1779 ("its form is that of a pastoral, easy, vulgar, and therefore disgusting"). C. A. Patrides, *Milton's "Lycidas": The Tradition and the Poem*, rev. ed. (Columbia: University of Missouri Press, 1983), collects many of the most important approaches, including the quoted selection from the Johnson essay (60–61). For works that pay attention to later trends in Milton studies by looking at *Lycidas*, see Michael Dietz, "'Thus Sang the Uncouth Swain': Pastoral, Prophecy, and Historicism in *Lycidas*," in *Milton Studies*, vol. 35, ed. Albert C. Labriola, 42–72 (Pittsburgh: University of Pittsburgh Press, 1997); and J. Martin Evans, *The Road from Horton: Looking Backwards in "Lycidas"* (Victoria: University of Victoria Press, 1998). For a summary of the poem's history and its current reception, see Gordon Teskey, "Dead Shepherd: Milton's *Lycidas*," in DuRocher and Thickstun, *Milton's Rival Hermeneutics*, 31–56, esp. 42–46.

31. J. Martin Evans, "Lycidas," in *The Cambridge Companion to Milton*, ed. Dennis Danielson, 39–53 (Cambridge: Cambridge University Press, 1999), sees in the verse of the poem's conclusion a move from pastoral to Christian epic, signaling a change in his own life, "animated no longer by the ideals of the pastoral eclogue but rather by those of the Christian epic" (52).

32. Teskey, "Dead Shepherd," 47.

33. Milton's experiences in Italy primed him for the task. See Susanne Woods, "'That Freedom of Discussion Which I Loved': Italy and Milton's Cultural Self-Definition," in *Milton in Italy: Contexts, Images, Contradictions*, ed. Mario A. Di Cesare, 9–18 (Binghamton, NY: Medieval & Renaissance Texts & Studies, 1991).

34. In May 1642 he married and brought to his house in London Mary Powell, the seventeen-year-old daughter of a royalist Oxfordshire landowner. By midsummer, when her celebratory friends and family had gone home to Oxford, she apparently found herself lonely in Milton's scholarly household, and he permitted her a visit home, expecting her return around the end of September. Once back in Oxfordshire, she stayed. They were not reconciled until the summer of 1645, possibly because at that point the royalist Powells could use Milton's support as the progress of the civil war saw the decline of royalist power (Lewalski, *Life of John Milton*, 184).

35. In David Norbrook's reading of the divorce tracts, "the woman's role is at once to provide dialogue and to listen to a monologue; she must become a vehicle for agency without achieving it" (*Writing the English Republic*, 118). It is true, as I argue, that Milton sees "a meet and happy conversation" as a vehicle for increasing a man's liberty by contributing to and extending his knowledge and choice within the domestic sphere. But for a different view of Milton's idea

of marriage, see Thomas H. Luxon, *Single Imperfection: Milton, Marriage, and Friendship* (Pittsburgh: Duquesne University Press, 2005). Luxon argues that Milton displaced the male friendship ideal with an ideal of marital companionship (2).

36. Besides two editions of *Doctrine and Discipline of Divorce*, Milton published *The Judgment of Martin Bucer*, a translation and commentary on a well-regarded Reformation scholar, in July 1944; in March 1645 he produced a reasoned explication of biblical texts on the subject of divorce, *Tetrachordon* (a reference to the four strings of the lyre), and *Colasterion*, a polemical attack on an anonymous response to *Doctrine and Discipline* (YP 2:416–79, 571–758). See Ernest Sirluck's summary of the occasion and arguments of the divorce tracts in YP 2:137–58. Lewalski, *Life of John Milton*, cites some of the responses to Milton (178–80, 202–03).

37. Kahn, "Metaphorical Contract," says that Milton makes clear in the *Tenure of Kings and Magistrates* (1648) that "Reading is a prophetic and ethical activity...because meaning is not simply or literally given but must be construed. The work of prophecy or interpretation is inseparable from the figurative dimension of scripture" (92). One can see Milton moving toward this position four years earlier as he grapples with that "figurative dimension of scripture" in the divorce tracts.

38. Ernest Sirluck's preface and notes to *Areopagitica* (YP 2:480–570) include most major commentary until 1959; and Lewalski's notes to her own discussion of *Areopagitica* in *Life of John Milton* (601) extend the discussion forward. See also Sharon Achinstein and Elizabeth Sauer, eds., *Milton and Toleration* (Oxford: Oxford University Press, 2007), including the essays by David Loewenstein, "Toleration and the Specter of Heresy in Milton's England" (45–71), and Thomas N. Corns, "John Milton, Roger Williams, and the Limits of Toleration" (72–85). Fallon, *Milton's Peculiar Grace*, uses *Areopagitica* on Milton's understanding of the prophet-poet (140–41). Fulton, *Historical Milton*, 82–114, situates *Areopagitica* in relation to Milton's developing ideas as evidenced in his Commonplace Book. *Milton Studies* frequently contains articles that concern all or part of *Areopagitica*, e.g., Eric Nelson, "'True Liberty': Isocrates and Milton's *Areropagitica*," in *Milton Studies*, vol. 40, ed. Albert C. Labriola, 201–21 (Pittsburgh: University of Pittsburgh Press, 2001).

39. Vincent Blasi, "Milton's *Areopagitica* and the Modern First Amendment," Third Annual Ralph Gregory Elliot First Amendment Lecture at Yale Law School, March 1995, www.law.yale.edu/documents/pdf/Milton.pdf. Norbrook, *Writing the English Republic*, 118–39, places *Areopagitica* firmly at the center of Milton's developing republicanism, which in turn became a model for others.

40. Sharon Achinstein, *Literature and Dissent in Milton's England* (Cambridge: Cambridge University Press, 2003), makes the interesting case that "the proximity of violence and grace [here, in John Bunyan's *Grace Abounding*] is a common feature of Dissenting writing, and that Dissenting writers deployed violence in order to solicit divine favor as well as to activate readers' desires for sympathy, solidarity and action" (84). The "cycles of defeat, persecution, and exile so dramatically recorded in the Bible could be assimilated and even ritually commemorated in the Puritan's imaginations" (85), she continues, suggesting they might even sanction political uprisings. Milton's imagery in his dissenting writings is generally more placid (until the 1660 effort to resist the Restoration), but the association of violence with grace is clearly a feature of Milton's *Samson* (162). See also chapter 5, below.

41. Stanley Fish, "Driving from the Letter: Truth and Indeterminacy in Milton's *Areopagitica*," in *Re-Membering Milton*, ed. Mary Nyquist and Margaret Ferguson (New York: Methuen, 1988), 234–54.

42. A point established by two essays in Dobranski and Rumrich, *Milton and Heresy*: Barbara K. Lewalski, "How Radical Was the Young Milton?" (49–74), and Stephen M. Fallon, "'Elect above the Rest': Theology as Self-Representation in Milton" (93–116). The editors summarize some of these articles' conclusions: "Until the early 1640s, as Barbara Lewalski's chapter indicates, the young Milton aligned himself with the Calvinist or Puritan side, though with what realization or endorsement of predestinarian theology remains unclear. The unmistakable Arminianism of the mature Milton, as Stephen Fallon's chapter demonstrates, is somewhat complicated by Calvinist vestiges—though these vestiges, as Fallon explains, are not without uncannily close precedent in Arminius himself. We are tempted to speculate that during the 1640s, the political and military defeat of the anti-Calvinists—or perhaps the rigid sanctimony of the Presbyterian victors, opened a space for Milton to adopt an Arminian advocacy of free will and valorization of rational choosing" (4).

43. Thomas Festa, *The End of Learning: Milton and Education* (New York: Routledge, 2006), makes a similar point in his analysis of Milton's developing sense of the importance of interpretive reading, evident in *Areopagitica:* "Individual conscience, guided by reason and the Holy Spirit, awakens the interpretive faculty to choice, serves as our connection to the divine *logos*" (41).

44. In his invocation to Parliament, Milton claims his "whole Discourse propos'd will be a certain testimony, if not a Trophy" of "joy and gratulation" for "all who wish and promote their Countries

liberty," since Parliament has presumably renewed this liberty for an England recently dominated by "tyranny and superstition." He assumes an attentive audience under this new dispensation: "For this is not the liberty which wee can hope, that no grievance should ever arrive in the Commonwealth, that let no man in this World expect; but when complaints are freely heard, deeply consider'd, and speedily reform'd, then is the utmost bound of civill liberty attrain'd, that wise men looke for. To which I now manifest by the very sound of this which I shall utter, that we are already in good part arrived" (YP 2:487).

45. See Corns, "John Milton, Roger Williams," 72–85, and Loewenstein, "Milton among the Religious Radicals," 45–71. Conversely, Norbrook, *Writing the English Republic*, 118–39, esp. 130, places Milton into a larger European discourse of republicanism.

46. John Illo, "Areopagiticus Mythic and Real," *Prose Studies* 11 (1988): 3–23; Fish, "Driving from the Letter," 234–54.

47. Skinner, *Liberty before Liberalism*, esp. "Free States and Individual Liberty" (59–99), and David Loewenstein, "Milton's Nationalism," in *Early Modern Nationalism and Milton's England*, ed. David Loewenstein and Paul Stevens, 25–50 (Toronto: University of Toronto Press, 2008).

48. Clement Fatovic, "The Anti-Catholic Roots of Liberal and Republican Conceptions of Freedom in English Political Thought," *Journal of the History of Ideas* 66 (Jan. 2005): 37–59: "Catholicism, or 'popery' as it was disparagingly called, played a constitutive role in the development of ideas about personal and collective autonomy that featured significantly in both liberal and republican theories of liberty.... When the leading figures of these two camps confronted Catholicism on the ideological field of battle, they devised many of the same rhetorical strategies and employed many of the same conceptual weapons to vanquish their common foe" (38).

49. According to Festa, *End of Learning*, "Milton advances his theory of education to rectify shortcomings that he believes inhibit the reformation of the spiritual and political nation" (12–13), but his educational project is much larger than what is contained in this small humanist treatise.

Notes to Chapter Four

1. In Lewalski's phrase. See her introduction to *Paradise Lost*, xvii; Lewalski, *Life of John Milton*, 460; and note 3 below. See also, e.g., Joseph Wittreich, *Why Milton Matters* (New York: Palgrave Macmillan, 2006): in *Paradise Lost*, "the authentic Milton, an

interrogator—and sometimes a transgressor—of orthodox opinion lurks in...sites of contestation from which he often reveals himself a sect of one, wherein he establishes precise inflections, makes crucial choices, all the while gently nudging us to do the same" (34); Stanley Fish, *How Milton Works* (Cambridge, MA: Harvard University Press, 2001): "The insecurity of Eden is its glory because it provides an arena of choice and testimony in which the free will can exercise itself for good or for ill" (547); John Rogers, *The Matter of Revolution: Science, Poetry, and Politics in the Age of Milton* (Ithaca: Cornell University Press, 1996): "As it threads through the wandering mazes of free will and providence, *Paradise Lost* broods continually on the problem of agency, both human and divine" (144).

2. Shore, *Milton and the Art of Rhetoric*, 60, notes that while "*Paradise Lost* is a poem primarily of the indicative rather than the subjunctive mood," based as it is on the Bible and not on the "counterfactual" imagination, "the Miltonic 'or'" is (as Herman, "Whose Fault," also argues) a crucial feature of its structure, preserving the possibility of counterfactual options. What I have called the "language of surmise," including conditional and subjunctive constructions, therefore remains essential to Milton's version of this biblical tale. Multiple ways of reading inhere in those constructions, as they do in Milton's structural choices and changes.

3. Norbrook, *Writing the English Republic*, 438–67, makes the case for Lucan as a model. Versions of a dramatic *Paradise Lost* are outlined in the Trinity manuscript; see description by Lewalski, *Life of John Milton*, 123–24.

4. See the "Textual Introduction" in the Lewalski, ed., *Paradise Lost*, xxx–xxxii; she speculates the original ten-book division was intended to resist "the Virgilian mode adopted by Dryden and many others in the early years of the reconstruction to celebrate Charles II as a new Augustus" (xxx).

5. See David Loewenstein's summary case in "The Radical Religious Politics of *Paradise Lost*," in *A Companion to Milton*, ed. Thomas N. Corns (Oxford: Blackwell, 2001), 348–62. Lewalski, *"Paradise Lost" and the Rhetoric of Literary Forms* (Princeton, NJ: Princeton University Press, 1986), outlines Milton's generic transformations: "*Paradise Lost* is preeminently a poem about knowing and choosing—for the Miltonic Bard, for his characters, for the reader....the ground for many of these choices is Milton's own choice and rhetorical use of a panoply of literary forms, with their accumulated freight of shared cultural significance" (3). Alastair Fowler, *Kinds of Literature: An Introduction to the Theory of Genres and Modes* (Cambridge, MA: Harvard University Press,

1982), also situates Milton as a poet singularly transformative in his use of genres. For Milton as provocateur, even trickster, see Stanley Fish, *Surprised by Sin: Milton and the Reader of "Paradise Lost"* (London: Macmillan, 1967), and *How Milton Works*, especially his chapters on various "temptations" (307 and following). I disagree with Fish's claim that Milton sees a "radical oneness of all things [as] a stable feature of the universe" (*How Milton Works*, 108) and will argue instead that Milton posits the unknowable individuality of each person's relationship with God. Milton's invitation to readerly choice extends from that premise, and his prophetic stance and theological certainty is always in some tension with his insistence that God works with individuals, not with dogmatic systems. His rhetoric and poetic reflect that tension.

6. Lewalski, ed., "The Verse," *Paradise Lost*, 10.

7. Susanne Woods, *Natural Emphasis: English Versification from Chaucer to Dryden* (San Marino, CA: Huntington Library Press, 1985), 276; a notable sixteenth century exception to rhymed narrative was Henry Howard, Earl of Surrey's translation of two books of Virgil's *Aeneid* in the 1540s. See Florence H. Ridley, ed., *The Aeneid of Henry Howard Earl of Surrey* (Berkeley and Los Angeles: University of California Press, 1963); see also Woods, *Natural Emphasis*, 89–91.

8. Derek Attridge, *Well-Weighed Syllables: Elizabethan Verse in Classical Metres* (Cambridge: Cambridge University Press, 1974); Woods, *Natural Emphasis*, 124–46, 197–205.

9. Lewalski in her edition of *Paradise Lost*, 10nn10–11, supposes quantity refers to syllabification and numbers to rhythm, but given the history of usage, the reverse is more likely true. For summary discussions of Milton's prosody in the shorter poems, see Edward R. Weismiller, "Studies of Verse Form in the Minor English Poems," in *A Variorum Commentary on the Poems of John Milton*, ed. A. S. P. Woodhouse and Douglas Bush (New York: Columbia University Press, 1972), 2.3:1007–87, and for Milton's blank verse, see Weismiller, "Studies of Style and Verse Form in *Paradise Regained*," in *A Variorum Commentary on the Poems of John Milton*, ed. Merritt Y. Hughes and Walter MacKellar (New York: Columbia University Press, 1975).

10. John Creaser, "Prosody and Liberty in Milton and Marvell," in *Milton and the Terms of Liberty*, ed. Graham Parry and Joad Raymond, 37–55 (Cambridge: D. S. Brewer, 2002), 39; Norbrook, *Writing the English Republic*, 225. See also John Creaser, "Prosodic Style and Conceptions of Liberty in Milton and Marvell," *Milton Quarterly* 34, no. 1 (2000): 1–13: Milton has "a rigorous commitment to the freedom of those fit to be free, but the means to that constant end can be diverse.... As in his prosody, so in his phi-

losophy" (5). In a complete misreading of Milton's intent, John Dryden famously asked and received permission from Milton to put "*Paradise Lost* into Rhime for the Stage." The result is Dryden's *State of Innocence* (1674), dedicated to the Catholic princess, Mary of Modena, the young wife of the future James II (Lewalski, *Life of Milton*, 508).

11. John Leonard provides a useful summary in "Language and Knowledge in *Paradise Lost*," in *The Cambridge Companion to Milton*, ed. Dennis Danielson (Cambridge: Cambridge University Press, 1999), 130–43; see also Kathleen Swaim, *Before and After the Fall: Contrasting Modes in "Paradise Lost"* (Amherst: University of Massachusetts Press, 1986), 158–267. The ambiguity of postlapsarian language is a premise of Fish, *Surprised by Sin*, and is at least a topic in most commentaries on the poem.

12. Hobbes anticipated a more literal-minded concept of poetic imitation of nature than Sidney implied or that Milton demonstrates, and thus anticipates the rationalist criticism of Dryden, Pope, and especially Samuel Johnson. See my discussion in chapter 6 on Thomas Hobbes, "The Answer of Mr. Hobbes to Sr. Will. Davenant's Preface before Gondibert," in William Davenant's *Gondibert: An Heroick Poem; written by Sir William D'avenant* (London, 1651), esp. D7, D7v.

13. As I noted in the introduction, note 12, Maritain (*Existence and the Existent*, 49–50) sees liberty as allowing a being to create itself through its own decisions. Like Jean-Paul Sartre's atheist existentialism in *Being and Nothingness*, trans. Hazel E. Barnes (New York: Philosophical Library, 1956); originally published in French as *L'Être et le néant* (1943), the Thomist Maritain insists that a conscious being's essence results from freely available decisions. For a similar Christian existentialist perspective, see Gabriel Marcel, *Philosophy and Existence* (London: Harvill Press, 1949).

14. E.g., Stephen Fallon, *Milton among the Philosophers: Poetry and Materialism in Seventeenth-Century England* (Ithaca, NY: Cornell University Press, 1991), 1–18; Rogers, *Matter of Revolution*, 110–11 (but Rogers is more interested in the vitalism that he sees underlying and pervading creation than in the materialist hierarchy suggested in book 5—see 112–22); Lewalski, *Life of John Milton*, 474–79; but see N. K. Sugimura, *Matter of Glorious Trial: Spiritual and Material Substance in "Paradise Lost"* (New Haven: Yale University Press, 2009), 48–57, in which she argues that metaphor itself is a way of knowing, one that suggests a kind of dualism in Milton's ontology.

15. As Joad Raymond, *Milton's Angels: The Early Modern Imagination* (Oxford: Oxford University Press, 2010), observes, "Milton's unorthodoxy on the matter of angelic digestion, often

understood to be an exceptionally literal-minded moment, is one aspect of a fuller theological picture of the creatureliness of angels, the spiritual congruity and legitimate sociability between humans and angels, and the continuity of matter across all creation" (282).

16. See note 14 above, though Sugimura, *Matter of Glorious Trial*, 284, disagrees, seeing instead an "ontological tension" signified by Milton's use of metaphor. . See also Wittreich, *Why Milton Matters*, 51–54, who notes Raphael's language of surmise ("What if Earth / Be but the shadow of Heav'n" [*PL* 5.574–74]) and argues that, like competing interpretations of the Bible, various voices in *Paradise Lost* invite various hermeneutics.

17. We have seen this as early as book 1, as in the logical construction: if the mind is its own place, then it can make a hell of heaven or a heaven of hell. This is only valid if "place" means the same thing in relation to the interior mind as to the external environment, and only true if the premise is true. By book 9 Satan reasons from false premises that earth must be better than heaven, "for what God after better worse would build?" (*PL* 9.102). Lewalski sees Satan using a "false narrative" to invite Eve into a similar misuse of discursive reason (*Life of John Milton*, 477).

18. Joseph Wittreich, "Sites of Contention in *Paradise Lost*," in DuRocher and Thickstun, *Milton's Rival Hermeneutics*, 101–34. Wittreich reads Adam's self-presentation in book 8 as self-centered and distorted, anticipating his fall (125–28). I think this pushes the evidence too far, but I agree that Adam's sin involves seeing Eve as so much a part of himself that choosing her over God is a sin of pride rather than uxoriousness. Additionally, it is possible to read Milton's brief presentation of Ptolemaic astronomy as dismissive or even parodic. After describing an apparently earth-centered cosmos to Adam, Raphael takes care to add: "Not that I so affirm, though so it seem / To thee who hast thy dwelling here on earth" (*PL* 8.117–18).

19. As Karen L. Edwards, "The 'World' of *Paradise Lost*," in *The Oxford Handbook of Milton*, ed. Nicholas McDowell and Nigel Smith, 496–509 (Oxford: Oxford University Press, 2009), puts it, "The 'World' of *Paradise Lost*, a creation responsible for readers' sense of being immersed in a wholly imagined reality when they read the poem, is in fact composed of the interaction of multiple imagined worlds" (497).

20. Wittreich, "Sites of Contention," 117.

21. Timothy Watt makes this argument extensively in "Milton's Visionary Obedience," Ph.D. diss., University of Massachusetts, 2011; see abstract at http://scholarworks.umass.edu/dissertations/AAI3482671/.

22. Barbara K. Lewalski, "Interpreting God's Word—and Words—in *Paradise Lost*," in DuRocher and Thickstun, *Milton's Rival Hermeneutics*, 77.

23. Teresa Feroli, "Rethinking 'shee for God in him': *Paradise Lost* and Milton's Quaker Contemporaries," in DuRocher and Thickstun, *Milton's Rival Hermeneutics*, 177.

24. Rogers, *Matter of Revolution*, argues that Adam's admiration of Eve's "female self-containedness," though properly rebuked, is "merely" Adam's transfer "to the realm of human relations [the vitalist] principle Raphael had already established as foundational to the material cosmos" (117).

25. Feroli, "Rethinking," argues the same point from Milton's theology of *imago Dei:* "man is in the image of God, and so he plays a role in creating woman" (162).

26. Fish, *Surprised by Sin* (throughout, and reiterated in the chapter headings of *How Milton Works*); the ominous tone comes from our knowledge of the biblical consequences of Adam following Eve's lead, but some argue that Raphael's admonition to Adam over his admiration of Eve is, at this point in the narrative, misplaced; see, for example, Shannon Miller, *Engendering the Fall: John Milton and Seventeenth-Century Women Writers* (Philadelphia: University of Pennsylvania Press, 2008), and Wittreich, "Sites of Contention," 127–28.

27. Paula Johnson, *Form and Transformation in Music and Poetry of the English Renaissance* (New Haven: Yale University Press, 1972), 14.

28. See, e.g., Mary Nyquist's pioneering essay, "Reading the Fall: Discourse and Drama in *Paradise Lost*," *English Literary Renaissance* 14, no. 2 (1984): 199–229; Catherine Belsey, *John Milton: Language, Gender, Power* (Oxford: Basil Blackwell, 1988); and Janet Halley, "Female Autonomy in Milton's Sexual Politics," in *Milton and the Idea of Woman*, ed. Julia Walker, 230–53 (Urbana: University of Illinois Press, 1988). Without negating these feminist concerns, Feroli explores the *imago dei* context in "Rethinking" (159–64).

29. Though Peter Herman argues that God, in fact, withholds from Adam and Eve information (notably, for example, that Satan is the source of Eve's disturbing dream at the end of book 4) that would presumably help them understand their exposure to temptation; see "'Whose Fault, Whose but His Own?': *Paradise Lost*, Negligence, and the Problem of Cause," in *The New Milton Criticism*, ed. Peter S. Herman and Elizabeth Sauer, 49–67 (Cambridge: Cambridge University Press, 2012). See also Peter Herman, *Destabilizing Milton: "Paradise Lost" and the Poetics of Incertitude* (London: Palgrave Macmillan, 2008), 120–25.

30. Diane McColley, *Milton's Eve* (Urbana: University of Illinois Press, 1983), makes a strong argument for Adam and Eve's full innocence until the actual moments of disobedience. See also Fish, *How Milton Works*, 550: at the end of the dispute between Adam and Eve

at the beginning of book 9, "the matter is still poised, as it always had been, between the sufficiency to stand and the freedom (not all compromised by mistakes that fall short of the fatal one) to fall" (550).

31. Herman, "'Whose Fault,'" makes a contrary case. I read the debate in this scene as a counter to Herman's claim that Adam and Eve are insufficiently informed and that God and Raphael have not given them enough information to avoid the Fall; both Adam and Eve clearly know that the enemy is out there.

32. Lewalski, "Interpreting God's Word," 78.

33. In the self-contemplation that began Satan's journey through Eden at the beginning of book 4, he unintentionally revealed himself to Uriel, whom he had fooled enough to gain entrance. Observing the multiple emotions that "marr'd [Satan's] borrow'd visage, and betrayed / Him counterfeit" (*PL* 4.116–17), Uriel knows them impossible for a "Spirit of happie sort" (4.128), reporting this to Gabriel, who sends Ithuriel and Zephon to find Satan.

34. See, e.g., Milton's much-lauded portrayal of Satan's descent from his rapturous observation of Eden into the hissing serpent in 9.99–179. His unwilled descent into serpent form (10.511–17) is the ultimate consequence of his self-delusion, as willful ignorance destroys his agency—his ability to will at all.

35. God's disquisition reflects Milton's theology and angelology as found in *On Christian Doctrine:* there are "both good and evil angels...for it is well known that a great many of them revolted from God of their own free will before the fall of man," and "the good angels stand by their own strength, no less than man did before his fall." The unfallen angels have an intuitive intelligence, though they "know by revelation only those things which God sees fit to show them, and they know other things by virtue of their very high intelligence" (*Christian Doctrine,* in YP 6:343, 344–45, 347–48). Erasmus, of whom Milton generally approved, argued that both human beings and the angels were formed with "an uncorrupted will, but which remained quite free...to choose also evil." After the "revolt against God by Lucifer and his followers....in those angels who fell, the will was so completely corrupted, that they could not perform any meritorious act. In those who remained faithful, their good will was so strengthened that it became henceforth impossible for them to choose evil." See Erasmus, "A Diatribe or Sermon concerning Free Will," in Winter, *Erasmus-Luther Discourse,* 22.

36. Augustine, *On Free Choice of the Will,* trans. Thomas Williams (Indianapolis: Hackett, 1993), 78: "Just as your memory does not force the past to have happened, God's foreknowledge does not force the future to happen."

37. Lucy Newlyn, *"Paradise Lost" and the Romantic Reader* (Oxford: Clarendon Press, 1993), traces the Romantic reception of Milton, including the general belief that he must have been of the devil's party. For a succinct version of the argument, see Joseph Wittreich, "'He Ever was a Dissenter': Milton's Transgressive Maneuvers in *Paradise Lost*," in *Arenas of Conflict: Milton and the Unfettered Mind*, ed. Kristin Pruitt McColgan and Charles W. Durham (Selinsgrove, PA: Susquehanna University Press, 1997), 21–40, and Michael Bryson, *The Tyranny of Heaven: Milton's Rejection of God as King* (Newark: University of Delaware Press, 2004). The founder of the modern controversy is William Empson, *Milton's God* (London: Chatto and Windus, 1961), e.g., Milton's "picture of God...[is] astonishingly like Uncle Joe Stalin" (146). Recovering Empson, and before him Denis Saurat, is a project of Herman and Sauer, *The New Milton Criticism*, especially Jeffrey Shoulson, "Denis Saurat and the Old New Milton Criticism," 194–211.

38. In *Surprised by Sin*, Fish argues that the emotive language given to Milton's God is an invitation to the reader to respond, not characteristic of the nature of God. Lieb, *Theological Milton*, 152, by contrast, insists that "The figure of God in *Paradise Lost* is portrayed as a fully passible being in whom is embodied a full spectrum of emotions," rather than as the "abstract principle" many readers prefer, citing, e.g., Dennis Danielson, *Milton's Good God: A Study in Literary Theodicy* (Cambridge: Cambridge University Press, 1982).

39. See Sanford Burdick, *The Dividing Muse: Images of Sacred Disjunction in Milton's Poetry* (New Haven: Yale University Press, 1985), 71: "In Milton's theodicy, the mind's relation to knowledge is represented as the struggle to attain a truthful image," and for Milton, "human knowledge, including even the knowledge of the divine...lies in the right perception and comprehension of images."

40. For summaries of reader attitudes toward Satan, see Merritt Y. Hughes, ed., *Milton: Complete Poems and Major Prose* (New York: Odyssey Press, 1957), 177–79; Roland Mushat Frye, "Satan," in Hunter, *A Milton Encyclopedia*, 7:166–69; John Carey, "Milton's Satan," in *The Cambridge Companion to Milton*, ed. Dennis Danielson, 160–74 (Cambridge: Cambridge University Press, 1999); and Stephen M. Fallon, "Satan," in *The Milton Encyclopedia*, ed. Thomas N. Corns, 330 (New Haven: Yale University Press, 2012).

41. Bryson, *Tyranny of Heaven*, 16–18.

42. Calvin, *Institutes*, 4.10.3, defined "conscience" etymologically as coming to knowledge with a sense of God's presence and judgment in the process: "when men, with the mind and intellect.

Apprehend the knowledge of things, they are thereby said to know, and hence the name of knowledge or science is used; so, when they have, in addition to this, a sense of the divine judgment, as a witness not permitting them to hide their sins, but bringing them before the tribunal of the judge, that sense is called conscience. For it occupies a kind of middle place between God and man, not suffering man to suppress what he knows in himself, but following him out until it bring him to conviction." This is consistent with Milton's use of the term. See, e.g., in his biographical preface to the second book of *Reason of Church-Government:* "neither envy nor gall hath entered me upon this controversy, but the enforcement of conscience only"; and "were it the meanest under-service, if God by his Secretary conscience injoyn it, it were sad for me if I should draw back" (YP 1:806, 822).

43. Milton often associates conscience with right choice, which he in turn defines as reason ("reason is but choosing" [YP 2:527]). In *Areopagitica,* for example, he notes that the earliest church authorities did not censure, but "were wont only to declare what Books were not commendable, passing no furder but leaving it to each ones conscience to read or let by" (YP 2:501). *A Treatise of Civil Power* is a virtual discourse on conscience, associating it with God-given individual choice; for example, with "the name of *Protestant*...hath ever been received this doctrine, which prefers the scripture before the church, and acknowledges none but the Scripture sole interpreter of itself to conscience.... But if any man shall pretend, that the scripture judges to his conscience for other men, he makes himself greater not only than the church, but also then the scripture, then the consciences of other men; a presumption too high for any mortal" (YP 7:243–44).

44. Mary Nyquist, "Slavery, Resistance, and Nation in Milton and Locke," in *Early Modern Nationalism and Milton's England,* ed. David Loewenstein and Paul Stevens, 356–97 (Toronto: University of Toronto Press, 2008), 365.

45. According to Scott, *Algernon Sidney,* "Applied politically, Platonism always...boiled down to the belief that knowledge, and liberty (the self-rule that knowledge made possible) were the property of those capable of achieving them, and not to be jeopardized by the ignorance and incapacity of those who were not. Those incapable of liberty, that is of ruling themselves, would have to be ruled by those capable of it. The thought of all the mid-seventeenth-century radicals strongly influenced by Platonism, prominently among them Milton, Sidney, Nedham, Stubbe, and Vane, always, despite the populism of their ideas in theory, pulled back to this position when the disappointing political behaviour of their liberated people pushed them to it in practice" (21).

46. Mary Ann Radzinowicz, "Politics of *Paradise Lost*," in *Politics of Discourse: The Literature and History of Seventeenth-Century England*, ed. Kevin Sharpe and Steven Zwicker, 204–29 (Berkeley and Los Angeles: University of California Press, 1987), 133.

Notes to Chapter Five

1. The texts of both *Samson* and *Paradise Regained* are taken from John Milton, *Complete Shorter Poems*, ed. Revard, with all quotations from this edition. There is some debate over when *Samson* was actually written (see Revard's summary, 451).

2. Achinstein, *Literature and Dissent in Milton's England*, 152.

3. Lewalski, *Life of John Milton*, 400–04, describes the tense period Milton endured in 1660, including his brief imprisonment. Lewalski argues further in "'To Try, and Teach the Erring Soul': Milton's Last Seven Years," in Parry and Raymond, *Milton and the Terms of Liberty*, 175–90, that both *Paradise Regained* and *Samson Agonistes* were part of Milton's continuing project to resist Restoration politics and values.

4. John Rogers, "*Paradise Regained* and the Memory of *Paradise Lost*," in McDowell and Smith, *Oxford Handbook of Milton*, 603–07, makes the point that Jesus understands that he is the Messiah and the Son of God, but in his position within linear time he does not recall the events of *Paradise Lost*. Similarly, Rogers notes, Satan seems to have repressed the war in heaven where he was "thunder-struck" and defeated by the Son (*PL* 6.858), just as, at the beginning of *Paradise Regained*, he is again "thunder-struck" (*PR* 1.36) by God's pronouncement at Jesus' baptism, the prelude to another defeat. Stella Revard, "Satan in *Paradise Regained*: The Quest for Identity," in DuRocher and Thickstun, *Milton's Rival Hermeneutics*, 205–24, notes that Rogers and others, including Mary Ann Radzinowicz and Barbara Lewalski, have pointed out that "there is no reason to suppose that Jesus remembers his superhuman Sonship in heaven" (206).

5. Jeffrey B. Morris, "Disorientation and Disruption in *Paradise Regained*," in *Milton Studies*, vol. 26, ed. James D. Simmonds (Pittsburgh: University of Pittsburgh Press, 1990), 219–37.

6. Mary Ann Radzinowicz, "*Paradise Regained* as Hermeneutic Combat," *University of Harvard Studies in Literature* 16 (1984): 99–107, makes a similar point. See also Radzinowicz, *Milton's Epics and the Book of Psalms* (Princeton, NJ: Princeton University Press, 1989), part 1.

7. Critics have had some difficulty with what seems to be Milton's rejection of his own lifelong love of classical learning in these passages, but as Lewalski points out, "Jesus's answer (and Milton's) does not repudiate learning as such, but flatly denies it is *necessary* to virtue, salvation, or the accomplishment of God's work in the world" (*Life of John Milton,* 521). Richard J. DuRocher, "Hermes's Blessed Retreat: Rival Views of Learning in *Paradise Regained,*" in Durocher and Thickstun, *Milton's Rival Hermeneutics,* 225–37, argues that what the Son is rejecting is "first and foremost the temptation itself. In tempting the Son with knowledge, Satan is not offering the Son knowledge itself; instead, the fallen angel casts knowledge as a political tool rather than a means to genuine enlightenment" (228).

8. Rogers, "*Paradise Regained* and the Memory," also points out that not even the New Testament Bible would have allowed Jesus to discover his role in the heavenly rout: "the only text whose revolving by the Son could have afforded him the information adequate to the truth of his status as the heroic 'debeller' of Satan is *Paradise Lost,* since it is that text alone in which the Son's role in the War in Heaven can be read" (604).

9. Revard, "Satan in *Paradise Regained,*" 205–24.

10. DuRocher, "Hermes's Blessed Retreat," 227.

11. Portions of the following argument appear in somewhat different form in Woods, "Inviting Rival Hermeneutics," 13–32, and in Woods, "Choice and Election in *Samson Agonistes,*" in Kelley, Lieb, and Shawcross, *Milton and the Grounds of Contention,* 274–87.

12. See Achinstein, *Literature and Dissent,* on Milton's choice to end the volume with violence: "The order of the poems in the volume, set by Milton, leaves us with a violent ending. Yet violence and Redemption are conjoined in Milton's thinking; Samson is not strictly to be relegated to the past, superseded by a New Covenant. Rather, the fiery ancient rage instills meaning for the present and future, spending a passion that will yet be spent in a final moment of revealed truth" (152). If the project of liberation, salvation, and redemption remains ongoing, there is no reason why the Danites should have a comprehensive liberation at the end of *Samson.*

13. For the former, see Lewalski, *Life of John Milton,* and Mary Ann Radzinowicz, *Toward "Samson Agonistes": The Growth of Milton's Mind* (Princeton, NJ: Princeton University Press, 1978); for the latter, see John Carey, *John Milton* (New York: Arco, 1970); and Joseph Wittreich, *Interpreting "Samson Agonistes"* (Princeton, NJ: Princeton University Press, 1986), and *Shifting Contexts: Reinterpreting "Samson Agonistes"* (Pittsburgh: Duquesne University Press, 2002).

14. John Carey, "A Work in Praise of Terrorism? September 11 and *Samson Agonistes*," *Times Literary Supplement*, September 6, 2002; Stanley Fish, "'There Is Nothing He Cannot Ask': Milton, Liberalism, and Terrorism," in *Milton in the Age of Fish: Essays on Authorship, Text, and Criticism*, ed. Michael Lieb and Albert C. Labriola, 243–64 (Pittsburgh: Duquesne University Press, 2006), 244.

15. Feisal G. Mohamed, "Confronting Religious Violence: Milton's *Samson Agonistes*," *PMLA* 120, no. 2 (2005): 327–40. This article sparked *PMLA* "Forum" responses from Joseph Wittreich and Peter Herman, with a reply by Mohamed; see *PMLA* 102, no. 5 (2005): 1641–44.

16. John Rumrich, "Samson and the Excluded Middle," in *Altering Eyes: New Perspectives on "Samson Agonistes,"* ed. Mark R. Kelley and Joseph Wittreich, 307–32 (Newark: University of Delaware Press, 2002), 307.

17. Radzinowicz, *Toward "Samson Agonistes,"* 184.

18. Lieb, *Theological Milton*, 204, 203; Wittreich, *Why Milton Matters*, 163.

19. Daniel Shore, "Why Milton Is Not an Iconoclast," *PMLA* 127, no. 1 (January 2012): 33.

20. Margaret Olofson Thickstun, "Fame, Shame, and the Importance of Community in *Samson Agonistes*," in DuRocher and Thickstun, *Milton's Rival Hermeneutics*, 202.

21. Shore, *Milton and the Art of Rhetoric*, 146–65.

22. Wittreich, *Why Milton Matters*, 170.

23. See Rumrich's discussion of Johnson's complaint in "Samson and the Excluded Middle" (315–19). Mohamed, "Confronting Religious Violence," argues that *Samson* "cannot have what Johnson would call a 'middle,'" because "in order for Samson's final act to be justified, it cannot be causally related to the fleshly, rational concerns of his three major dialogues [with Manoa, Dalila, and Harapha]; it must instead take its impulse from the immediate divine illumination residing entirely outside the events with which we are presented" (334).

24. Thickstun, "Fame, Shame," makes the case that "the Samson Milton imagines is a man who cares about reputation and is highly sensitive to how he appears in the world" (186).

25. "Of that sort of Dramatic Poem which is call'd Tragedy," Milton's introduction to *Samson Agonistes* (*Complete Shorter Poems*, 461).

26. Ibid., 461.

27. That is, a poetics that invites God's elect to choose and therefore fulfill their proper vocations; see Woods, "Choice and Election," 174–87.

28. See, e.g., Susanne Woods, "How Free Are Milton's Women?," in *Milton and the Idea of Woman*, ed. Julia M. Walker, 11–30 (Urbana: University of Illinois Press, 1988). However, the tendency of modern criticism is simply to dismiss Dalila's motives along with her rhetoric; see, e.g., Fish, "Milton, Liberalism, and Terrorism": offering a rhetorical clue to her bad intentions, "she says...I did it for this reason, no, for that reason, for the reason of civil duty, for the reason of religion, because the priests urged me to, because the maxims of 'wisest men' urged me to, and on and on.... It is sincerity, the intention to do good and be true to one's deepest loyalties, that justifies, not some confected heap of tried-on and cosmetically applied reasons" (251).

29. For Milton's thinking on a drama about the Fall, see the Trinity manuscript notes reproduced in Lewalski's edition of *Paradise Lost* (341–43).

30. As Joan Bennett notes, citing John Hale, "As a tragic hero, Samson is not constructed nor held up as an examplar for readers to emulate; rather tragic heroes relate to us as 'persons like ourselves..., doing or suffering terrible things, with respect to those dearest to them.'" Bennett, "Reading *Samson Agonistes*," in *The Cambridge Companion to Milton*, ed. Dennis Danielson, 219–35 (Cambridge: Cambridge University Press, 1999), 221; John K. Hale, *Milton's Languages: The Impact of Multilingualism on Style* (Cambridge: Cambridge University Press, 1997), 193.

31. Aristotle, *Poetics*, trans. S. H. Butcher, ed. Francis Fergusson (New York: Hill and Wang, 1961). In accounting characters in comedy or tragedy as worse or better "than in real life," Aristotle assumes a common standard (52); the character of writers affects the character of what they choose to imitate and the genres (preeminently tragedy) that they choose (56); our common values inform our individual response to a good tragedy, for "pity is aroused by unmerited misfortune, fear by the misfortune of a man like ourselves," requiring [as in Samson's case] a tragic hero who is "not eminently good and just, yet whose misfortune is brought about not by vice or depravity, but by some error or frailty" (76) in someone who is "above the common level" (82); fear and pity are best aroused from "the inner structure of the piece" (78). Milton places Aristotle and his Renaissance Italian interpreters, along with Horace, in his syllabus in "Of Education" (YP 2:404–05). Milton was long thoughtful about genres, the poet's skills, and the relation of poet and poetry to the good of the community, as in his self-presentation in *The Reason of Church-Government*. Sounding something like a Christianized Aristotle, Milton concludes his reverie about potential genres and topics by pronouncing the poet's gifts from God, and "of power beside the office of the pulpit, to imbreed and cherish in

a great people the seeds of vertu, and publick civility, to allay the perturbations of the mind, and to set the affections in right tune" (YP 1:816–17).

32. Preface to *Samson* (*Complete Shorter Poems*, 461).

Notes to Chapter Six

1. Thomas Holt White, ed., *Areopagitica: A Speech to the Parliament of England, for the Liberty of Unlicensed Printing*, by John Milton; with prefatory remarks, copious notes, and excursive illustrations, by T. Holt White, Esq., to which is subjoined, A Tract sur la Liberté de la Presse, imité de L'Angloise de Milton, par Le Comte de Mirabeau (London, 1819), liv.

2. Thomas Hobbes, *Leviathan*, ed. Richard Tuck (Cambridge: Cambridge University Press, 1996), 91; hereafter cited in the text.

3. John Locke, *Two Treatises of Government*, ed. Peter Laslett (1960; repr., Cambridge: Cambridge University Press, 1988), 269; hereafter cited in the text.

4. In *Philosophicall Rudiments concerning Government and Society* (London, 1651), Hobbes notes that "the greatest part of those men who have written ought concerning Commonwealths, either suppose, or require us, or beg of us to believe, That Man is a Creature born fit for society," a position he heartily rejects. Rather than forming societies out of mutual good will, they form them out of mutual fear, which "consists partly in the natural equality of men, partly in their mutuall will of hurting: whence it comes to pass that we can neither expect from others, nor promise to our selves the least security" (C5v). Since even the weakest person is able to kill the strongest, all are essentially equal and choose by contract to limit their rights mutually. A contract becomes a covenant when those rights are conveyed not just for a single occasion, but as an agreement into the future (Dv, D2).

5. Tuck records an addition in a scribal manuscript reading that makes the point more explicit: "They beare downe not onely Religion w[hich] they reduce to Private fancy but also the Civill government that would uphold it reducing it to the naturall Condition of Private force" (*Leviathan*, 86n2).

6. Tufte, *Artful Sentences*, 208.

7. Hobbes argues for the privacy of personal belief, since "Faith hath no relation to, nor dependence at all upon Compulsion, or Commandement," and even if civil power were to forbid a belief in Christ, "such forbidding is of no effect; because Beleef, and Unbeleef never follow mens Commands. Faith is a gift of God, which Man can neither give, nor take away by promise of rewards or menace of

torture" (*Leviathan*, 342, 343). Private belief stems from faith, and "*Faith* is a part of Christian Doctrine, which is not comprehended under the title of a *Law*; for Lawes are made, and given, in reference to such *actions* as follow our will, not in order to our *opinions*, and *Beliefs*, which being out of our power, follow not the Will" (Hobbes, *Philosophicall Rudiments*, E12–E12v).

8. *Civil Power*'s full title sums up Milton's position: *A Treatise of Civil Power in Ecclesiastical causes: A Shewing that it is not lawfull for any power on earth to compel in matters or Religion* (1659) (YP 8:238).

9. Locke's *Two Treatises of Government* have the effect of countering many of Hobbes's arguments, but its immediate response was to Robert Filmer's popular monarchist arguments in *Patriarcha* (1680). In the *First Treatise*, Locke takes on Filmer's claim that monarchal authority descends from the fatherhood of Adam, noting (among other things) that the argument from fatherhood should include mothers, who have "an equal share, if not the greater" in bringing forth and raising children (180). Throughout, Locke seems dismissive of biblical arguments, believing they are too often twisted to suit the prejudices of the moment. His arguments about and on behalf of political society are secular; religion is not a part of them. See, e.g., 2.8, "Of the Beginning of Political Societies" (*Two Treatises*, 330–49). Nothing in Locke parallels Hobbes's "Christian Commonwealth," the extended subject of *Leviathan*, part 3.

10. In *Eikonoklastes*, Milton assumes something like Locke's view of private property, taking it as a given that "those fruits, which our industry and labours have made upon our own," are no "Privilege" granted by the king, but the product of legal rights made by "free born Englishmen." Milton scorns the audacity of a king known to favor those who preached "that the Subject had no property of his own goods, but that all was the Kings right" (YP 3:573–74). In the same work, even as Milton berates the king's borrowing of Pamela's prayer from that "vain amatorious Poem of Sr *Philip Sidneys Arcadia*," he asserts the right of authors to their own work: "But leaving what might justly be offensive to God, it was a trespass also more then usual against human right, which commands that every Author have the property of his own work reservd to him after death as well as living" (YP 3:362, 364–65). Milton's awareness of national political economies is evident throughout the "State Papers" he produced for the commonwealth government between 1549 and 1559 (YP 5, part 2).

11. For example, *Leviathan*, chapter 9, "Of the Severall Subjects of Knowledge," 60–61.

12. John Locke, *An Essay concerning Human Understanding* (London, 1694), F3–F3v.

13. John Locke, *Some Thoughts concerning Education* (London, 1693), O8.

14. Scott, *Algernon Sidney*, 1–2. Algernon Sidney's *Discourses*, like Locke's *First Treatise*, was a response to Filmer's *Patriarcha*. Sidney's views were in many ways closer to Milton's than to Locke's, as Scott suggests, esp. 21–31.

15. Hobbes, "The Answer of Mr. Hobbes," D7, D7v. For Sir Philip Sidney's very different view of imitating nature, see my chapter 2 above.

16. As famously stated by Alexander Pope's *Essay on Man*: "Know then thyself, presume not God to scan; / The proper study of mankind is Man" (2.1.1–2). Samuel Johnson's *Life of Milton* takes Milton to task on many fronts, from his religion to his perceived inconsistencies, and includes the disparagement of *Lycidas* that sounds like Hobbes's appreciation for both realism and novelty: "in this poem there is no nature, for there is no truth; there is no art, for there is nothing new"; see Samuel Johnson, *The Lives of the Most Eminent English Poets* (London, 1783), 1.218.

17. The first decade of the new millennium saw a number of books arguing for Milton's continuing relevance, as I do here. But I would also be cautionary: the figure of Milton, like the idea of freedom, is multidimensional and ultimately elusive. In addition to Wittreich, *Why Milton Matters*, and Fish, *How Milton Works*, see Nigel Smith, *Is Milton Better Than Shakespeare?* (Cambridge, MA: Harvard University Press, 2008). This last got some of the popular notice its title was meant to provoke, but the book itself makes a serious case for the continuing importance of Milton alongside Shakespeare.

18. Lewalski, *Life of John Milton*, 244–46.

19. Alien largely in their avoidance of religion: "It was generally held that to offer religion to a Whig was the equivalent of offering garlic to a vampire…. [Whigs were] not so much against religion as oblivious to it"; see L. G. Mitchell, *The Whig World: 1760–1837* (New York: Hambledon London, 2005), 115. Religious "enthusiasm" was distrusted both as a relic of the troubled civil wars and as alien to eighteenth century rationalism. Milton certainly would have approved the republican tendencies of the Whigs, however. See Skinner, *Liberty before Liberalism*, 72–76.

20. Lewalski, *Life of John Milton*, 541.

21. That is, between a neo-Roman view of liberty as free citizens constructing free states whose laws ensure the general good and maximize personal agency, versus "the liberal analysis of negative

liberty in terms of the absence of coercive impediments," a definition derived from Hobbes, and essentially Isaiah Berlin's "negative liberty," which he separates from ideas of justice and equality (Skinner, *Liberty before Liberalism*, 112–13). See note 52 below.

22. *Milton: Areopagitica*, ed. with introduction by John W. Hales (1875; repr., Oxford: Clarendon Press, 1928). Other editions include 1878, 1882, 1927, and 1949; citations will be taken from the introduction to the 1928 edition. Hales was a professor of English language and literature (one of the first) at King's College, University of London, and had been a fellow and tutor at Cambridge, as well as a barrister of Lincoln's Inn. His introduction argues for at least some influence of the text during the seventeenth century, and for the work's continuing importance to freedom of thought. For the Grolier club edition, see *Areopagitica, a Speech of Mr. John Milton*, with introduction by James Russell Lowell (New York: Grolier Club, 1890). Though Lowell acknowledges that "no man was farther from being a democrat in the modern sense" than Milton, he cannot help but admire the poetic "spirit that pours through the 'Areopagitica' as through a trumpet sounding the charge against whatever is base and recreant, whether in the world about us or in the ambush of our own natures" (xxxii, xlvi–xlvii). For a full list of editions, see Ernest Sirluck's preface in YP 2:480–81.

23. John Milton, *Areopagitica: A Speech to the Parliament of England, for the Liberty of Unlicens'd Printing*. First Published in the Year 1644. With a preface, by another hand [James Thomson] (London: Printed for A. Millar, 1738). Millar was a Whig publisher and Thomson's own, and also did a complete collected *Prose Works* of Milton in 1738; the definitive 1749 edition of Milton's poetical works, edited by Thomas Newton and printed by the Tonson heirs, was dedicated to the Earl of Bath, who as Sir William Pulteney had been the long-time leader of the reform wing of the Whig party and was himself a great advocate of a free press, even though he was often mercilessly ridiculed by it.

24. William Levine, "Collins, Thomson, and the Whig Progress of Liberty," *Studies in English Literature* 34, no. 3 (Summer 1994): 553.

25. James Sambrook, *James Thomson, 1700–1748: A Life* (Oxford: Clarendon Press, 1991), 36, 173–74. See also Sambrook's editions of Thomson's *The Seasons* (Oxford: Clarendon Press, 1981), and Thomson's *Liberty, The Castle of Indolence and Other Poems* (Oxford: Clarendon Press, 1986). Citations of the relevant poems are from these editions.

26. Sambrook, *James Thomson*, 173.

27. Adam Smith, *An Inquiry into the Nature and Causes of the Wealth of Nations* (London, 1776).

28. From Cato Institute, "Cato's Mission," www.cato.org/mission; and American Enterprise Institute, "AEI's Organization and Purpose," www.aei.org/about.

29. Catharine Macauley, *A Modest Plea for the Property of Copyright* (Bath, 1774), 26. L. Bently and M. Kretschmer, eds., *Primary Sources on Copyright (1450–1900)*, www.copyrighthistory.org. Macauley's interpretation of freedom has a neo-republican flavor, as she rejects the idea that a dependent author can be relied upon: "If literary property becomes common, we can have but two kinds of authors, men in opulence and men in dependance" (37), and "can that instruction be edifying which falls from a venal pen, exerted merely to earn the favor of a patron?" (42).

30. *Dictionary of National Biography* (Oxford: Oxford University Press, 2004), Brydges (K. A. Manley, 8:416–18); Nott (Rosemary Mitchell, 41:213–14); Todd (D. A. Brunton, 54:879–82). Todd's edition of Milton, *Poetical Works of John Milton* (London, 1801) is dedicated to Francis, Duke of Bridgewater, "in humble but grateful acknowledgement of the assistance afforded him by his Grace's library, and of other favors conferred." The Huntington Library in California now has that library, including the Bridgewater copies of Todd's various editions.

31. Todd, *Poetical Works of John Milton*, 1:a1r; 1:x (b5v).

32. Ibid., 1:xlviii (d8v), lv–lvi (e4–e4v). Newton's edition of *Poetical Works of John Milton* (London, 1749) had been the standard through most of the eighteenth century.

33. William Wordsworth, *Poems in Two Volumes, and Other Poems, 1800–1807*, ed. Jared Curtis (Ithaca, NY: Cornell University Press, 1983), 165.

34. The European view of English liberty by this time was that "it was a personal possession, something somehow private." See, e.g., Langford, *Englishness Identified*, 275.

35. Percy Bysshe Shelley, "Sonnet: England in 1819," in *The Complete Poetical Works of Percy Bysshe Shelley*, ed. Thomas Hutchinson (Oxford: Oxford University Press, 1919), 570.

36. *Letters to William Paley, M.A. Archdeacon of Carlisle, on His Objections to a Reform in the Representation of the Commons, And on His Apology for the Influence of the Crown in Parliament, being strictures on the Essay upon the British Constitution introduced in his principles of Moral and Political Philosophy*. Published anonymously, but the Huntington copy is bound with Thomas Holt White's *Review of Johnson's Criticism on the Style of Milton's English Prose* (London: R. Hunter, 1818); interestingly, this volume concludes with an advertisement: "Speedily will be published, by R. Hunter, *Areopagitica* [etc.])." The attribution of the *Letters* is confirmed by Algernon Holt White, who has written his father's

name on the title page of the Huntington copy and described the two works on an endpaper with his signature. In *Review of Johnson's Criticism*, Holt White takes on Samuel Johnson for not appreciating Milton's style, particularly the Latinate diction and structures to which Johnson objects in his *Life of Milton*.

37. Houghton Library MS Eng. 731, and Hampshire Public Record Office, papers associated with Gilbert White and Family.

38. *Dictionary of National Biography*, 8:739.

39. White, introduction to *Areopagitica*, xxv–xxvi, li.

40. By 1819 parliamentary reform movements, including those associated with Burdett and another with James Mill (John Stuart Mill's father) and Jeremy Bentham, rejected the Whig party itself along with the Tories. According to Major Cartwright, "Whatever may be the language of partisans, from either direct selfishness or egregious folly, the nation at large has no hope whatever, in respect of its liberties, from either party." Cited in A. D. Harvey, *Britain in the Early Nineteenth Century* (New York: St. Martin's Press, 1978). Burdett's group attacked the "borough-mongering oligarchy" rather than the crown, though Bentham's group saw the monarchy as the greater evil; see J. R. Dinwiddy, *Radicalism and Reform in Britain, 1780–1850* (London: Hambledon Press, 1992), 281. From a broader perspective, though, White's politics may be seen in the light of the Whig-led reforms of the earlier nineteenth century that accomplished the abolition of slavery, Catholic enfranchisement, and the "constituency networks" that led to electoral reform. William Anthony Hay, *The Whig Revival, 1808–1830* (Basingstoke: Palgrave Macmillan, 2005), 8.

41. White, introduction to *Areopagitica*, lv–lvi. To show how well entrenched this view was to become, see the Hales introduction to his Victorian (and after) *Areopagitica*: "The attempt made to reimpose restrictions upon freedom of expressed thought, against which [Milton] raises his voice in the *Areopagitica* with so noble a vehemence, so that it will still be heard to the very end of time, was only too significant of the temper and tendencies of the Presbyterian rule that then lay on the country" (xiv).

42. Center for American Progress, "What We Believe," www.americanprogress.org/about/mission, accessed May 2013; emphasis mine.

43. Edward Arber, *English Reprints*, vol. 7, Milton's *Areopagitica*, ed. [Sir] R[ichard] C[laverhouse] (London: A. Murray and Son, 1868); R. C. Jebb, *Milton's Areopagitica: A Commentary* (Cambridge: Privately printed by C. J. Clay, M.A., at the University Press, 1872). The quote is written in Jebb's hand in the page after the title page in the Huntington Library copy.

44. Lewalski, *Life of John Milton*, 541.

45. Hales, introduction to *Areopagitica*, xxv.
46. Ibid., xliii. I have focused on the English tradition, but it is worth noting that an American edition from the 1920s also illustrates the pattern I have been suggesting, of Milton's invitational poetics allowing editorial interpretation suited to the editor's own opinions. *Areopagitica and Other Prose Writings*, ed. William Haller (New York, 1927), offers a can-do 1920s American individualism, as Haller reads *Areopagitica's* main points in his introduction: "we must be ever on the alert to know and understand the truth about ourselves and our world, not one man or one class of men at any one time for other men but each man for himself in every age by his own effort during each moment of existence. This is fate. Life is by necessity one continued act of choice between freedom and slavery. It is not enough that truth is; truth must be sought and chosen, and the whole of experience must be kept open to each man that he may seek and choose for himself." Haller appreciates Milton's radical individualism, but surely it would have surprised Milton to see it as "fate."
47. James Mill, John Stuart's influential father, was a colleague of Bentham and other free thinkers. Interestingly, in 1810 when John Stuart was about four, "the family lived briefly in the poet John Milton's former house." See Nicolas Capaldi, *John Stuart Mill: A Biography* (Cambridge: Cambridge University Press, 2004), 3. James Mill, who was responsible for his son's education, was not a fan of poetry, which John Stuart regretted in his *Autobiography*, but he did have the "highest admiration" for Milton (16–17).
48. John Stuart Mill, *On Liberty* (London: John W. Parker and Son, 1859), 7, 100, 119, 134–35. Vincent Blasi, the Corliss Lamont Professor of Civil Liberties at Columbia University, notes that Mill's argument in this work in favor of a wide-ranging free press is a "secular reformulation" of Milton's *Areopagitica* (1644). See Blasi, "Milton's *Areopagitica* and the Modern First Amendment," *Ideas of the First Amendment* (Toronto: Thomson/West, 2006), 102–07.
49. John Stuart Mill, *On Liberty* (1859), ed. David Bromwich and George Kateb (New Haven: Yale University Press, 2003), 102.
50. George Lakoff, *Whose Freedom? The Battle over America's Most Important Idea* (New York: Farrar, Straus and Giroux, 2006), 29, 36.
51. Philip Pettit, *Republicanism: A Theory of Freedom and Government* (Oxford: Oxford University Press, 1997), 2, 4.
52. Isaiah Berlin, *Liberty*, ed. Henry Hardy (Oxford: Oxford University Press, 2002), 170, 178, 172. For differences with Berlin, see, e.g., Orlando Patterson, who finds "positive" and "negative" freedoms simplistic and ahistorical, and instead posits tensions among three kinds of freedom that he calls "personal, civic and

sovereignal," in *Freedom and the Making of Western Culture* (New York: Basic Books, 1991), 5, and Lakoff, *Whose Freedom?*, 76, who sees social conditions such as fairness and justice as essential to freedom.

53. Michael J. Sandel, *Justice: What's the Right Thing to Do?* (New York: Farrar, Straus and Giroux, 2009), 220–21. Acknowledging that we live in a culture that defines and values freedom as individual choice, Sandel argues that "freedom of choice—even freedom of choice under fair conditions—is [not] an adequate basis for a just society."

54. Pettit, *Republicanism*, 271.

55. Steven Pinker, *How the Mind Works* (New York: W. W. Norton, 1997), and *The Blank Slate: The Modern Denial of Human Nature* (New York: Penguin Putnam, 2002); Penrose, *Shadows of the Mind*; Richard Dawkins, *The Blind Watchmaker* (1986; repr., New York: W. W. Norton, 1991); and Michael Gazzinaga, *Who's in Charge? Free Will and the Science of the Brain* (New York: Ecco Press, 2011). Sam Harris, *Free Will* (New York: Free Press, 2012), draws on this work and states simply, "free will is an illusion" (5). A belief in free will in the face of determinism is called "compatibilism," which philosophers trace to Thomas Hobbes in *Leviathan* (1651) and later to David Hume. The atheist David Dennett, *Freedom Evolves* (New York: Viking, 2003), a specialist in philosophy of mind and philosophy of science, makes the modern compatibilist argument. For a philosophical analysis of the origins and issues of free will and compatibilism, see Michael McKenna, "Compatibilism," in *Stanford Encyclopedia of Philosophy*, 2004, plato.stanford.edu/entries/compatibilism.

56. Lewalski describes "Milton's epic universe" as "monist, exhibiting the 'animist materialism' that Milton sketched out in *De Doctrina Christiana* as a response to Hobbesian mechanistic and deterministic materialism" (*Life of John Milton*, 475). See also, e.g., Regina Schwartz, *Remembering and Repeating: On Milton's Theology and Poetics* (Chicago: University of Chicago Press, 1988), and Rogers, *Matter of Revolution*, 112–22, which argues for Milton's monistic vitalism. For a contrasting argument, see Sugimura, *Matter of Glorious Trial*, xxiii–xxiv, 55.

57. E. J. Lowe, *An Introduction to the Philosophy of Mind* (Cambridge: Cambridge University Press, 2000), 257.

58. Gazzinaga, *Who's in Charge?*, 141, argues that although free will is illusory, we do have responsibility to the social group because our brains "are wired from birth for social interactions" (144), so that we need to "incorporate social dynamics into personal choice" (178). Similarly, Pinker in *The Blank Slate* argues against the Lockean *tabula rasa* on the grounds that the evolutionary

human brain is at once complex, individual, and active (see, e.g., 197–98). See also Harris, *Free Will*, and the response by Michael Shermer, "Free Won't: Volition as Self-Control Exerts Veto Power over Impulses," *Scientific American* (Aug. 2012): 86, and the follow-up discussion in the comments at www.scientificamerican.com/article.cfm?id=how-free-will-collides-with-unconscious-impulses.

59. Lowe, *An Introduction*, 175, 183.

60. As a result, "Science is guaranteed to eat away at the will, *regardless* of what it finds, because the scientific mode cannot accommodate the mysterious notion of uncaused causation that underlies the will.... Free will is an idealization of human beings that makes the ethics game playable.... Science and morality are separate spheres of reasoning" (Pinker, *How the Mind Works*, 54–55).

61. Elizabeth Fowler, *Literary Character: The Human Figure in Early English Writing* (Ithaca, NY: Cornell University Press, 2003), 1–5; Marshall Grossman, *"Authors to Themselves": Milton and the Revelation of History* (Cambridge: Cambridge University Press, 1987), 179. Grossman describes how Milton's poetic narrative seeks to negotiate the intersections of time and eternity, ultimately in service of creating characters, and I would add readers, free to create themselves: "Two stories—one of 'man's first disobedience' and the other of 'one greater man'—are entwined so that each provides the hermeneutic necessary for the interpretation of the other in a dialectic of personal and apocalyptic eschatologies. The rhetoric that accomplishes this suturing of two stories performs the conflation of reading and writing implied by the notion of 'self-authorship.' The rhetorical pivots at which Milton's narrative turns from a temporally situated vision to an eternal and universal one locate the privileged moments at which the Miltonic subject authors itself by freely enacting the judgments and choices it makes in accord with its providential role" (178–79).

Works Cited

Achinstein, Sharon. *Literature and Dissent in Milton's England.* Cambridge: Cambridge University Press, 2003.

Achinstein, Sharon, and Elizabeth Sauer, eds. *Milton and Toleration.* Oxford: Oxford University Press, 2007.

Alvis, John, ed. *Areopagitica and Other Political Writings of John Milton.* Chicago: Liberty Fund, 1999.

Arber, Edward. *English Reprints.* London: A. Murray and Son, 1868.

Aristotle. *Poetics.* Translated by S. H. Butcher. Edited by Francis Fergusson. New York: Hill and Wang, 1961.

———. *The Politics.* Translated by T. A. Sinclair. New York: Penguin, 1981.

Ascham, Roger. *The scholemaster or plaine and perfite way of teaching children, to vnderstand, write, and speake, the Latin tong, but specially purposed for the priuate bringing vp of youth in jentlemen and noble mens houses, and commodious also for all such, as haue forgot the Latin tonge.* London, 1570.

———. *The Scholemaster.* Edited by Lawrence V. Ryan. Ithaca, NY: Cornell University Press for the Folger Shakespeare Library, 1967.

Attridge, Derek. *Well-Weighed Syllables: Elizabethan Verse in Classical Metres.* Cambridge: Cambridge University Press, 1974.

Augustine, Saint. *On Free Choice of the Will.* Translated by Thomas Williams. Indianapolis: Hackett, 1993.

Aylmer, John. *An Harborowe for Faithfull and Trewe Subjects.* Strasburg, 1559.

Baker, John H. *The Legal Profession and the Common Law.* London: Hambledon Press, 1986.

Bellarmine, Cardinal Robert. *Catechism.* Translated by Richard Haydock. 1602.

Belsey, Catherine. *John Milton: Language, Gender, Power.* Oxford: Basil Blackwell, 1988.

Bennett, Joan. "Reading *Samson Agonistes.*" In *The Cambridge Companion to Milton*, ed. Dennis Danielson, 219–35. Cambridge: Cambridge University Press, 1999.

Bently, L., and M. Kretschmer, eds. *Primary Sources on Copyright (1450–1900).* www.copyrighthistory.org.

Berlin, Isaiah. *Liberty.* Edited by Henry Hardy. Oxford: Oxford University Press, 2002.

Berry, Lloyd E. *John Stubbs's Gaping Gulf, with Letters and Other Relevant Documents.* Charlottesville: University of Virginia Press for the Folger Shakespeare Library, 1968.

Blake, N. F. *A History of the English Language.* New York: New York University Press, 1996.

Blasi, Vincent. *Ideas of the First Amendment.* Toronto: Thomson/West, 2006.

———. "Milton's *Areopagitica* and the Modern First Amendment." Third Annual Ralph Gregory Elliot First Amendment Lecture at Yale Law School. March 1995. www.law.yale.edu/documents/pdf/Milton.pdf.

Brown, Cedric. *Milton's Aristocratic Entertainments.* Cambridge: Cambridge University Press, 1985.

———. "Milton's Ludlow Mask." In *The Cambridge Companion to Milton*, ed. Dennis Danielson. Cambridge: Cambridge University Press, 1999.

Brown, Eric C. "'The Melting Voice through Mazes Running': The Dissolution of Borders in *L'Allegro* and *Il Penseroso.*" In *Milton Studies*, vol. 40, ed. Albert C. Labriola, 1–18. Pittsburgh: University of Pittsburgh Press, 2001.

Bryson, Michael. *The Tyranny of Heaven: Milton's Rejection of God as King.* Newark: University of Delaware Press, 2004.

Burdick, Sanford. *The Dividing Muse: Images of Sacred Disjunction in Milton's Poetry.* New Haven: Yale University Press, 1985.

Burgess, Glenn. *British Political Thought, 1500–1660: The Politics of the Post-Reformation.* New York: Palgrave Macmillan, 2009.

———. *The Politics of the Ancient Constitution: An Introduction to British Political Thought, 1603–1642.* University Park: Pennsylvania State University Press, 1993.

Bury, J. B. *A History of the Freedom of Thought.* Cambridge: Cambridge University Press, 1913.

Calvin, John. *Cathechisme.* London, 1582.

———. *Institutes of the Christian Religion.* Translated by Henry Beveridge. Grand Rapids, MI: Eerdmans, 1989.

———. *Sermons of John Calvin upon the Epistle to the Ephesians.* Translated by Arthur Golding. London, 1577.

Capaldi, Nicolas. *John Stuart Mill: A Biography.* Cambridge: Cambridge University Press, 2004.

Carey, John. *John Milton.* New York: Arco, 1970.

———. "Milton's Satan." In *The Cambridge Companion to Milton,* ed. Dennis Danielson, 160–74. Cambridge: Cambridge University Press, 1999.

———. "A Work in Praise of Terrorism? September 11 and *Samson Agonistes.*" *Times Literary Supplement,* September 6, 2002.

Castiglione, Count Baldessar. *The Courtyer of Count Baldessar Castilio.* Translated by Thomas Hoby. London, 1561.

Chambers, A. M. *A Constitutional History of England.* London: Methuen, 1909.

Coiro, Ann Baynes. "'A Thousand Fantasies': The Lady and the Maske." In *The Oxford Handbook of Milton,* ed. Nicholas McDowell and Nigel Smith. Oxford: Oxford University Press, 2009.

Collinson, Patrick. "The Monarchical Republic of Queen Elizabeth I." *Bulletin of the John Rylands University Library of Manchester* 69 (1987): 394–424.

Corns, Thomas N. "John Milton, Roger Williams, and the Limits of Toleration." In *Milton and Toleration,* ed. Sharon Achinstein and Elizabeth Sauer, 72–85. Oxford: Oxford University Press, 2007.

Corns, Thomas N., ed. *The Milton Encyclopedia.* New Haven: Yale University Press, 2012.

Creaser, John. "Prosodic Style and Conceptions of Liberty in Milton and Marvell." *Milton Quarterly* 34, no. 1 (2000): 1–13.

———. "Prosody and Liberty in Milton and Marvell." In *Milton and the Terms of Liberty*, ed. Graham Parry and Joad Raymond, 37–55. Cambridge: D. S. Brewer, 2002.

Cressy, David. *England on Edge: Crisis and Revolution, 1640–1642*. Oxford: Oxford University Press, 2006.

Cummings, Brian. "Metalepsis: The Boundaries of Metaphor." In *Renaissance Figures of Speech*, ed. Sylvia Adamson et al., 217–33. Cambridge: Cambridge University Press, 2007.

Cummins, Juliet, ed. *Milton and the Ends of Time*. Cambridge: Cambridge University Press, 2003.

Danielson, Dennis. *Milton's Good God: A Study in Literary Theodicy*. Cambridge: Cambridge University Press, 1982.

Danielson, Dennis, ed. *The Cambridge Companion to Milton*. Cambridge: Cambridge University Press, 1999.

Davenant, William. *Gondibert: An Heroick Poem*. London, 1651.

Dawkins, Richard. *The Blind Watchmaker*. 1986. Reprint, New York: W. W. Norton, 1991.

Dennett, David. *Freedom Evolves*. New York: Viking, 2003.

Dietz, Michael. "'Thus Sang the Uncouth Swain': Pastoral, Prophecy, and Historicism in *Lycidas*." In *Milton Studies*, vol. 35, ed. Albert C. Labriola, 42–72. Pittsburgh: University of Pittsburgh Press, 1997.

Dinwiddy, J. R. *Radicalism and Reform in Britain, 1780–1850*. London: Hambledon Press, 1992.

Dobranski, Stephen B., and John P. Rumrich, eds. *Milton and Heresy*. Cambridge: Cambridge University Press, 1998.

Duncan-Jones, Katherine. *Sir Philip Sidney, Courtier Poet*. New Haven: Yale University Press, 1991.

Duncan-Jones, Katherine, ed. *Sir Philip Sidney*. Oxford: Oxford University Press, 1989.

DuRocher, Richard J. "Hermes's Blessed Retreat: Rival Views of Learning in *Paradise Regained*." In *Milton's Rival Hermeneutics: "Reason Is But Choosing,"* ed. Richard J. DuRocher and Margaret Thickstun, 225–37. Pittsburgh: Duquesne University Press, 2012.

DuRocher, Richard J., and Margaret Thickstun, eds. *Milton's Rival Hermeneutics: "Reason Is But Choosing."* Pittsburgh: Duquesne University Press, 2012.

Dzelzainis, Martin. "Milton's Classical Republicanism." In *Milton and Republicanism*, ed. David Armitage, Armand Himy, and

Quentin Skinner. Cambridge: Cambridge University Press, 1995.

Dzelzainis, Martin, ed. *Milton: Political Writings.* Cambridge: Cambridge University Press, 1991.

Eccles, Mark. "Burghley." In *The Spenser Encyclopedia,* ed. A. C. Hamilton et al. Toronto: University of Toronto Press, 1990.

Edwards, Karen L. "The 'World' of *Paradise Lost."* In *The Oxford Handbook of Milton,* ed. Nicholas McDowell and Nigel Smith, 496–509. Oxford: Oxford University Press, 2009.

Elizabeth I, Queen. *Elizabeth I: Autograph Compositions and Foreign Language Original.* Edited by Janel Mueller and Leah S. Marcus. Chicago: University of Chicago Press, 2003.

———. *Queen Elizabeth I: Selected Works.* Edited by Steven May. New York: Washington Square Press, 2004.

Elton, G. R. *The Parliament of England, 1559–1581.* Cambridge: Cambridge University Press, 1986.

———. "The Rule of Law in Sixteenth-Century England." *Studies in Tudor and Stuart Politics.* Cambridge: Cambridge University Press, 1974.

Elyot, Sir Thomas. *The Boke Named the Governour.* London, 1531.

Empson, William. *Milton's God.* London: Chatto and Windus, 1961.

Erasmus. *Erasmus-Luther Discourse on Free Will.* Translated and edited by Ernst F. Winter. 1961. Reprint, London: Continuum 1999.

Evans, J. Martin. "Lycidas." In *The Cambridge Companion to Milton,* ed. Dennis Danielson, 39–53. Cambridge: Cambridge University Press, 1999.

———. *The Road from Horton: Looking Backwards in "Lycidas."* Victoria: University of Victoria Press, 1998.

Fallon, Stephen M. "'Elect above the Rest': Theology as Self-Representation in Milton." In *Milton and Heresy,* ed. Stephen B. Dobranski and John P. Rumrich, 93–116. Cambridge: Cambridge University Press, 1998.

———. *Milton among the Philosophers: Poetry and Materialism in Seventeenth-Century England.* Ithaca, NY: Cornell University Press, 1991.

———. *Milton's Peculiar Grace: Self-Representation and Authority.* Ithaca, NY: Cornell University Press, 2007.

———. "Satan." In *The Milton Encyclopedia,* ed. Thomas N. Corns, 330. New Haven: Yale University Press, 2012.

———. "'The Strangest Piece of Reason': Milton's *Tenure of Kings and Magistrates.*" In *The Oxford Handbook of Milton*, ed. Nicholas McDowell and Nigel Smith, 241–51. Oxford: Oxford University Press, 2009.

Fatovic, Clement. "The Anti-Catholic Roots of Liberal and Republican Conceptions of Freedom in English Political Thought." *Journal of the History of Ideas* 66 (Jan. 2005): 37–59.

Feroli, Teresa. "Rethinking 'shee for God in him': *Paradise Lost* and Milton's Quaker Contemporaries." In *Milton's Rival Hermeneutics: "Reason Is But Choosing,"* ed. Richard J. DuRocher and Margaret Thickstun, 159–81. Pittsburgh: Duquesne University Press, 2012.

Finch, Casey, and Peter Bowen. "The Solitary Companionship of *L'Allegro* and *Il Penseroso.*" In *Milton Studies*, vol. 26, ed. James D. Simmonds, 3–24. Pittsburgh: University of Pittsburgh Press, 1990.

Fish, Stanley. "Driving from the Letter: Truth and Indeterminacy in Milton's *Areopagitica.*" In *Re-Membering Milton*, ed. Mary Nyquist and Margaret Ferguson, 234–54. New York: Methuen, 1988.

———. *How Milton Works.* Cambridge, MA: Harvard University Press, 2001.

———. "Problem Solving in *Comus.*" In *Illustrious Evidence: Approaches to English Literature of the Earlier Seventeenth Century*, ed. Earl Miner, 93–113. Berkeley and Los Angeles: University of California Press, 1975.

———. *Surprised by Sin: Milton and the Reader of "Paradise Lost."* London: Macmillan, 1967.

———. "'There Is Nothing He Cannot Ask': Milton, Liberalism, and Terrorism." In *Milton in the Age of Fish: Essays on Authorship, Text, and Criticism*, ed. Michael Lieb and Albert C. Labriola, 243–64. Pittsburgh: Duquesne University Press, 2006.

Fisher, David Hackett. *Liberty and Freedom: A Visual History of America's Founding Ideas.* New York: Oxford University Press, 2005.

Fletcher, Anthony. *Gender, Sex and Subordination in England, 1500–1800.* New Haven: Yale University Press, 1995.

Fowler, Alastair. *Kinds of Literature: An Introduction to the Theory of Genres and Modes.* Cambridge, MA: Harvard University Press, 1982.

Fowler, Elizabeth. *Literary Character: The Human Figure in Early English Writing.* Ithaca, NY: Cornell University Press, 2003.

Fraunce, Abraham. *The Arcadian Rhetoricke.* London, 1588.

Frye, Roland Mushat. "Satan." In *A Milton Encyclopedia,* ed. William B. Hunter et al., 7:166–69. Lewisburg, PA: Bucknell University Press, 1978–81.

Friedman, Donald. "Comus and the Truth of the Ear." In *The Muses Common-Weale,* ed. Claude Summers and Ted-Larry Pebworth, 119–32. Columbia: University of Missouri Press, 1989.

Fulton, Thomas. *Historical Milton: Manuscript, Print, and Political Culture in Revolutionary England.* Amherst: University of Massachusetts Press, 2010.

Gascoigne, George. *Certayne Notes of Instruction.* London, 1575.

Gazzinaga, Michael. *Who's in Charge? Free Will and the Science of the Brain.* New York: Ecco Press, 2011.

Goodman, Christopher. *How Superior Powers Ought to Be Obeyed.* 1558.

Griffiths, Jane. *John Skelton and Poetic Authority: Defining the Liberty to Speak.* Oxford: Oxford University Press, 2006.

Grossman, Marshall. *"Authors to Themselves": Milton and the Revelation of History.* Cambridge: Cambridge University Press, 1987.

Hadfield, Andrew. *Shakespeare and Republicanism.* Cambridge: Cambridge University Press, 2005.

Hadow, G. E., ed. *Sir Walter Raleigh: Selections from His Historie of the World, His Letters, etc.* Oxford: Clarendon Press, 1917.

Hale, John K. *Milton's Languages: The Impact of Multilingualism on Style.* Cambridge: Cambridge University Press, 1997.

Hales, John W., ed. and intro. *Milton: Areopagitica.* 1875. Reprint, Oxford: Clarendon Press, 1928.

Halley, Janet. "Female Autonomy in Milton's Sexual Politics." In *Milton and the Idea of Woman,* ed. Julia Walker, 230–53 (Urbana: University of Illinois Press, 1988.

Hamilton, A. C. *Sir Philip Sidney: A Study of His Life and Works.* Cambridge: Cambridge University Press, 1977.

Hamilton, A. C. et al., ed. *The Spenser Encyclopedia.* Toronto: University of Toronto Press, 1990.

Hannay, Margaret P. *Philip's Phoenix.* New York: Oxford University Press, 1990.

Harrington, Sir John, trans. "Preface, or rather a Brief Apology of Poetry" to Ariosto's *Orlando Furioso*. London, 1591.

Harris, Sam. *Free Will*. New York: Free Press, 2012.

Harvey, A. D. *Britain in the Early Nineteenth Century*. New York: St. Martin's Press, 1978.

Hay, William Anthony. *The Whig Revival, 1808–1830*. Basingstoke: Palgrave Macmillan, 2005.

Helgerson, Richard. *Self-Crowned Laureates: Spenser, Jonson, Milton, and the Literary System*. Berkeley and Los Angeles: University of California Press, 1983.

Herman, Peter. *Destabilizing Milton: "Paradise Lost" and the Poetics of Incertitude*. London: Palgrave Macmillan, 2008.

———. *Royal Poetrie: Monarchic Verse and the Political Imaginary of Early Modern England*. Ithaca, NY: Cornell University Press, 2010.

———. "When Is a Defense Not a Defense? Sidney's Paradoxical *Apology for Poetry*." *Squitter-wits and Muse-haters: Sidney, Spenser, Milton, and Renaissance Antipoetic Sentiment*. Detroit: Wayne State University Press, 1996.

———. "'Whose Fault, Whose but His Own?': *Paradise Lost*, Negligence, and the Problem of Cause." In *The New Milton Criticism*, ed. Peter S. Herman and Elizabeth Sauer, 49–67. Cambridge: Cambridge University Press, 2012.

Herman, Peter S., and Elizabeth Sauer, eds. *The New Milton Criticism*. Cambridge: Cambridge University Press, 2012.

Hill, Christopher. *The Century of Revolution, 1603–1714*. Rev. ed. London: Routledge, 1980.

———. *Liberty against the Law*. London: Allen Lane, 1996.

———. *Milton and the English Revolution*. London: Macmillan, 1977.

———. *The World Turned Upside Down*. London: Penguin, 1984.

Hobbes, Thomas. "The Answer of Mr. Hobbes to Sr. Will. Davenant's Preface before Gondibert." In William Davenant, *Gondibert: An Heroick Poem*. London, 1651.

———. *Leviathan*. Edited by Richard Tuck. Cambridge: Cambridge University Press, 1996.

———. *Leviathan; or, The Matter, Forme and Power of a Common-Wealth Ecclesiastical and Civil*. London: Printed for Andrew Crooke, 1651.

———. *Philosophicall Rudiments concerning Government and Society.* London, 1651.

Hughes, Merritt Y., ed. *Milton: Complete Poems and Major Prose.* New York: Odyssey Press, 1957.

Hunter, William B. et al. *A Milton Encyclopedia.* Lewisburg, PA: Bucknell University Press, 1978–81.

Hurstfield, Joel. *Freedom, Corruption and Government in Tudor England.* London: Jonathan Cape, 1973.

Illo, John. "Areopagiticus Mythic and Real." *Prose Studies* 11 (1988): 3–23.

James VI and I, King. *Basilikon Doron; or, His Majesties Instructions to his Dearest Sonne, Henry the Prince.* Edinburgh: Printed by Robert Walde-grave, Printer to the Kings Majestie, 1603.

———. *The Lawe of Free Monarchies; or, The Reciprock and mutuall dutie betwixt a free King, and his naturall Subjectes.* London: Printed by [Thomas Creede for] Robert Waldengrave, Printer to the Kings most excellent Majestie, 1603.

———. *A remonstrance of the most gratious King Iames I. King of Great Brittaine, France, and Ireland, defender of the faith, &c. For the right of kings, and the independance of their crownes. Against an oration of the most illustrious Card. of Perron, pronounced in the chamber of the third estate. Ian. 15. 1615. Translated out of his Maiesties French copie.* Cambridge: Printed by Cantrell Legge, printer to the Universitie of Cambridge, 1616.

Jebb, R. C. *Milton's Areopagitica: A Commentary.* Cambridge: Privately printed by C. J. Clay, M.A., at the University Press, 1872.

Johnson, Paula. *Form and Transformation in Music and Poetry of the English Renaissance.* New Haven: Yale University Press, 1972.

Johnson, Samuel. *The Lives of the Most Eminent English Poets.* London, 1783.

Jonson, Ben. *Ben Jonson.* Edited by Ian Donaldson. Oxford: Oxford University Press, 1985.

Joseph, Sister Miriam. *Shakespeare's Use of the Arts of Language.* New York: Hafner, 1947.

Judson, Alexander Corbin. *A Biographical Sketch of John Young, Bishop of Rochester, with Emphasis on His Relations with Edmund Spenser.* Bloomington: Indiana University Studies, 103:21, March 1934.

Juvenal. *The Sixteen Satires of Juvenal.* Translated by Peter Green. London: Penguin, 1982.

Kahn, Victoria. "The Metaphorical Contract in Milton's *Tenure of Kings and Magistrates*." In *Milton and Republicanism*, ed. David Armitage, Armand Himy, and Quentin Skinner, 82–105. Cambridge: Cambridge University Press, 1995.

Kelley, Mark R., Michael Lieb, and John T. Shawcross, eds. *Milton and the Grounds of Contention*. Pittsburgh: Duquesne University Press, 2003.

Knox, John. *First Blast of the Trumpet against the Monstruous Regiment of Women*. Geneva, 1558.

Lake, Peter. "'The Monarchical Republic of Queen Elizabeth I' (and the Fall of Archbishop Grindal) Revisited." In *The Monarchical Republic of Early Modern England*, ed. John F. McDiarmid, 129–47. Aldershot: Ashgate, 2007.

Lakoff, George. *Whose Freedom? The Battle over America's Most Important Idea*. New York: Farrar, Straus and Giroux, 2006.

Langford, Paul. *Englishness Identified: Manners and Character, 1650–1850*. Oxford: Oxford University Press, 2000.

Lanham, Richard. *A Handlist of Rhetorical Terms*. Berkeley and Los Angeles: University of California Press, 1991.

Leishman, J. B. *Milton's Minor Poems*. Pittsburgh: University of Pittsburgh Press, 1969.

Leonard, John. "Language and Knowledge in *Paradise Lost*." In *The Cambridge Companion to Milton*, ed. Dennis Danielson, 130–43. Cambridge: Cambridge University Press, 1999.

Levao, Ronald. *Renaissance Minds and Their Fictions: Cusanus, Sidney, Shakespeare*. Berkeley and Los Angeles: University of California Press, 1985.

Levin, Stanley R. *The Semantics of Metaphor*. Baltimore: Johns Hopkins University Press, 1977.

Levine, William. "Collins, Thomson, and the Whig Progress of Liberty." *Studies in English Literature* 34, no. 3 (Summer 1994): 553–77.

Lewalski, Barbara K. "How Radical Was the Young Milton?" In *Milton and Heresy*, ed. Stephen B. Dobranski and John P. Rumrich, 49–74. Cambridge: Cambridge University Press, 1998.

———. "Interpreting God's Word—and Words—in *Paradise Lost*." In *Milton's Rival Hermeneutics: "Reason Is But Choosing,"* ed. Richard J. DuRocher and Margaret Thickstun, 77–99. Pittsburgh: Duquesne University Press, 2012.

———. *The Life of John Milton: A Critical Biography.* Oxford: Blackwell, 2000.

———. *"Paradise Lost" and the Rhetoric of Literary Forms.* Princeton, NJ: Princeton University Press, 1986.

———. *Protestant Poetics.* Princeton, NJ: Princeton University Press, 1979.

———. "'To Try, and Teach the Erring Soul': Milton's Last Seven Years." In *Milton and the Terms of Liberty,* ed. Graham Parry and Joad Raymond, 175–90. Cambridge: D. S. Brewer, 2002.

Lewis, C. S. "The New Learning and the New Ignorance." *Sixteenth-Century English Literature.* Oxford: Oxford University Press, 1954.

Lieb, Michael. "Milton and the Socinian Heresy." In *Milton and the Grounds of Contention,* ed. Mark R. Kelley et al., 234–83. Pittsburgh: Duquesne University Press, 2003.

———. *Theological Milton: Deity, Discourse, and Heresy in the Miltonic Canon.* Pittsburgh: Duquesne University Press, 2006.

Lieb, Michael, and John Shawcross, eds. *Achievements of the Left Hand: Essays on the Prose of John Milton.* Amherst: University of Massachusetts Press, 1974.

Locke, John. *An Essay concerning Human Understanding.* London, 1694.

———. *Some Thoughts concerning Education.* London, 1693.

———. *Two Treatises of Government.* Edited by Peter Laslett. 1960. Reprint, Cambridge: Cambridge University Press, 1988.

Loewenstein, David. "Milton among the Religious Radicals and Sects: Polemical Engagements and Silences." In *Milton Studies,* vol. 40, ed. Albert C. Labriola, 222–47. Pittsburgh: University of Pittsburgh Press, 2001.

———. "Milton's Nationalism." In *Early Modern Nationalism and Milton's England,* ed. David Loewenstein and Paul Stevens, 25–50. Toronto: University of Toronto Press, 2008.

———. "The Radical Religious Politics of *Paradise Lost.*" In *A Companion to Milton,* ed. Thomas N. Corns, 348–62. Oxford: Blackwell, 2001.

———. "Toleration and the Specter of Heresy in Milton's England." In *Milton and Toleration,* ed. Sharon Achinstein and Elizabeth Sauer, 45–71. Oxford: Oxford University Press, 2007.

Loewenstein, David, and James Grantham Turner. *Politics, Poetics and Hermeneutics in Milton's Prose.* Cambridge: Cambridge University Press, 1990.

Loewenstein, David, and John Marshall, eds. *Heresy, Literature and Politics in Early Modern English Culture.* Cambridge: Cambridge University Press, 2006.

Loewenstein, David, and Paul Stevens, eds. *Early Modern Nationalism and Milton's England.* Toronto: University of Toronto Press, 2008.

Lowe, E. J. *An Introduction to the Philosophy of Mind.* Cambridge: Cambridge University Press, 2000.

Luxon, Thomas H. *Single Imperfection: Milton, Marriage, and Friendship.* Pittsburgh: Duquesne University Press, 2005.

Macauley, Catharine. *A Modest Plea for the Property of Copyright.* Bath, 1774.

MacCaffrey, Wallace T. *Elizabeth I.* London: Edward Arnold, 1993.

———. *The Shaping of the Elizabethan Regime.* Princeton, NJ: Princeton University Press, 1968.

MacCormac, Earl R. *A Cognitive Theory of Metaphor.* Cambridge, MA: MIT Press, 1988.

Maitland, F. W. Preface to Thomas Smith, *De republica Anglorum*, ed. L. Alston. Cambridge: Cambridge University Press, 1906.

Marcel, Gabriel. *Philosophy and Existence.* London: Harvill Press, 1949.

Maritain, Jacques. *Existence and the Existent: An Essay on Christian Existentialism.* Translated by Lewis Galantière and Gerald B. Phelan. New York: Pantheon, 1948.

McColley, Diane. *Milton's Eve.* Urbana: University of Illinois Press, 1983.

McCoy, Richard. *Rebellion in Arcadia.* New Brunswick, NJ: Rutgers University Press, 1979.

McDowell, Nicholas, and Nigel Smith, eds. *The Oxford Handbook of Milton.* Oxford: Oxford University Press, 2009.

McGuire, Maryann Cale. *Milton's Puritan Masque.* Athens: University of Georgia Press, 1983.

Mill, John Stuart. *On Liberty.* London: John W. Parker and Son, 1859.

———. *On Liberty.* Edited by David Bromwich and George Kateb. New Haven: Yale University Press, 2003.

Miller, Shannon. *Engendering the Fall: John Milton and Seventeenth-Century Women Writers.* Philadelphia: University of Pennsylvania Press, 2008.

Milton, John. *Areopagitica: A Speech to the Parliament of England, for the Liberty of Unlicens'd Printing.* First Published in the Year 1644. With a preface, by another hand [James Thomson]. London: Printed for A. Millar, 1738.

———. *Areopagitica.* Edited by [Sir] R[ichard]. C[laverhouse]. In *English Reprints*, vol. 7, ed. Edward Arber. London: A. Murray and Son, 1868.

———. *Areopagitica.* Edited with introduction by John W. Hales. 1875. Reprint, Oxford: Clarendon Press, 1928.

———. *Areopagitica, a Speech of Mr. John Milton.* Introduction by James Russell Lowell. New York: Grolier Club, 1890.

———. *Areopagitica and Other Political Writings of John Milton.* Edited by John Alvis. Chicago: Liberty Fund, 1999.

———. *Areopagitica and Other Prose Writings.* Edited by William Haller. New York, 1927.

———. *The Complete Prose Works of John Milton.* 8 vols. Edited by Don M. Wolfe et al. New Haven: Yale University Press, 1953–82.

———. *A Defence of the People of England, by John Milton: In Answer to Salmasius's Defence of the King.* London, 1692.

———. *John Milton: Complete Shorter Poems.* Edited by Stella Revard. Oxford: Wiley-Blackwell, 2009.

———. *John Milton: Paradise Lost.* Edited by Barbara K. Lewalski. Oxford: Blackwell, 2007.

———. *Milton: Complete Poems and Major Prose.* Edited by Merritt Y. Hughes. New York: Odyssey Press, 1957.

———. *Poetical Works of John Milton.* Edited by Henry John Todd. London, 1801.

———. *Poetical Works of John Milton.* Edited by Thomas Newton. London, 1749.

Mitchell, L. G. *The Whig World: 1760–1837.* New York: Hambledon London, 2005.

Mohamed, Feisal G. "Confronting Religious Violence: Milton's *Samson Agonistes.*" *PMLA* 120, no. 2 (2005): 327–40.

Mohl, Ruth. *John Milton and His Commonplace Book.* New York: Frederick Ungar, 1969.

More, Thomas. "The History of King Richard the Thirde." 1513? London: Richard Rastell, 1557.

Morris, Jeffrey B. "Disorientation and Disruption in *Paradise Regained.*" In *Milton Studies,* vol. 26, ed. James D. Simmonds, 219–37. Pittsburgh: University of Pittsburgh Press, 1990.

Mueller, Janel. "Milton on Heresy." In *Milton and Heresy,* ed. Stephen B. Dobranski and John P. Rumrich, 21–38. Cambridge: Cambridge University Press, 1998.

Myers, Benjamin. *Milton's Theology of Freedom.* Berlin: Walter de Gruyter, 2006.

Myrick, Kenneth. *Sir Philip Sidney as a Literary Craftsman.* 1935. 2nd ed. Lincoln: University of Nebraska Press, 1965.

The Myrrour for Magistrates. Edited by Lily B. Campbell. Cambridge: Cambridge University Press, 1938.

Nelson, Eric. "'True Liberty': Isocrates and Milton's *Areropagitica.*" In *Milton Studies,* vol. 40, ed. Albert C. Labriola, 201–21. Pittsburgh: University of Pittsburgh Press, 2001.

Nelson, William. *The Poetry of Edmund Spenser.* New York: Columbia University Press, 1963.

Newlyn, Lucy. *"Paradise Lost" and the Romantic Reader.* Oxford: Clarendon Press, 1993.

Norbrook, David. "John Milton, Lucy Hutchinson, and the Republican Biblical Epic." In *Milton and the Grounds of Contention,* ed. Mark R. Kelley et al., 37–63 Pittsburgh: Duquesne University Press, 2003.

———. *Writing the English Republic: Poetry, Rhetoric and Politics, 1627–1660.* Cambridge: Cambridge University Press, 1999.

Nowottny, Winifred. *The Language Poets Use.* London: University of London Athlone Press, 1962.

Nyquist, Mary. "Reading the Fall: Discourse and Drama in *Paradise Lost.*" *English Literary Renaissance* 14, no. 2 (1984): 199–229.

———. "Slavery, Resistance, and Nation in Milton and Locke." In *Early Modern Nationalism and Milton's England,* ed. David Loewenstein and Paul Stevens, 356–97. Toronto: University of Toronto Press, 2008.

Olmsted, Wendy. *The Imperfect Friend: Emotion and Rhetoric in Sidney, Milton and Their Contexts.* Toronto: University of Toronto Press, 2008.

Orgel, Stephen. *The Illusion of Power: Political Theatre in the English Renaissance.* Berkeley and Los Angeles: University of California Press, 1975.

Orwell, George. *Why I Write.* 1946. Reprint, New York: Penguin, 2005.

Osborn, James M. *Young Philip Sidney.* New Haven: Yale University Press, 1972.

Parry, Graham, and Joad Raymond, eds. *Milton and the Terms of Liberty.* Cambridge: D. S. Brewer, 2002.

Patrides, C. A. *Milton's "Lycidas": The Tradition and the Poem.* Rev. ed. Columbia: University of Missouri Press, 1983.

Patterson, Orlando. *Freedom and the Making of Western Culture.* New York: Basic Books, 1991.

Peltonen, Markku. "Rhetoric and Citizenship in the Monarchical Republic of Queen Elizabeth I." In *The Monarchical Republic of Early Modern England: Essays in Response to Patrick Collinson,* ed. John F. McDiarmid, 109–27. Aldershot, Hamps: Ashgate, 2007.

Penrose, Roger. *Shadows of the Mind: A Search for the Missing Science of Consciousness.* Oxford: Oxford University Press, 1994.

Perkins, William. *Works.* London, 1605.

Pettit, Philip. *Republicanism: A Theory of Freedom and Government.* Oxford: Oxford University Press, 1997.

Pinker, Steven. *The Blank Slate: The Modern Denial of Human Nature.* New York: Penguin Putnam, 2002.

———. *How the Mind Works.* New York: W. W. Norton, 1997.

Plato. *Republic.* Rev. ed. Edited and translated by Desmond Lee. New York: Penguin, 1974.

Pocock, J. G. A. *The Ancient Constitution and the Feudal Law: A Study of English Historical Thought in the Seventeenth Century.* 1957; rev. ed., Cambridge: Cambridge University Press, 1987.

Poole, Kristen. *Radical Religion from Shakespeare to Milton: Figures of Nonconformity in Early Modern England.* Cambridge: Cambridge University Press, 2000.

Puttenham, George. *Arte of English Poesie.* London, 1589; facsimile reprint, Kent, OH: Kent State University Press, 1970.

———. *The Art of English Poesy.* Edited by Frank Whigham and Wayne Rebhorn. Ithaca, NY: Cornell University Press, 2007.

Radzinowicz, Mary Ann. *Milton's Epics and the Book of Psalms.* Princeton, NJ: Princeton University Press, 1989.

———. "*Paradise Regained* as Hermeneutic Combat." *University of Harvard Studies in Literature* 16 (1984): 99–107.

———. "Politics of *Paradise Lost.*" In *Politics of Discourse: The Literature and History of Seventeenth-Century England,* ed. Kevin Sharpe and Steven Zwicker, 204–29. Berkeley and Los Angeles: University of California Press, 1987.

———. *Toward "Samson Agonistes": The Growth of Milton's Mind.* Princeton, NJ: Princeton University Press, 1978.

Raitiere, Martin. *Faire Bitts: Sir Philip Sidney and Renaissance Political Theory.* Pittsburgh: Duquesne University Press, 1984.

Raymond, Joad. *Milton's Angels: The Early Modern Imagination.* Oxford: Oxford University Press, 2010.

Revard, Stella. "*L'Allegro* and *Il Penseroso:* Classical Tradition and Renaissance Mythography." *PMLA* 101 (1986): 338–50.

———. "Satan in *Paradise Regained:* The Quest for Identity." In *Milton's Rival Hermeneutics: "Reason Is But Choosing,"* ed. Richard J. DuRocher and Margaret Olofson Thickstun, 205–24. Pittsburgh: Duquesne University Press, 2012.

Ridley, Florence H., ed. *The Aeneid of Henry Howard Earl of Surrey.* Berkeley and Los Angeles: University of California Press, 1963.

Ringler, William A. *The Poems of Sir Philip Sidney.* Oxford: Clarendon Press, 1962.

Rogers, John. *The Matter of Revolution: Science, Poetry, and Politics in the Age of Milton.* Ithaca, NY: Cornell University Press, 1996.

———. "Milton and the Heretical Priesthood of Christ." In *Heresy, Literature and Politics in Early Modern English Culture,* ed. David Loewenstein and John Marshall, 203–20. Cambridge: Cambridge University Press, 2006.

———. "*Paradise Regained* and the Memory of *Paradise Lost.*" In *The Oxford Handbook of Milton,* ed. Nicholas McDowell and Nigel Smith, 603–07. Oxford: Oxford University Press, 2009.

Rumrich, John. "Samson and the Excluded Middle." In *Altering Eyes: New Perspectives on "Samson Agonistes,"* ed. Mark R. Kelley and Joseph Wittreich, 307–32. Newark: University of Delaware Press, 2002.

Russell, Conrad. *The Crisis of Parliaments: English History, 1509–1660.* Oxford: Oxford University Press, 1971.

———. *The Fall of the British Monarchies, 1637–1642.* Oxford: Oxford University Press, 1991.

Sambrook, James. *James Thomson, 1700–1748: A Life.* Oxford: Clarendon Press, 1991.

Sandel, Michael J. *Justice: What's the Right Thing to Do?* New York: Farrar, Straus and Giroux, 2009.

Sandoz, F. Ellis. "Fortescue, Coke, and the Anglo-American Constitution." In *The Roots of Liberty: Magna Carta, Ancient Constitution, and the Anglo-American Rule of Law,* ed. Ellis Sandoz, 1–21. Columbia: University of Missouri Press, 1993.

Sartre, Jean-Paul. *Being and Nothingness.* Translated by Hazel E. Barnes. New York: Philosophical Library, 1956. Originally published in French as *L'Être et le néant,* 1943.

Schwartz, Regina. *Remembering and Repeating: On Milton's Theology and Poetics.* Chicago: University of Chicago Press, 1988.

Scott, Jonathan. *Algernon Sidney and the English Republic, 1623–1677.* Cambridge: Cambridge University Press, 1988.

Sharpe, Kevin. *The Personal Rule of Charles I.* New Haven: Yale University Press, 1992.

Shelley, Percy Bysshe. "Sonnet: England in 1819." In *The Complete Poetical Works of Percy Bysshe Shelley,* ed. Thomas Hutchinson. Oxford: Oxford University Press, 1919.

Shermer, Michael. "Free Won't: Volition as Self-Control Exerts Veto Power over Impulses." *Scientific American* (Aug. 2012). www.scientificamerican.com/article.cfm?id=how-free-will-collides-with-unconscious-impulses.

Shore, Daniel. "'Fit though Few': *Eikonoklastes* and the Rhetoric of Audience." In *Milton Studies,* vol. 45, ed. Albert C. Labriola, 129–48. Pittsburgh: University of Pittsburgh Press, 2006.

———. *Milton and the Art of Rhetoric.* Cambridge: Cambridge University Press, 2012.

———. "Why Milton Is Not an Iconoclast." *PMLA* 127, no. 1 (Jan. 2012): 22–37.

Shoulson, Jeffrey. "Denis Saurat and the Old New Milton Criticism." In *The New Milton Criticism,* ed. Peter Herman and Elizabeth Sauer, 310–34. Cambridge: Cambridge University Press, 2012.

Shullenberger, William. *Lady in the Labyrinth: Milton's "Comus" as Initiation.* Madison, NJ: Fairleigh Dickinson University Press, 2008.

Sidney, Algernon. *Discourses concerning Government*. London, 1680.

Sidney, Sir Philip. *An Apology for Poetry; or, The Defence of Poesy*. Edited by Geoffrey Shepherd. London: Nelson, 1965.

———. *The Countess of Pembroke's Arcadia [The New Arcadia]*. Edited by Victor Stretkowicz. Oxford: Clarendon Press, 1987.

———. *The Poems of Sir Philip Sidney*. Edited by William A. Ringler Jr. Oxford: Clarendon Press, 1962.

———. *The Prose Works of Sir Philip Sidney*. Edited by Albert Feuillerat. 1912. Reprint, Cambridge: Cambridge University Press, 1963.

———. *Sir Philip Sidney*. Edited by Katherine Duncan-Jones. Oxford: Oxford University Press, 1989.

Simpson, James. *Reform and Cultural Revolution*. Vol. 2, 1350–1547. Oxford: Oxford University Press, 2002.

Sinfield, Alan. "Power and Ideology: An Outline Theory and Sidney's *Arcadia*." *ELH* 52 (1985).

Skinner, Quentin. *The Foundations of Modern Political Thought*. 2 vols. Cambridge: Cambridge University Press, 1978.

———. "John Milton and the Politics of Slavery." In *Milton and the Terms of Liberty*, ed. Graham Parry and Joad Raymond, 1–22. Cambridge: D. S. Brewer, 2002.

———. *Liberty before Liberalism*. Cambridge: Cambridge University Press, 1998.

Smith, Adam. *An Inquiry into the Nature and Causes of the Wealth of Nations*. London, 1776.

Smith, Nigel. *Is Milton Better Than Shakespeare?* Cambridge, MA: Harvard University Press, 2008.

Smith, Thomas. *De republica Anglorum, The maner of Governement or policie of the Realme of England, compiled by the honorable man Thomas Smyth*. London, 1583.

———. *De republica Anglorum*. Edited by L. Alston. Cambridge: Cambridge University Press, 1906.

———. *De republica Anglorum*. Edited by Mary Dewar. Cambridge: Cambridge University Press, 1983.

Sommerville, Johann P. "English and Roman Liberty in the Monarchical Republic of Early Stuart England." In *The Monarchical Republic of Early Modern England*, ed. John F. McDiarmid. Aldershot: Ashgate, 2007.

———. *Royalists and Patriots: Politics and Ideology in England, 1603–1640.* 2nd ed. London: Longman, 1999.

Sommerville, J. P., ed. *James VI and I, Political Writings.* Cambridge: Cambridge University Press, 1994.

Spenser, Edmund. *The Poetical Works of Edmund Spenser.* Edited by J. C. Smith and Ernest De Selincourt. London: Oxford University Press, 1912.

———. *The Spenser Encyclopedia.* Edited by A. C. Hamilton et al. Toronto: University of Toronto Press, 1990.

Spink, Ian. *Henry Lawes: Cavalier Songwriter.* Oxford: Oxford University Press, 2000.

Stevens, Paul. *Imagination and the Presence of Shakespeare in "Paradise Lost."* Madison: University of Wisconsin Press, 1985.

Stillman, Robert E. "The Truth of a Slippery World: Poetry and Tyranny in Sidney's *Defence.*" *Renaissance Quarterly* 55 (2002): 1287–1319.

Stubbs, John. *The Discoverie of a Gaping Gulf whereunto England Is Likely to Be Swallowed.* London, 1579.

Sugimura, N. K. *Matter of Glorious Trial: Spiritual and Material Substance in "Paradise Lost."* New Haven: Yale University Press, 2009.

Swaim, Kathleen. *Before and After the Fall: Contrasting Modes in "Paradise Lost."* Amherst: University of Massachusetts Press, 1986.

Teskey, Gordon. "Dead Shepherd: Milton's *Lycidas.*" In *Milton's Rival Hermeneutics: "Reason Is But Choosing,"* ed. Richard J. DuRocher and Margaret Thickstun, 31–56. Pittsburgh: Duquesne University Press, 2012.

Thickstun, Margaret Olofson. "Fame, Shame, and the Importance of Community in *Samson Agonistes.*" In *Milton's Rival Hermeneutics: "Reason Is But Choosing,"* ed. Richard J. DuRocher and Margaret Olofsun Thickstun, 183–203. Pittsburgh: Duquesne University Press, 2012.

Thomson, James. *Liberty, The Castle of Indolence and Other Poems.* Edited by James Sambrook. Oxford: Clarendon Press, 1986.

———. *The Seasons.* Edited by James Sambrook. Oxford: Clarendon Press, 1981.

Todd, Henry John, ed. *Poetical Works of John Milton.* London, 1801.

Tufte, Virginia. *Artful Sentences: Syntax as Style.* Cheshire, CT: Graphics Press, 2006.

Turner, James Grantham. *One Flesh: Paradisal Marriage and Sexual Relations in the Age of Milton.* Oxford: Oxford University Press, 1987.

———. "The Poetics of Engagement." In *Politics, Poetics, and Hermeneutics in Milton's Prose,* ed. David Loewenstein and James Grantham Turner, 257-75. Cambridge: Cambridge University Press, 1990.

Tuve, Rosamund. *Images and Themes in Five Poems by Milton.* Cambridge, MA: Harvard University Press, 1957.

Watt, Timothy. "Milton's Visionary Obedience." Ph.D. diss., University of Massachusetts, 2011. Abstract available at scholarworks.umass.edu/dissertations/AAI3482671/.

Webbe, William. *Discourse of English Poetrie.* London, 1586.

Weismiller, Edward R. "Studies of Style and Verse Form in *Paradise Regained.*" In *A Variorum Commentary on the Poems of John Milton,* ed. Merritt Y. Hughes and Walter MacKellar. New York: Columbia University Press, 1975.

———. "Studies of Verse Form in the Minor English Poems." In *A Variorum Commentary on the Poems of John Milton,* ed. A. S. P. Woodhouse and Douglas Bush. New York: Columbia University Press, 1972.

White, Thomas Holt, ed. *Areopagitica: A Speech to the Parliament of England, for the Liberty of Unlicensed Printing,* by John Milton; with prefatory remarks, copious notes, and excursive illustrations, by T. Holt White, Esq., to which is subjoined, A Tract sur la Liberté de la Presse, imité de L'Angloise de Milton, par Le Comte de Mirabeau. London, 1819.

———. *Letters to William Paley, M.A. Archdeacon of Carlisle, on His Objections to a Reform in the Representation of the Commons, And on His Apology for the Influence of the Crown in Parliament, being strictures on the Essay upon the British Constitution introduced in his principles of Moral and Political Philosophy.* Bound with *Review of Johnson's Criticism on the Style of Milton's English Prose.* London: R. Hunter, 1818.

Wiener, Andrew D. *Sir Philip Sidney and the Poetics of Protestantism.* Minneapolis: University of Minnesota Press, 1978.

Wilson, Thomas. *Art of Rhetorique.* London, 1553.

———. *Rule of Reason.* London, 1551.

Wittreich, Joseph. "'He Ever was a Dissenter': Milton's Transgressive Maneuvers in *Paradise Lost.*" In *Arenas of Conflict: Milton and the Unfettered Mind,* ed. Kristin Pruitt McColgan and Charles W. Durham, 21–40. Selinsgrove, PA: Susquehanna University Press, 1997.

———. *Interpreting "Samson Agonistes."* Princeton, NJ: Princeton University Press, 1986.

———. *Shifting Contexts: Reinterpreting "Samson Agonistes."* Pittsburgh: Duquesne University Press, 2002.

———. "Sites of Contention in *Paradise Lost.*" In *Milton's Rival Hermeneutics: "Reason Is But Choosing,"* ed. Richard J. DuRocher and Margaret Olofsun Thickstun, 101–34. Pittsburgh: Duquesne University Press, 2012.

———. *Why Milton Matters.* New York: Palgrave Macmillan, 2006.

Woods, Susanne. "Choice and Election in *Samson Agonistes.*" In *Milton and the Grounds of Contention,* ed. Michael R. Kelley, Michael Lieb, and John T. Shawcross, 274–87. Pittsburgh: Duquesne University Press, 2003.

———. "Elective Poetics and Milton's Prose: *A Treatise of Civil Power* and *Considerations Touching the Likeliest Means to Remove Hirelings Out of the Church.*" In *Politics, Poetics, and Hermeneutics in Milton's Prose,* ed. David Loewenstein and James Grantham Turner, 193–212. Cambridge: Cambridge University Press, 1990.

———. "Freedom and Tyranny in Sidney's *Arcadia.*" In *Sir Philip Sidney's Achievements,* ed. M. J. B. Allen et al., 165–75. New York: AMS Press, 1990.

———. "How Free Are Milton's Women?" In *Milton and the Idea of Woman,* ed. Julia M. Walker, 11–30. Urbana: University of Illinois Press, 1988.

———. "Inviting Rival Hermeneutics: Milton's Language of Violence and the Invitation to Freedom." In *Milton's Rival Hermeneutics: "Reason Is But Choosing,"* ed. Richard J. DuRocher and Margaret Olofsun Thickstun, 3–16. Pittsburgh: Duquesne University Press, 2012.

———. "Making Free with Poetry: Spenser and the Rhetoric of Choice." *Spenser Studies* 15 (2001): 1–16.

———. *Natural Emphasis: English Versification from Chaucer to Dryden.* San Marino, CA: Huntington Library Press, 1985.

———. "'That Freedom of Discussion Which I Loved': Italy and Milton's Cultural Self-Definition." In *Milton in Italy: Contexts, Images, Contradictions*, ed. Mario A. Di Cesare, 9–18. Binghamton, NY: Medieval & Renaissance Texts & Studies, 1991.

Worden, Blair. *Literature and Politics in Cromwellian England: John Milton, Andrew Marvell, Marchamont Nedham*. Oxford: Oxford University Press, 2007.

———. *The Sound of Virtue: Sir Philip Sidney's Arcadia and Elizabethan Politics*. New Haven: Yale University Press, 1996.

Wordsworth, William. *Poems in Two Volumes, and Other Poems, 1800–1807*. Edited by Jared Curtis. Ithaca, NY: Cornell University Press, 1983.

Zwicker, Steven N. *Lines of Authority: Politics and English Literary Culture, 1649–1689*. Ithaca, NY: Cornell University Press, 1993.

Index

Achinstein, Sharon, 144, 161, 231n40, 242n12
Adam and Eve: choice of, 105–06, 112, 115, 126, 129–30, 135–38; freedom of, 138, 140; and knowledge, 105–06, 138; marriage of, 113–19, 121–23, 131, 133, 136–38, 236n18; in *Paradise Lost*, 105–06, 129–30, 135; and reason, 113, 122–24, 131; redemption of, 139–40, 142; and Satan, 118–19
Ad Patrem, 87, 224n4
Agamemnon (Thomson), 182
agency, 32, 115, 196, 247n21; in *Paradise Lost*, 232n1; in *Samson Agonistes*, 164, 167
American Enterprise Institute, 183
American Revolution, 185–86
Andrews, Lancelot (bishop of Winchester), 223n1
"Answer" (Hobbes), 178–79
An Apology against a Pamphlet, 6, 201n11
An Apology for Poetry (Sidney), 221n51, 221n55
An Apology for Smectymnuus, 87
appearance: of Eve, 114, 116, 121–22, 126; favoring poetry and song over, 82, 227n21
Arber, Edward, 190
Arcades, 73, 79–80, 87, 226n15

Arcadia (Sidney). See *The Countess of Pembroke's Arcadia*
Areopagitica, 70, 106, 166, 230nn38–39, 231n43; choice in, 2, 4; editions of, 181–87, 189–90, 248n22, 248n23; on free press, 46–47, 95, 97, 185; on free thought and expression, 6, 74, 95, 97, 191; on freedom, 2, 35, 102, 189, 250n41; influence of, 10, 173; invitational poetics in, 94, 195, 251n46; moral of, 95–96; questions raised in, 85–86; and political culture, 10; reception of, 14, 179–81, 190, 197; writing style in, 7–8, 41, 98–99, 134
Arians, 36
Aristotle, 57–58, 61, 86, 170, 244n31
Arminianism, Milton's, 35–36, 96, 212n58, 231n42
Arminius, Jacobus, 32, 212n58
Art of Logic, 64–65
Art of Poetry (Horace), 57–58
The Arte of English Poesie (Puttenham), 43–44
Ascham, Roger, 49–50, 216n22
atheists, 100, 179, 252n55
audience, 3, 92, 98, 200n6
Augustine, Saint, 127, 238n36

authority: 14–15, 86, 92–93, 101, 215n16

Bacon, Francis, 28
Baldwin, William, 19, 44–48, 51, 207n22
Basilikon Doron (James I), 27, 30
beauty, 129
Bellarmine, Robert, 33
Bentham, Jeremy, 250n40, 251n47
Berlin, Isaiah, 193–95, 247n21, 251n52
Bible, 69, 222n60; authority of, 35, 85–86, 101; clarity of, 35, 37, 129, 228n27; interpretation of, 37, 96, 214n8; Jesus' childhood in, 149–50; knowledge from study of, 77–78, 156–57; on marriage and divorce, 42, 92–94, 230n36; poetics of, 58–60, 62–63; reading of, 230n37, 231n43; as source of truth, 85–86, 92–93
Bishops' War, 90
Blake, Norman, 39
blindness, Milton's, 13, 145, 197
Bowen, Peter, 224n8
Brown, Eric, 77
Brydges, Egerton, 184
Bryson, Michael, 138
Burdett, Francis, 186–87, 250n40

Calvin, John, 31–33, 239n42
Calvinism, 64, 86, 211n53, 231n42
Campion, Thomas, 105
capitalism, 183
Carey, John, 162
Cartwright, Major John, 186–87, 250n40
Catholic Church, 32–33, 232n48; and freedom, 57, 73, 101–02, 219n39; and James I and popes' authority, 28–30; and Jesuits, 67–68; and religious tolerance, 100–02, 179
Cato Institute, 183
Cecil, William (Lord Burghley), 21, 44, 50
censorship, 95, 100, 179, 180
Center for American Progress, 188–89
Chambers, A. M., 204nn8–9
Charles I, King, 14–15, 27, 30–31, 210n45
choice, 9, 87, 96, 100, 231n43, 240n43; Adam and Eve's, 105–06, 112, 115, 126, 129–30, 135–38; consequences of, 115, 145, 161; freedom and, 2, 4, 38, 103, 172, 252n53; and God, 2, 78, 113, 201n16; happiness and, 130–31; and individual, 97–98, 134, 170, 192; Jesus as model for, 160–61; knowledge and, 88, 107, 118–19, 156, 192, 233n5; limitations of, 76–77; neuroscience of, 196–97; *Paradise Lost* and, 104; readers', 79, 116–17, 129–31, 162–66; reason in, 2–3; and knowledge and freedom, 81, 107, 113–15, 123–24, 126, 139–40, 145, 149–50, 159, 196; in salvation, 31–32, 35, 37; in *Samson Agonistes*, 161, 165–66; vocation and, 144, 159
church and state separation, 4, 37–38, 174, 195, 246n8
Civil Power, 6–7, 246n8
civil rights, 18, 25, 30, 188, 204n8
civil society, 43
civil wars, 13, 53–54
Clarke, Charles Cowden, 186–87
class, social, 22, 53–56
classics, 59; in education, 49, 102; Greek and Roman models in,

48, 61, 63, 69; Sidney's use of, 57–58
Coiro, Ann, 83, 226n15, 227n22
Coke, Edward, 28, 206n20
Colasterion, 230n36
commissions, Milton's, 72–73
Commonwealth of England (Smith), 16
community, 194, 197, 245n4, 252n58
compatibilism, 252n55
conscience, 3, 37, 225n11, 239n42, 240n43; importance of, 4, 6–7, 195; reason and, 142–43
Council of Trent, 29
Counter-Reformation, 9, 11, 32–33
The Countess of Pembroke's Arcadia (Sidney), 50–57, 63, 218n32, 219n41, 220n44, 220n46
Creaser, John, 105
creation, 109–12, 114–15, 117, 121
Cromwell, Oliver, 4, 13, 28, 180
Cummings, Brian, 40–41

D'Alençon, Duc, 43
Daniel, Samuel, 105
De copia (Erasmus), 40
De doctrina Christiana, 36
De republica Anglorum (Smith), 16
death, 111, 124, 134–36
The Defence of Poetry (Sidney), 53, 57–66
A Defence of the People of England, 13, 212n59
democracy, 193
Dennett, David, 252n55
depravity, 32, 34
Discourses concerning Government (Sidney), 220n48, 247n14

dismemberment, poetics of, 88, 95–97
Dissenting writers, 231n40
divorce, 42, 92–94, 96. *See also* marriage
divorce tracts, Milton's, 42, 91, 96, 179–80, 229n35, 230n36
The Doctrine and Discipline of Divorce, 91–94, 230n36
drama, 170
Dryden, John, 105, 234n10
DuRocher, Richard, 10, 160

economy, 16
education, 209n37, 232n49; benefits of, 51–54, 56; choice and, 51–54, 79, 87; knowledge versus, 156–57; Milton's, 212n58, 242n7; need for, 82–83; as ongoing process, 143, 150; recommended content of, 48, 226n20; treatises on, 49, 102
Edward VI, King, 17
Egerton, Alice, 226n16, 227n22
Egerton, Thomas (earl of Bridgewater), 73, 226n16, 227n23
Eikon Basilike (Charles I), 18
Eikonoklastes, 18, 190, 194, 206n18, 246n10
elective poetics, 6
Elizabeth I, Queen, 17, 44, 49–50; claim to throne, 210n43, 217nn24–25; on monarchs' authority, 49–50, 208n32; Pope Pius V and, 28, 101; Sidney and, 50–51, 67, 217nn28–29, 218nn30–31
Elton, G. R., 204n10
Elyot, Thomas, 209n37
England, 23, 34, 67; freedom in self-definition of, 2, 13–14, 16, 22, 31, 35, 42, 188; freedom in traditions of, 180, 187–88,

204n10; and God and servants, 4–5
English language, 39, 65. *See also* language; poetic language
entertainments, 73, 79–82, 87
episcopacy, 95, 203n2
equality, social, 194
Erasmus, 32, 40, 209n37, 238n35
Essay concerning Human Understanding (Locke), 176–77
existentialism, 107, 201n16
experience: interpretation of, 140, 225n11; knowledge and, 107–08, 124; leading to virtue, 51–54

The Faerie Queen (Spenser), 44, 83
faith, 32–33, 245n7
Fall, the, 102; choices in, 126, 131; effects of, 32, 34, 98, 106, 130, 138–42, 145; in *Paradise Lost*, 105–06; prohibiting salvation, 31–32; and reason, 109, 114, 133, 147; Satan's, 125–26; and tyranny, 141–42
Fall of Princes (Boccaccio), 19–20
Fallon, Stephen, 231n42
Fatovic, Clement, 101–02, 232n48
Felton, Nicholas (bishop of Ely), 223n1
Feroli, Teresa, 113
Ferrers, George, 19, 207n22
Festa, Thomas, 231n43, 232n49
Filmer, Robert, 220n48, 246n9, 247n14
Finch, Casey, 224n8
Fish, Stanley, 11, 95–96, 116, 162, 233n5, 239n38
"fit-though-few," 3, 92, 98, 200n6
foreign policy, monarchs' power in, 16, 30
Fortescue, John, 18, 206n20

Fowler, Elizabeth, 197
Francis, Duke of Bridgewater, 249n30
Frederick, Prince of Wales, 182
free markets, 180–83, 193
free press: *Areopagitica* on, 95, 97, 185; Milton's and, 46–47, 179–80, 182–84
free speech, 2, 38, 95, 172, 177, 216n23; danger of exercising, 42–43; in English self-definition, 22, 180, 188; in Parliament, 18, 42; as poets' prerogative, 44–45, 47–48
free will, 9, 34, 127, 192, 196, 231n42; as gift from God, 6, 27, 78; Milton on, 5–6, 31, 35, 96; neuroscience and, 252n55, 252n58, 253n60; nonsalvific, 212n57; in *Paradise Lost*, 104, 107; Reformation debate about, 18, 22, 85; salvific, 34–35, 62, 96
freedom, 91, 192, 204n9, 211n47, 235n13; Adam and Eve's, 138, 140; *Areopagitica* on, 102, 180, 191, 250n41; as birthright, 173–74, 200n3; Catholic Church and, 101–02, 232n48; changing meanings of, 172, 193, 249n34; economic, 181–83, 193; in Elizabethan era, 45–46, 48; in English self-definition, 13–14, 16, 31, 35, 42; English tradition of, 180, 187–88, 204n10; God and, 31, 162, 211n54; government and, 101, 189, 247n21; groups' special liberties, 21, 35; in *Il Penseroso* and *L'Allegro*, 74–75; individual, 37, 193–94, 252n53; liberty and, 199n1; "licence" versus, 15–16; limits on, 22, 140–41, 154–55, 158, 192, 204n10; Milton's

definition of, 1–2, 4, 15, 38, 196; Milton's ideas on, 3, 10, 102; Milton's influence on ideas of, 172–73, 179, 185, 187–88; Milton's rhetoric of, 85, 173; modern science's contribution to, 195; Parliament supposed to ensure, 231n44; poetic, 62, 64, 67, 71, 73–74, 95, 140, 178; poetics of, 41, 104, 196; of poets, 68–69, 104–05; political, 16, 18–19, 35, 140–42; positive versus negative, 194–95, 247n21, 251n52; and private property, 183, 249n34; as process, 96, 103; progressive versus conservative notions of, 192–93; reason and, 141–42; relation of to choice and knowledge, 107, 113–15, 123–24, 126, 139–40, 145, 149–50, 159, 196; religion and, 57, 175; responsibilities of, 54–55; in *Samson Agonistes*, 161, 164, 166; Satan trying to destroy, 118–19, 124; sources of, 31, 52, 101, 154, 189, 247n21; threats to, 19, 31, 101–02
French Revolution, 181, 185
Friends of Parliamentary Reform, 187

Gazzunaga, Michael, 195–97, 252n58
George III, King, 186
Gibson, James, 26
Gil, Alexander, 212n58
God, 4–5, 25, 80, 172, 238n35, 239n38; Adam and, 111–13; and choice, 2, 113; foreknowledge of, 127, 238n36; and free will, 9, 27, 31, 78, 100; freedom and, 31, 107, 162, 201n16; grace and, 22, 86; individual relationships with, 162, 233n5; Mary's trust in, 151–52, 154; monarchs and, 27, 210n43, 215n17; offering redemption, 139–40, 142; poets and, 62, 68, 70; portrayals of, 119–20, 128–29, 138, 158; salvation and, 32–33; service to, 144, 211n54; Son's trust in, 151, 154; telling Adam and Eve about Satan, 118–19; trust in, 147, 159. *See also* religion
good and evil, 119, 121, 124, 131–32, 135–36
good works, 33
Gosson, Stephen, 57–58, 177
Gostlin, John, 223n1
government, 15, 27, 101, 183–84, 187, 246n10; good versus bad, in Sidney's *Arcadia*, 53, 55–56; inner versus outer, 155–56; parliamentary, 16–17, 42, 98; relation to freedom, 189, 194–95; self-, 155, 192; as social contract, 56–57, 174, 176
grace, 86, 231n40
Greville, Fulke, 217n29, 218n32
Grossman, Marshall, 197, 253n61

Hales, John, 190–91, 248n22, 250n41
Hall, Joseph, 6
Haller, William, 251n46
Hamilton, A. C., 52
Harris, Sam, 252n55
Henrietta Maria, Queen, 73
Henry, Prince, 23, 27, 30
Henry IV (Henry of Navarre), 28
Henry VI, King, 18
Henry VIII, King, 21–22
heresy, 36–37, 92

Herman, Peter, 10, 221n55,
    222n61, 237n29, 238n31
History of the World (Ralegh),
    27–28
Hobbes, Thomas, 208n33,
    235n12, 245n4, 245n7,
    246n9; on church and state
    separation, 174–75; on human
    nature, 173–74; Milton
    compared to, 173, 176, 178;
    mistrust of poetic language,
    178–79
Holland, 67
Holt White, Thomas, 173,
    184–90, 249n36
Horace, 57–58
House of Commons, 22. *See also*
    Parliament
human nature, 9, 31, 108–09,
    173–74, 212n57
humanism, 48, 49
humanities, 48, 62–63
humility, 6
Hunt, Leigh, 187
Hurstfield, Joel, 204n10
hypocrisy, 81

ignorance and knowledge, 80–81
Il Penseroso, 72, 74–78, 87, 224n8
incompleteness, 88, 95, 166
individualism, 16, 179, 183,
    190–92, 196, 251n46
individuals, 2, 22, 37, 95, 159;
    autonomy of, 176–77; choices
    of, 27, 134, 146, 192; and
    different readings of stories,
    153–54, 158; in *Il Penseroso*
    and *L'Allegro*, 74, 76–77;
    religion of, 38, 233n5
interrogative, rhetorical forms
    of, 7–8
invitational poetics, Milton's,
    9–10, 80, 94; in *Areopagitica*,
    189, 195, 251n46; effects
    of, 86, 88, 173, 179, 189;
    goals of, 5–6, 77, 98–99; in
    Paradise Lost, 104, 120–21,
    178; in *Paradise Regained*
    and *Samson Agonistes*, 144,
    146–48, 171. *See also* poetics;
    writing style
invitational rhetoric, 95, 116
Italy, 67–68, 90

James I, King, 174, 209n39,
    223n1; denying right to rebel,
    25, 208n32; on monarchs'
    power, 16, 22–23, 28; Prince
    Charles compared to, 30–31,
    210n45; treatises on monar-
    chy, 23–25, 27–30, 208n30
Jebb, R. C., 190
Jeremiah, 68
Jesus: childhood of, 149–50; as
    model of choosing, 160–61;
    and Satan, 146–48, 152–53,
    156–59, 241n4, 242n7;
    vocation of, 146–47, 150–51,
    158
John, King, 18
Johnson, Paula, 116
Johnson, Samuel, 162, 165,
    228n30, 247n16
Jonson, Ben, 65, 72, 223n2,
    226n19
The Judgment of Martin Bucer,
    230n36
judicial system, 19–20, 28, 42,
    209n40

Kahn, Victoria, 42, 214n8
Keats, John, 187
Kelley, Maurice, 36
King, Edward, 87, 228n30
knowledge, 80, 85, 110, 127,
    155, 239n39; of Adam and
    Eve, 105–06, 138; choice and,
    81, 88; education versus,
    156–57; experience's relation
    to, 107–08; individuals', 177,

192; kinds of, 106–07, 112; limits of, 125, 169; Locke and Hobbes compared to Milton on, 176–77; need for, 82–83; in *Paradise Lost*, 103, 136, 233n5; reason in reaching, 108–09, 113–14, 124, 147; relation of to choice and freedom, 107, 113–15, 123–24, 126, 139–40, 145, 149–50, 159, 196; of Satan, 118–19, 237n29, 238n31; Satan on, 153, 242n7; self-, 150–51, 153, 157, 163–65; sources of, 77–78, 86–87, 108, 121, 140, 147–48

Lakoff, George, 192, 194
L'Allegro, 72, 74–78, 87, 224n8
Lamb, Charles and Mary, 187
language, 40, 55, 65, 127, 214n11; effects of Fall on, 106, 138–39; Elizabethan exaltation of, 43–44; in humanism, 48–49; safety in indirect, 45–47, 55; Satan's, in *Paradise Lost*, 132–33. *See also* English language; poetic language
Languet, Hubert, 56, 219n39, 220n44
Lanham, Richard, 41
law, 18–21, 24–27, 101
The Law of Free Monarchies (James I), 23–26, 30
Lawes, Henry, 83, 85, 223n3, 224n4, 226n15; Milton collaborating with, 73, 79, 227n23
Letters to William Paley (Holt White), 186, 249n36
Levellers, religious tolerance of, 100–01
Leviathan (Hobbes), 26, 173, 208n33
Lewalski, Barbara, 83, 180, 212n58, 226n15, 242n7; on Milton, 65, 231n42, 241n3, 252n56; on *Paradise Lost*, 113, 233n5, 234n9
Lewis, C. S., 9
libel, 42
liberalism, 181, 183
libertarianism, 191–92
"licence," 15–16
Lieb, Michael, 162–63
Likeliest Means to Remove Hirelings, 37, 157, 195
Lilburne, John, 100–01
literary criticism, 39, 57
literary culture, 40
Locke, John, 173–77, 179, 183, 246nn9–10, 247n14
Lodge, Thomas, 57
Lowe, E. J., 196
Lowell, James Russell, 181, 248n22
Luther, Martin, 31–33
Lycidas, 87–90, 134, 166, 229n31; criticisms of, 228n30, 247n16; structure of, 88–89
Lydgate, John, 19
Lyrical Ballads (Wordsworth and Coleridge), 185

Macauley, Catharine, 249n29
MacCormac, Earl R., 213n2
Magna Carta, 18
Maguire, Mary Ann, 83
Manso, Giovanni Baptista, 223n1, 224n9
Maritain, Jacques, 235n13
marriage, 91–93; Adam and Eve's, 113–19, 121–23, 131, 133, 136–38, 236n18; Milton's unhappy, 91, 229n34. *See also* divorce
Mary, Queen of Scots, 28
Mary of Modena, 234n10
A Mask Presented at Ludlow Castle, 73, 79–87, 134, 226n16, 227nn22–23

masques, 73, 83–84
materialism, 252n56
Macauley, Catharine, 184
McCoy, Richard, 50, 56
meritocracy, 49–50, 52, 54–56, 143, 196
Mill, James, 250n40, 251n47
Mill, John Stuart, 191–92, 251n47
Millar, A., 248n23
Milton, John (father), 72, 224n4
Milton, Mary Powell (wife), 229n34
Mirabeau, Le Comte de, 181, 186
Model Parliament (1295), 18
Mohamed, Feisal, 162, 243n23
Mohl, Ruth, 65
monarchs/monarchy, 31, 209n37; authority of, 28, 49; claims to throne, 210n43, 217n24; corrupt judges serving, 19–20; individuals dependent on "grace" of, 22, 25; James I's treatises on, 16, 23–25, 28–30, 208n30; limits on power of, 22–23, 26–27; opposition to, 173, 250n40; and Parliament, 16, 18, 22–25, 42, 95, 207n21; and people, 14, 174, 215n17; regicide of, 13–15; religion and, 21–22, 27–30, 65–67, 215n17; responsibilities of, 26–27, 30, 51; rights of, 23, 206n19; and right to depose, 15, 21, 215n18; source of power of, 14, 23–24, 49, 173, 246n9; subjects and, 23, 25–26, 174, 215n17; and tyrants, 17, 46, 205n12
monism, 108–09, 115, 195–96, 252n56
More, Thomas, 17–18, 206n17
Mornay, Philip de, 56, 219n39
Morris, Jeffrey, 148
music, 82, 86, 226n16, 226n20, 227n21

Myers, Benjamin, 211n47
Myrick, Kenneth, 55
A Myrrour for Magistrates, 19, 22, 44–48, 51, 191, 207n22

Napoleonic wars, 185–86
nationalism, 181–82
natural rights, 14–15
nature, 9, 58, 61–62, 68–69, 235n12
neo-Roman republicanism, 1, 194, 247n21
neo-Stoicism, and Puritanism, 52
Netherlands, 56, 219n39
neuroscience, 195–97, 252n55, 252n58, 253n60
Newton, Thomas, 185, 248n23
Norbrook, David, 105, 216n23, 229n35
Nott, George Frederick, 184
Nowottny, Winifred, 40, 213n5
Nyquist, Mary, 142

obedience, 107, 111, 113, 120, 128, 130
Of Civil Power, 4
Of Education, 80, 102, 226n20
Of Reformation, 35, 65–67, 80
Of True Religion, 36–37
Olmsted, Wendy, 219n37
On Christian Doctrine, 238n35
On Liberty (Mill), 191–92
order, 25, 27, 174
Orwell, George, 213n61
Overton, Richard, 100–01
Oxford, Earl of, 51

Paley, William, 186, 188, 249n36
pamphlet wars, 3–4
pamphlets, Milton's, 37, 134, 225n13; antiprelatical, 35, 65–66, 71, 87, 185; divorce tracts, 42, 91, 96, 179–80, 229n35, 230n36

Paradise Lost, 25, 31, 36, 96, 232n1; Adam and Eve in, 105–06, 129–30, 135; creation in, 109–12, 114–15, 117, 121; death in, 111, 124, 134–36; and Dryden, 234n10; God in, 128–29, 239n38; good and evil in, 119, 121, 124, 135–36; influences on, 65; invitational poetics in, 104, 116, 120–21, 178; and knowledge, 106–07; knowledge and choice in, 103, 233n5; obedience in, 107, 111, 113, 120, 128, 130; *Paradise Regained* compared to, 145–46, 159–60; readers and, 99, 115–17, 120–21, 129–33; reason in, 108–10; reception of, 14, 197; Satan in, 82, 117–19, 123–28, 132, 236n17, 238nn33–34; structure of, 104–05, 117, 233nn2–3, 234n9; writing of, 197; writing style of, 8, 99, 120–22, 126, 129–33, 213n5

Paradise Regained, 6; *Paradise Lost* compared to, 145–46, 159–60; *Samson Agonistes* and, 144, 161; Satan and Jesus in, 146–48, 152–55, 156–59, 241n4, 242n7; vocation in, 145–46; writing style in, 144, 148, 160

Parliament, 91–92; in English traditions, 42, 98; in English understanding of freedom, 18–19, 204n10; free speech in, 18, 42; James I versus, 22–23, 28–30; Milton on, 98–99, 201n11, 231n44; monarchs' relations with, 16, 18, 42, 207n21; monarchy's relation to, 20, 22–25, 95; reform movements and, 181, 186–90, 250n40; religion and, 30, 90. *See also* House of Commons

passions/pleasures, 8, 15–16
Patriarcha (Filmer), 220n48, 246n9, 247n14
patronage, 72, 223n1
Perkins, William, 34, 212n56, 212n57
Perron, Jacques du, 29
personality, Milton's, 6, 75–76, 224n9
Pettit, Philip, 193
Pinker, Steven, 252n58, 253n60
Pius V, Pope, 28–30, 101
Plato, 155–56, 221n55, 222n56
Platonism, 240n45
pluralism, 36–37
Poems (1645), 72, 73, 224n4
Poems of Mr. John Milton (1645), 228n30
poetic indirection, 10
poetic language, 60, 71; Hobbes's mistrust of, 178–79; radicalism of, 40, 42–44; as safer mode of expression, 45–47, 177. *See also* English language; language; poetry
Poetical Works of John Milton, 184–85
Poetices (Scaliger), 58
poetics, 104–05, 196. *See also* invitational poetics
Poetics (Aristotle), 57–58, 61, 170
poetry, 95, 144, 177, 223n2; biblical, 58–60, 62; blank verse, 104–05; education in, 49, 216n20; Elizabethan, 43, 50; as imitation of nature, 58, 61; Milton on, 65, 226n16; revealing knowledge, 86–87; Sidney and, 64, 221n55; techniques of, 64, 134, 213n5, 216n20; versus other branches of learning, 62–64. *See also* poetic language
poetry, Milton's, 1, 10–11

poets, 43, 112, 222n61; court, 73; experimenting with structure and rhyme, 104–05; freedom of, 44–45, 47–48, 62, 64, 68–69, 178; Milton on, 65, 70; Milton's career as, 73, 87, 91, 224n4, 224n6; in *A Myrrour for Magistrates*, 44–48; as prophets, 58–60, 69, 106; responsibilities of, 66–67, 90, 244n31; Sidney on, 58–60; status of, 61–63, 220n49; as teachers, 69–70
politics, 11, 38, 186; freedom in, 2, 35, 56; spiritual and political realms of, 21–22; writers and, 213n61, 220n49
politics of popularity, 213n62
Pope, Alexander, 105
popes, 21–22, 28–30
power, 21–22
predestination, 31, 84, 212n57
prelates, 91; pamphlets opposed to, 35, 65–66, 71, 87, 185
Prelatical Episcopacy, 225n13
Presbyterian Westminster Assembly, 91
private property, 175–76, 183–84, 193, 246n10, 249n29, 249n34
Pro populo anglicano defensio, 15
progress, 188
Prose Works, 248n23
Protestantism, 30, 73; freedom and, 57, 216n23; resistance tracts of, 203n2, 208n29; Sidney and, 50–51, 67
Protestants vs. Catholics, 29
Pulteney, William, 248n23
Puritanism, 22, 52, 67, 212n58, 231n42
Puttenham, George, 43–44, 214n12

Quintillian, on metaphor, 40–41

Radzinowicz, Mary Ann, 143, 162
Ralegh, Walter, 27–28, 209n39
Ramus, Peter, 64–65, 126
Raymond, Joad, 235n15
reason, 2–3, 15, 32, 96, 148; Adam and Eve's, 113, 122–24, 131; conscience and, 142, 240n43; effects of Fall on, 106, 114, 130, 133, 138–42, 147; leading to social contracts, 173–74; limits of, 82, 169; in *Paradise Lost*, 108–10; reaching knowledge through, 108–09, 113–14, 147
The Reason of Church-Government, 91, 239n42; and audience, 98, 200n6; on virtue, 78, 156–57; writing of, 65, 68, 203n21
reform movements, 181, 186–90, 250n40
Reform Protestant tradition, English, 34
Reformation, 2, 8, 11, 21–22, 33; and free will, 9, 18, 22, 85
religion, 175, 215n18, 216n23, 246n9, 247n19; in antiprelatical treatises, 35, 65–66, 185; effects of Reformation on, 2, 21–22; episcopacy not essential to monarchies, 65–67; individual, 2–3, 38, 245n7; Milton on, 90, 188; separation from state, 4, 37–38, 174, 195, 246n8. *See also* God
religious tolerance, 36–37, 100–02, 179
Remonstrance... for the right of kings (James I), 28–30
Renaissance, 9, 48, 54–55
Reply to Stephen Gosson Touching Plays (Lodge), 57
republicanism, 54, 56, 143, 177, 189, 247n19, 247n21; and

Algernon Sidney, 177, 220n48; in *Arcadia*, 220n46; Milton's, 145, 189–90, 203n5, 230n39
Restoration, 145, 163, 231n40, 241n3
Revard, Stella, 160
rhetoric, 55; Milton's, 173, 179, 191, 253n61; power of, 191, 219n37; Sidney's, 58–59; study of, 49, 214n11
Richard II, King, 19–21, 207n25
Richard III, King, 17–18, 45
Richard III (Shakespeare), 18, 206n17
Ringler, William A., 217n28
Romanticism, British, 186, 239n37
Rumrich, John, 162

salvation, 82, 84, 86, 96, 147; choice in, 31–32, 35, 37; Fall prohibiting, 31–32; as gift of God, 32–33
Samson Agonistes, 6, 79, 244n28; choice in, 145, 165–66; differing interpretations of ending, 161–63; heroism in, 161–63, 167, 170, 244n30; *Paradise Regained* and, 144, 161; readers' decisions about, 162–66; violence in, 161–62, 164, 167–68, 242n12, 243n23; writing style in, 144, 162, 168–71
Sandel, Michael, 194, 252n53
Sauer, Elizabeth, 10
Scaliger, Julius Caesar, 58
scholemaster, The (Ascham), 49–50
School of Abuse (Gosson), 57–58
Scotland, 23, 26
Seasons, The (Thomson), 181–82
Second Defence, The, 102, 190, 204n8
Second Defense of the English People, 13, 37

Second Treatise (Locke), 173, 175–76
Secretary for Foreign Tongues, Milton as, 13
sedition, 42
self-determination and nationalism, 181–82
Shakespeare, William, 18
Shepheardes Calendar (Spenser), 58
Shore, Daniel, 3, 7, 11, 163, 200n6, 233n2
Sidney, Algernon, 57, 177, 220n48, 240n45, 247n14
Sidney, Philip, 10, 39, 41, 219n39, 221n55, 222n56; *The Countess of Pembroke's Arcadia* by, 50–57, 63; *The Defence of Poesy* by, 52, 57–63; Elizabeth and, 50–51, 67, 217n28, 217n29, 218nn30–31; Milton and, 56–57, 64–65, 68, 219n37; poets and, 56, 61–63, 220n49; religion of, 52, 64; writing of, 57–58, 69–71, 105, 222n60
Simpson, James, 22
Sinfield, Alan, 56
Sirluck, Ernest, 101, 230n38
Skelton, John, 215n16
Skinner, Quentin, 1, 194, 204n10
Smith, Adam, 183
Smith, Thomas, 16–17, 205nn11–12, 206n15
social contracts, 56–57, 172–74, 176, 186, 245n4
Socinians, 36
Some Thoughts concerning Education (Locke), 177
Spain, 67, 182–83, 219n39
Spenser, Alice (countess dowager of Derby), 73, 79–80
Spenser, Edmund, 44, 58, 80, 83, 105, 213n3; influence on Milton, 64, 70–71, 223n65

State of Innocence (Dryden), 234n10
Stillman, Robert, 57
Stuart, Mary, 101
Stubbs, John, 42–43
suffrage, 188

temptation, 161; cautions against, 20, 82–83; of Eve and Adam, 127, 131–33, 135; of Jesus, 146–48, 152–53, 155–56; knowledge for choice in, 100, 107, 118
Tenure of Kings and Magistrates, 16, 26, 31, 200n3, 230n37; and Milton's political beliefs, 14–15, 20–21, 173, 194
terrorism, 162
Teskey, Gordon, 89
Tetrachordon, 230n36
Thickstun, Margaret, 10, 163–64
Thomson, James, 181–83, 185–86, 189
Todd, John Henry, 184–85, 249n30
tragedy, 170
Treatise on Civil Power, 195, 240n43
Tresilian, Robert, 19–20, 22, 42, 191
Trinitarian doctrine, 36
truth, 85, 136; dismembered, 96–97; individuals', 95, 134, 177; looking beyond received, 2–3, 97; and test against falsehood, 99–100; pursuit of, 143, 177
Tudor dynasty, 17–18, 21, 42, 55, 215n18
Tufte, Virginia, 7–8, 175
Two Treatises of Government (Locke), 177, 246n9
tyrants/tyranny, 20, 25, 57, 91–92, 194, 207n25, 219n39; and bad men's servility, 15–16; in Elizabethan era, 45–46, 48; and the fallen condition, 141–42; James I and, 25, 208n32; peoples' right to depose, 15, 17, 21, 37, 204n8, 206n15; as preferable to chaos, 25, 27; of prelacy, 66–67; rebellion against, 54–55; Richard III portrayed as, 17–18; vs. legitimate monarchs, 17, 205n12

United States, 180–81, 251n46

violence: Dissenting writers using, 231n40; in *Samson Agonistes*, 161–62, 164, 167–68, 242n12, 243n23
virtue, 52, 82, 86; chastity as, 84–85, 201n10, 228n26; choice and, 51–52, 96; sources of, 156–57
vitalism, monist, 108–09, 115, 252n56
vocation, 159; God working through, 158–59, 172; of Jesus, 146–47, 150–51, 158; in *Paradise Regained* and *Samson Agonistes*, 144–46, 167

Walpole, Robert, 182
Wealth of Nations (Smith), 183
Whigs, 180–84, 186, 247n19, 248n23, 250n40
Williams, Roger, 100–01
Wilson, Thomas, 214n11
Wittreich, Joseph, 112–13, 163, 236n18
Wolfe, Don, 201n11
Worden, Blair, 16, 50, 54–55
Wordsworth, William, 185, 190
writers, 213n61, 244n31; Dissenting, 231n40; politics of, 213n61, 215n16, 220n49; responsibilities of, 68, 70,

215n16; works of, 11–12, 249n29
writing style, Milton's, 65; ambiguities in, 89–90, 145, 148, 161, 168–70; assumption of speaking to knowing readers, 98–99, 115–16; clarifying or obfuscating through language, 126–27; encouraging readers' involvement, 88, 99, 129–33, 134, 146–48, 160, 162–66, 168, 170–71, 200n8; genres and, 233n5, 244n31; hermeneutics of, 197–98; increasing facility of, 72, 92, 102; influence due to, 179; interrogative forms in, 7–8, 144; "litotes" in, 168, 200n8; metaphoric, 4–5, 40–44, 94–95, 129, 213n2, 213n5; of *Paradise Lost,* 104, 122, 126, 129–33, 233n2; persuasive strategies in, 7, 21, 38, 126–27; poetics in, 4, 65–66, 71; structure and, 74–75, 88–89, 213n5; surmise in, 99, 144, 233n2; tentativeness in, 69–71, 134. *See also* invitational poetics

Young, John, 21–22
Young, Thomas, 72, 212n58